# SISTERHOOD OF WAR

# SISTERHOOD OF WAR

*Minnesota*
*Women*
*in Vietnam*

## Kim Heikkila

Minnesota Historical
Society Press

The publication of this book was supported though a generous grant from the Eugenie M. Anderson Women in Public Affairs Fund.

www.mhspress.org

The Minnesota Historical Society Press is a member of the Association of American University Presses.

Manufactured in the United States of America

10 9 8 7 6 5 4 3 2 1

∞ The paper used in this publication meets the minimum requirements of the American National Standard for
Information Sciences—Permanence for Printed Library Materials, ANSI Z39.48-1984.

International Standard Book Number
ISBN: 978-0-87351-637-2 (paper)
ISBN: 978-0-87351-839-0 (e-book)

Library of Congress Cataloging-in-Publication Data
Heikkila, Kim, 1968–
    Sisterhood of war : Minnesota women in Vietnam / Kim Heikkila.
        p. cm.
    Includes bibliographical references and index.
    ISBN 978-0-87351-637-2 (pbk. : alk. paper)
    ISBN 978-0-87351-839-0 (e-book)
    1. Vietnam War, 1961–1975—Women—United States. 2. Vietnam War, 1961–1975—Medical care. 3. Nurses—Vietnam—Biography. 4. Nurses—Guam—Biography. 5. Nurses—United States—Minnesota—Biography. 6. Vietnam War, 1961–1975—Veterans—United States—Biography. 7. Women veterans—United States—Biography. 8. Women—Minnesota—Biography. I. Title. II. Title: Minnesota women in Vietnam.
    DS559.8.W6H45 2011
    959.704'37—dc23
                                                                    2011018546


Photo on page 41 by A. Schneider, courtesy U.S.O. Photo/Vietnam

Photo on page 155 from Library of Congress, Prints and Photographs Division, HABS DC, WASH, 643-90

*This book is dedicated to the memory of my mother,*
*Sharon Lee Moore Wikstrom, the first and most important*
*of the many strong women who have shaped my life.*

# CONTENTS

# SISTERHOOD OF WAR

# Introduction

I don't go off to war
So they say
I'm a woman.
Who then
Has worn my boots?
  *Diane Carlson Evans, "Our War," 1983*

But this too is true: stories can save us.
  *Tim O'Brien,* The Things They Carried [1]

**VETERANS DAY 2008** was chilly but sunny in Washington, D.C. As they do every November, Vietnam veterans from across the country gathered at the Wall to pay their respects to those who had served and died in the United States' longest and most controversial war. Flowers adorned the pathway along which visitors descend into the earth, swallowed by the seemingly endless listing of names of the war's dead. A stage stood on the grassy lawn in front of the Wall. News trucks lined the nearby streets as cameras captured the swelling throngs, military color guard, musical performers, and featured speakers. Filling the hundreds of chairs in front of the stage were the day's honorees—veterans who had encountered in Vietnam the heights of human bravery and depths of human depravity and had come home to a divided, sometimes indifferent and sometimes hostile, nation. The veterans wore jackets and ties, jeans and sweatshirts, black leather vests and boonie hats. They sported clean-shaven faces and crew cuts or beards and ponytails, mellowed and graying with the passing of time. But clustered among this crowd of men were women who had also served in Vietnam, for on this day, they were the special guests of honor at the annual celebration.

Veterans Day 2008 marked the fifteenth anniversary of the dedication of the Vietnam Women's Memorial. Standing just south of the eastern tip of the Wall, the memorial statue depicts three uniformed women in various expressions of women's service in the war. The campaign to build the memorial had spanned ten years, but women's battle to be recognized as soldiers and veterans had lasted even longer than that, and their struggle to come to terms with their wartime service longer still. Those struggles receded on this occasion, however, as women Vietnam veterans were feted not just by each other but also by their admiring brother veterans and civilian supporters. For four days, these women assembled to reconnect with each other, to share laughter and tears, to remember and be remembered. Among those who gathered in the nation's capital for this celebration was a group of women from Minnesota who had served in the war as military nurses and whose efforts had helped bring the Memorial to fruition fifteen years earlier. It is their stories that this book tells.

More than a quarter million women served in the U.S. armed forces during the Vietnam War era, and about 7,500 of those women served in Vietnam. Of the twenty-three thousand women veterans living in Minnesota in September 2009, almost four thousand of them had served during the Vietnam era, whether in Vietnam itself, in the surrounding area of operations, or at other overseas or stateside bases. Military women who went to Vietnam worked as officers in military intelligence; as clerk-typists, administrative assistants, and communications specialists in the Women's Army Corps; as photojournalists and historians in the Air Force; and as line officers in the Navy and enlisted Women Marines. Women also went to Vietnam as civilians, working for the American Red Cross, the United Service Organizations (USO), and the Army Special Services. They were journalists, U.S. government secretaries, nurses employed by the Agency for International Development (AID), and missionary doctors. In short, American women served in a wide variety of capacities during the U.S. war in Vietnam. Sixty-eight of them—eight military nurses and sixty civilian women—did not make it home alive. By far the largest number of military women to serve "in-country" in Vietnam were nurses. Nurses made up approximately 80 percent—six thousand or so—of female military personnel who served in Vietnam.[2]

*Sisterhood of War* focuses on the experiences of fifteen nurses from Minnesota who went to war in Vietnam. It is a story of venturesome women who chose to practice their traditionally feminine career in a decidedly masculine setting. The story told in the following chapters rises to heights of excitement as they embarked on their generation's defining adventure, falls to depths of despair as they experienced the carnage of war, ascends again as they eagerly left the war zone and returned home, only to descend once more as they encountered public hostility, institutional indifference, and psychological stress in the aftermath of war. It ends somewhere between these peaks and valleys as they found some measure of peace through their participation in a support group for nurse war veterans and their work on behalf of the Vietnam Women's Memorial. The embrace of women Vietnam veterans by the American public that had taken place at the 1993 dedication of the Memorial had represented the culmination of these women's long search for identity as veterans. Although this search had become explicit with the launching of the Vietnam Women's Memorial Project in 1984, it had begun years before as women grappled with the conflicts inherent not just in being veterans of such a divisive war but in being women who had gone to war.[3]

This book has its origins in a study I had planned to conduct about military women who had been part of the antiwar G.I. movement during the Vietnam War. In my search for women to interview, I posted a message about my project to an online group of women Vietnam veterans. Within twenty-four hours, eight women responded and said they would be happy to talk to me—but they didn't know anything about the antiwar G.I. movement, in fact had never heard of it. Why had these women responded so quickly and been so eager to share their stories, even when they weren't about the topic I had identified? As I began to contact the women who had responded, it was clear they felt that their contributions to the war had faded into the background of the dominant narrative that focused on male veterans.[4]

After transforming this original interest into a study of Minnesota women who had served in Vietnam as nurses, I again encountered among the women I interviewed an eager willingness to share their stories, even if they did not relish reliving their wartime experiences. They wanted to provide other Minnesotans with a glimpse into their lives as nurses both during and after the war and to share their stories with young people who otherwise might not look past the wrinkles of this older generation. They thought it was worth resurrecting war-related nightmares if they could ensure that women's service would be recognized and remembered. Thus the driving interest behind this project became an exploration of why women Vietnam veterans had felt so invisible for so long after the war's end. That male Vietnam veterans felt overlooked and neglected after they came home is part of the common lore of the war, but I wondered if there was something about being female that also contributed to women veterans' sense of displacement.

The answer, I learned from these women, is that being female absolutely did matter. In many ways, women in uniform blended in with their male counterparts, sharing an identity based on generation, nation, and loyalty born of a shared ordeal. But in other important ways, women's gender set them apart from the standard—i.e., male—experience as soldiers and then as veterans. Sometimes their gender had made them invisible—outnumbered and overshadowed by men, expected to adapt to the male norm in all but trivial ways. At other times, being women had made them hypervisible—objects of attention and (often unwanted) affection, emblems of home and American femininity, incomprehensible gender deviants. In either case, being female had mattered. It affected their decision to become nurses and then join the military; it shaped their experiences in Vietnam, from the jobs they did to the way they were treated by male colleagues and patients; it influenced their postwar lives because they were not assumed to be veterans at all, much less war veterans struggling with post-traumatic stress; and ultimately it mattered in how they came to terms with their wartime service. It wasn't all that mattered, but it mattered nonetheless.[5]

And in large part it mattered because, in so many ways, their identity as "women" was supposed to be something very different and separate from the other identities—as "soldiers," "citizens," "veterans"—that come into play when one goes to war. The tensions between being female and being soldiers and veterans affected military women regardless of their rank, branch of service, or job. For nurses, however, some of these contradictions were mitigated by their role as professional caregiver. Although the women I interviewed may have chosen an atypical career path for women in midcentury America by joining the military, they had also taken a common one in becoming nurses. Nursing thus allowed them to retain their feminine status in the military, even while the military afforded them opportunities not otherwise widely available to women: the chance to travel the world, experience another culture, serve their country—and go to war.[6]

The women I met had wanted to share with the men of their generation the burden of national service. So they, too, had endured the culture shock of living in a poor, war-torn country during their yearlong tours of duty. They worked long, stressful hours as they tried to repair the broken bodies of young G.I.s. They hated the violence of war but remained firmly committed to their patients. The professional selflessness of nursing led them to stifle their own emotions in deference to the well-being of the scared young men for whom they cared. In return, their male patients referred to them as "angels," symbols of home in the midst of war. Although it could be wearisome, sometimes even dangerous, to be an American woman surrounded by so many lonely young men, nurses spoke more often of the brotherly protectiveness of male G.I.s.

For a time, nursing had also allowed these women to avoid the political fray surrounding the war. They had seen themselves as nurses first, soldiers second; their job was to heal, not to kill. It didn't matter whether the war was justified or not, because their job—saving the lives of American G.I.s—was always beyond reproach. As their year in Vietnam wore on, however, many nurses found that they could no longer insulate themselves from the political and moral questions surrounding U.S. involvement in Vietnam. By the time they came home as experienced nurses and weary war veterans, many of them, like their male counterparts, had lost faith in the war and their government.

When met with a troubling reception upon their return to the United States, wherein troops were often blamed for the failings of the war they had themselves come to doubt, the nurses I met had retreated into a long silence about their wartime experiences. They attempted to resume lives comparable to the civilian women around them. They found jobs, married, raised children, all the while doing their best to conceal their veteran status and to repress memories of their year in a war zone. By the 1980s, however, those memories had begun to bubble to the surface in unexpected and unwelcome ways, leaving many of the women veterans feeling scared and alone. Post-traumatic stress disorder (PTSD) had only recently been recognized as a bona fide mental health issue among war veterans, and what attention it received centered on combat veterans.

When the Veterans Administration (VA) proved unresponsive to women veterans' mental and physical health concerns, the nurses I interviewed turned to each other for help in dealing with lingering war-related stress. If no one else would care for the caregivers, they would do it themselves. With the help of a committed counselor at the Minneapolis VA hospital, nurses from Minnesota and Wisconsin formed a PTSD support group. They began talking about the war, about the trauma of being surrounded by war's victims on a daily basis, about the incredible sense of responsibility for their patients they had shouldered. As they began to heal on an individual, psychological level, they also began to seek recognition and reconciliation in the public sphere. In 1984—two years after the Wall had been dedicated to the nation's Vietnam veterans and the same year that a statue of three infantrymen was added to the Vietnam Veterans Memorial—women veterans from Minnesota founded the Vietnam Women's Memorial Project. They marshaled the efforts of women (and men) veterans from across the country to build a memorial to the women who had served in Vietnam. It was these collective efforts that led to the anniversary celebration in 2008, when women veterans could rest in the knowledge that their place in the national memory of the war had been secured.

The stories contained in this book are the stories of individual women, each with a unique tale to tell about her time in Vietnam. But those individual stories also represent the collective story of a tight-knit group of women who came to know and rely on each other in the aftermath of war. Most of them did not know one another while they were in Vietnam; instead, they had found each other in the mid-1980s through word-of-mouth among women looking for help in dealing with the aftereffects of war. My entry into this project came through this group some years later; my network of interviewees reflects its network of veterans. They are "Minnesota women" not because they were all born and raised here but because they formed their identities as Vietnam veterans through their associations with each other in the Twin Cities area. They are Vietnam veterans because their job was taking care of soldiers wounded in the war. Finding each other in their postwar search for community helped these women make sense of their past, united them across differences in experience and background, and charted a forward course for them as sister veterans. They still gather as a group several times a year to reconnect. They are a warm, gracious bunch who agreed to share their stories with me in interviews that lasted anywhere from two to five hours. They have welcomed me into their lives, included me in their reunions, and invited me into their homes. They held a baby shower for me when my husband and I adopted our son and brought me homemade soup while I cared for my dying mother. They have spoken at my college courses on the war and tolerated countless follow-up e-mail queries. Their courage and generosity have been inspiring.[7]

Who, then, are these women? All fifteen of them served as military nurses during the Vietnam War. All but one of them lived in Minnesota before and/or after their time in Vietnam; the other grew up and still lives in central Wisconsin. They came from small towns and large cities, working- and middle-class families, Catholic and Protestant backgrounds. Like the majority of nurses, civilian and military, and of women who went to Vietnam in the mid-1960s, they are white. Five of them were born during the early years of the baby boom that began in 1946, the rest slightly earlier than that. They came of age under the guidance of those who had survived the Great Depression and won the Good War. The America of their youth was a nation defined by contradiction, where proclamations of freedom and equality rested uneasily against the realities of Jim Crow segregation; in which unprecedented prosperity accompanied increasing poverty; when happy conformity to the "American Dream" concealed brewing dissatisfaction among women, gays and lesbians, and cultural rebels; and in which claims of America's inherent moral righteousness would shatter on the shores of a tiny country half a world away. They landed squarely in the middle of their generation's cultural zeitgeist, both participants in and observers of the social, cultural, and political changes afoot in sixties America.

The women whose stories are told here had joined the military nurse corps—twelve signed on with the Army Nurse Corps, two with the Navy Nurse Corps, and one with the Air Force Nurse Corps—for a variety of reasons, including to help pay for nursing school, to share with their brothers the obligation of serving their nation, and to put their nursing skills to good use on behalf of American wounded. Two of them had become military nurses in 1958, before most Americans had ever even heard of Vietnam. The rest joined the corps in the 1960s. The first to go to Vietnam arrived in September 1965, just six months after the Marines had landed in Da Nang. The last of them to leave Vietnam came home in 1971, as U.S. ground troops were gradually withdrawing so that the war could be "Vietnamized." Thirteen of them served one-year tours at hospitals in South Vietnam, from the southernmost tip of the country to just below the demilitarized zone (DMZ); one served two one-year tours in Vietnam, and another worked at the U.S. Naval Hospital on Guam for eighteen months. All nurses were commissioned officers, and while some of the women in this study left the military when their two-year commitment expired, some opted to expand their military service. Two women rejoined the Army Nurse Corps after their original discharge, and six women served anywhere from five to twenty years in the Reserves. Eleven of them acknowledged having suffered some degree of PTSD, and the majority of them helped in some way to build the Vietnam Women's Memorial. It was through their efforts to deal with PTSD and build the Memorial that these individual women had become a group of sisters.

And it is their stories that drive the narrative of the book. Such a focus distinguishes *Sisterhood of War* from other literature about women Vietnam veterans. Though this book is based on oral history interviews, it is more than a collection of edited interview transcripts. And although all of these women were military nurses, this book is not a history of nursing, the military, or even military nursing. Other fine books tackle all of these issues. Instead, this book weaves the strands of individual women's stories into a collective whole and locates them within a broader historical context. We get to know these nurses; we see them evolve from spirited young women into isolated war survivors and then proud Vietnam veterans. We come to understand how history shaped them and how they shaped history. As such, we realize that their stories are the story of an entire generation, told through the unique tale of a specific group of women.[8]

We can learn a lot from these women. On the most basic level, we learn a new story about the Vietnam War. Nurses' stories are as dramatic as any combat veteran's. They engaged in life-and-death struggles, if in the operating room rather than on the battlefield. They confronted the quandary of how to behave morally in the morally ambiguous context of war. Is it worth it to save a young man's life if he would have to live that life without his limbs, or vision, or sexual function? Is it right to restore a G.I.'s health enough so that he could be sent back into battle, thus risking his life all over again? Is it okay to provide the same level of care for a captured Vietnamese enemy as for a wounded American soldier? The women formed strong bonds with the colleagues with whom they shared the burden of mending the wounds of war, hour after hour, day after day, month after month. They, too, lost their youthful idealism and faith in American leaders as they discovered the gap between what officials claimed was happening in the war and what they saw in front of them. In short, theirs are compelling war stories.

But rather than simply offering slight adjustments to the dominant, male-centered story, these are stories with more substantial differences, too, because they are women's stories. As the following chapters will show, nurses' experiences were both similar to and different from men's; their gender affected them positively at times, negatively at other times, and sometimes not at all. Accordingly, this book suggests that gender is not the tidy identity we sometimes assume it to be. We give gender too much credit if we view it as the sole determinant of an individual's experience of war, but too little if we grant it no role whatsoever. Nurses' stories are not merely interesting additions to men's stories of the war—though they are that. They are also part and parcel of the war story itself.

We also learn something about the nature of storytelling. Any work that relies on oral history as a research method engages issues surrounding the fallibilities of memory. Memories fade and change, stories are lost to the ravages of time or become solidified in the retelling. Some of the women I interviewed were sharing their war experiences for the first time. Others were seasoned narrators, having told their stories numerous times over the years. Some recounted tales that have been widely reported in other literature and confirmed by research, while others described events that seemed hard to believe and were, anyway, impossible to verify. Although the stories recounted here are intended to be read as nonfiction, we would do well to heed the distinction Vietnam veteran and author Tim O'Brien draws between "happening-truth" and "story-truth." Happening-truth, he writes, is the literal truth of occurrence. Story-truth, on the other hand, is the emotional truth of subjective experience.[9]

While oral historians must attend to the literal facts of occurrence and weed out blatant falsities in a way that a novelist need not, the value of the method is lost if that becomes the only focus. As oral historian Alessandro Portelli writes, "Oral sources tell us not just what people did, but what they wanted to do, what they believed they were doing, and what they now think they did." Historical narratives built from personal memories, even erroneous ones, are "themselves events, clues for the work of desire and pain over time." In the case of nurses who served in Vietnam, even the most incredible-seeming, unverifiable stories tell us something about how these women have come to understand their wartime and postwar lives. Those stories may be factually accurate as well, however. Sometimes story-truth and happening-truth are one and the same. Truth doesn't always depend on plausibility and verifiability, especially in the chaotic setting of war.[10]

More timely lessons can be gained from these women as well. At the time of this book's writing, the war in Afghanistan was on the verge of supplanting Vietnam as the United States' lengthiest war, even while the drawdown in Iraq continues. Women are serving in greater numbers and in a wider variety of capacities in the wars in the Middle East than they did in Vietnam. Though these wars have provided greater opportunities for uniformed women, they have also led to increased risk: women are more directly involved in combat, and sexual harassment and assault continue to be serious problems in the U.S. military. It seems that the more involved in combat women become and the further they get from traditionally feminine jobs, the higher their risk of sexual assault. Add to these stressors the persistent cultural stereotypes about women in uniform, and today's military women still face a daunting set of challenges. Although the military and the Department of Veterans Affairs are making increased efforts to help veterans, male and female, deal with trauma-related stress, women still frequently struggle in silent anonymity.

Though the wars are different and the context has changed, women Vietnam veterans understand what it is to feel isolated in their fear. *Sisterhood of War* tells how they were able to break free from that isolation by reaching out to each other. They built a network of support where none had existed because no one else would do it for them. Today's women veterans may find this story useful, as it offers hope that recovery from war and trauma, however halting and hard won, is possible.

One of the key events at the fifteenth anniversary celebration of the Vietnam Women's Memorial in 2008 was storytelling. From nine o'clock in the morning until five o'clock in the evening, with a two-hour break for the ceremony at the Wall, women (and a handful of men) Vietnam veterans gathered at the statue to share their war stories with the crowd. They spoke about their time in Vietnam and their struggles after the war; they spoke as nurses and line officers and Red Cross workers. Some of them spoke because they were asked to, others because they wanted to. They all spoke because they had to, because in telling their stories, they confirmed their own existence and validated their own identities. And with the sharing of their stories—whether they stood in front of the microphone that day or had gathered in a support group years before—they were healing themselves. Letting go of the memories they once held so closely to their hearts released them from their burden, for a burden shared is a burden relieved. As Tim O'Brien has written, "Stories can save us." They save us by bringing the dead back to life, even when the dead are the selves we once were and may never be again. By telling our stories, however, that former self—the young, the innocent, the unscarred—can become part of who we are now. For nurses who served in Vietnam, the war was a transformative experience in their lives, the dividing point between who they once were and who they became. For a long time, it had seemed impossible to integrate their "before" and "after" selves. Telling their stories about the war helped them do so. The following chapters share the stories of fifteen women whose experiences, together with those of thousands of other women Vietnam veterans across the nation, are the story behind the Vietnam Women's Memorial.[11]

# 1

## "I Knew I Had Something I Could Contribute"

### Nurses and Soldiers

**VALERIE BUCHAN** is a soft-spoken woman whose reserved exterior belies her venturesome spirit. In a crowd, Buchan tends to dwell in the background, doing more listening than talking. When she does speak, however, she is forthright and good humored. She seemed younger than her seventy years when I met her in 2005 in her quiet apartment in St. Paul. Three years later she was in Washington, D.C., for the fifteenth anniversary of the Vietnam Women's Memorial. From September 1968 to September 1969, Valerie Buchan worked as an Army nurse at the 12th Evacuation Hospital in Cu Chi, Vietnam. She spent a total of twenty-one and a half years in the Army and Army Reserves, retiring with the rank of colonel.

This chapter explores the factors that inspired women such as Buchan to become nurses and then to become soldiers. As girls growing up in an era of gradually escalating change, they were surrounded by mixed messages, some telling them that their future destinies were at home with husband and children, others modeling the possibilities for independence and personal achievement. A combination of idealistic notions and practical considerations, shaped by both family and culture, led these women to nursing, the military, and, eventually, Vietnam. Buchan's recollections of her path to war revealed themes that emerged in many military nurses' stories.

Born in 1935, Valerie Buchan grew up on a farm in Henning, Minnesota. While her father tended the fields, her mother worked as a teacher in a small country school. Even as a little girl, Buchan knew she wanted to be a nurse. She recalled seeing an ad for a nursing program in her church bulletin that featured a beautiful nurse "standing in a ray of sunlight." Instantly, Buchan knew that she, too, wanted to be a nurse. In June 1954, she began the official pursuit of this long-held dream when she enrolled in Hamline University's three-year nursing diploma program. After graduating in 1957, she worked for nine years as a nurse, during which time the Cold War standoff between the United States and Soviet Union escalated dramatically. Fearing, even hating, communism seemed as American as apple pie and baseball, and Buchan and her family were good Americans. They and their fellow citizens in Henning firmly believed that the United States was the "best place in the world" and that communism posed a very serious threat to their way of life.

No wonder, then, that Buchan "never had a second thought about going to Vietnam." When she began getting letters from the armed forces in late 1965, asking her to help care for wounded soldiers, she didn't hesitate. Despite the fact that some people believed military women to be "immoral," "sexually loose," defeminized women who used bad language, Buchan responded to the Army's entreaties by joining its nurse corps in 1966. "It was a personal means of doing some service for my country," she said. "We were all girls in our family. We didn't have any brothers to go. So I thought it was my job to do that. I knew I had something that I could contribute."

### From Florence Nightingale to Cherry Ames: Becoming Nurses

What did little girls in postwar America dream of becoming when they grew up? For many, the vision of their future lives included a husband, children, and a comfortable home. Raised by parents who had suffered the privations of the Great Depression, baby boomer children grew up in a culture that, understandably, valued material comfort and the security of family life; for girls, this usually meant being a housewife. Still, like Valerie Buchan, many women who served in Vietnam knew from an early age that they wanted to be nurses, too. Their heads were filled with romantic images of nurses as angels in white, tenderly caring for those in need. "I don't ever remember not wanting to be a nurse," recalled Edy (Thompson)

Johnson of her midwestern childhood. As a young girl, she would ask her mother to make a nurse's hat for her out of tissue and pin it in her hair: "I thought they must be angels, and I wanted to be an angel." This Florence Nightingale, "lady with the lamp" persona took on a more modern glow in two popular novel series aimed at girls in midcentury America. Nurses Sue Barton and Cherry Ames encountered romance and adventure as they tended to the ill and injured, adding a touch of glamour to the image of nurses as gentle caregivers. Mary Breed remembered that she and her girlfriends in Brooklyn Center "were all reading" Cherry Ames, drawn in by the combination of high adventure and merciful caregiving. "I'm laughing to this day at what this [fictional] nurse did," she said. "So we all wanted to be nurses."

The desire to be a nurse was not a substitute for the home and family that so many girls also wanted, however. Indeed, one of the attractions of nursing was that it allowed women both job and family. For Buchan and Johnson, the shift work that was part of the nursing life meant that they could tend to children during the day and work at night. Mary O'Brien Tyrrell also envisioned a future that combined nursing and family. "When I grow up," she had declared as an elementary school student in Mankato, Minnesota, "I want to be a nurse and when my husband dies, I want to go back and be a nurse again." Tyrrell's second-grade view of the life that awaited her reflected middle-class Americans' ideas about women's relative roles as workers and wives: they could be workers until they married, at which point they would devote their energies to being wives. Nevertheless, it also was an expression of her personal desire to have a career of her own, and a recognition that a woman needed to have a backup plan in case something happened to her husband.

In many ways, the women in this study represented the "average" American nurse of the mid-twentieth century: mostly white young women who came from working- or middle-class Christian families and earned three-year nursing diplomas. They were products of a culture that suggested that proper women were to marry young and stay home to raise children. If they were to work outside the home at all, it was only to supplement their husbands' income so that the family could achieve middle-class status. Their jobs—as waitresses, or cashiers, or maids—were to be secondary to their primary roles as wife and mother. Yet this cultural rhetoric was undercut by a reality that was more complex, one in which women's income was crucial to the survival of the family and in which women embraced their professional identities as much as their maternal roles. In both cases, the women I interviewed described as role models female family members who successfully combined work and family, in spite of cultural, and sometimes familial, discouragement.[1]

Despite popular media images to the contrary, most of the women I interviewed had mothers who combined paid work, either consistently or intermittently, with child care duties. The postwar period saw significant increases in the number of women who worked outside the home, especially among married women with children. Still, day care facilities were virtually nonexistent in the 1950s, and so women with large families often had to delay their entry into the workforce until the children were in school. Kay (Wilhelmy) Bauer's mother, for example, stayed home to rear her fourteen children in St. Paul, taking part-time jobs here and there as needed for extra income. Edy Johnson's and Mary O'Brien Tyrrell's mothers, with eight and seven children respectively, worked on and off according to the ebb and flow of child-rearing demands. Even women with fewer children tended to stay home while their children were small before returning to work they had enjoyed prior to becoming mothers. Valerie Buchan's mother had been a teacher but took an eleven-year sabbatical while her three daughters were young. Once they were all in school, however, she returned to teaching full time. Buchan's mother's income contributed to the family's middle-class standing, as did the earnings of Diane Carlson Evans's mother. Evans grew up on a dairy farm in Buffalo, Minnesota, and her mother worked full time outside of the home as a registered nurse. "We had a working mother, and all our friends didn't," Evans recalled. "She worked because, I think, she felt she had to. She had six kids, and she wanted a good life for us." She also loved nursing, however, and practiced it with a passion. For increasing numbers of women during the 1940s and 1950s, professional work became a source not only of income but also of self-development and pride.[2]

Working-class families relied on women's income as a matter of survival, however. Although the middle-class ethos was so prevalent in the postwar United States that even children who grew up in poor or working-class families often didn't see themselves as poor, their parents confronted the economic realities head on. This usually meant that mothers had no choice but to work, regardless of whether such paid employment provided personal fulfillment. Army nurse veteran Donna-Marie (D-M) Boulay's parents both worked in the textile industry in rural Massachusetts, but being poor was "absolutely not" part of her self-consciousness as a child; it wasn't until many years later that she came to the realization that her family was "very poor." Lynn Bower's family also relied on her mother's earnings. Finding ways to care for their young children presented Bower's parents with a challenge, but nursing provided her mother with a way to balance both child rearing and gainful employment: for a number of years, she cared for terminally ill children in her own home. Bower served as an informal nurse's assistant for her mother. As a junior high student, she couldn't participate in any after-school activities because she had to come home and help tend to sick children ranging in age from infancy to eight years. Over the years, Bower had "eleven foster brothers and sisters who all eventually died" from their illnesses. "It was just the way life was, and you just did it," she remembered.

Like Bower, many daughters also worked, both outside and inside the home. Employment rates for teenagers began to rise after the end of World War II. Mary O'Brien Tyrrell was one of the growing number of teenage girls who held part-time jobs while still in school. She started working as a nurse's assistant in eighth grade but left that job as a senior in high school to take a higher-paying position with the telephone company, where she worked four to six hours a night after school. She saved most of her earnings for her college education. Daughters' work within families reflected both practical necessity and cultural ideas about gender. When asked if there were different expectations for boys and girls within their families, most women responded by talking about household duties. For those who grew up on farms, work was constant. Although girls were assigned household chores rather than duties in barn or field, they worked as long and as hard as their fathers and brothers. "Everything on a farm is hard," Diane Carlson Evans explained. "There really is no such thing as women's work and men's work." Women who grew up in urban or suburban homes also recalled that household duties were generally allocated along gender lines but that both boys and girls contributed to the functioning of the household.[3]

Despite differences in household chores, most of the women I interviewed recalled that their parents treated them and their brothers fairly equitably. Such messages about gender egalitarianism often began in the examples parents set for their children. Mary Lu (Ostergren) Brunner's mother and father both worked outside the home, her father as a box cutter at Flour City Paper Box Company in North Minneapolis and her mother in various restaurants and grocery stores in their South Minneapolis neighborhood. After long days at work, her parents shared the cooking and cleaning responsibilities at home. Ann (Benson) Rudolph's parents both had degrees from St. Olaf College in Northfield, Minnesota, and expected Rudolph and her two younger brothers to attend college as well. In other families, postsecondary education for girls was considered practical, a safeguard against economic hardship and life's unforeseen challenges. Even though Lynn Bower's parents assumed she would marry and have a family, they encouraged her to pursue some kind of vocational training because "*never* could you depend on your husband to support you. It wasn't like you'll marry a bum, but it was more that something might happen and you've got to be prepared, so you've got to have something that you can do."

Of course, not every woman I met had parents with such liberal-minded ideas about girls' education. Penny Kettlewell and her two brothers grew up in Midland, Texas. From an early age, her parents told her that they couldn't afford to put both her and her brothers through college so she would have to pay her own tuition. She said that this arrangement seemed unfair, "but it was a fact of life." Fortunately for Kettlewell, her grandmother provided her with support and inspiration: "She was the kind of woman that just said, 'You can do anything. You don't have to be a man to make it in this world.'" With her grandmother as a role model, Kettlewell went on to put herself through nursing school, join the Army Nurse Corps, and serve two tours in Vietnam.

Thus, the decision to pursue nursing satisfied many desires: it was a fulfillment of a childhood dream, it would offer an economic safety net, and it would provide enough flexibility to raise a family. Nursing also was one of the few vocations—along with teaching and secretarial work—that women could pursue without violating too many cultural taboos. It was considered by many an extension of women's supposedly natural caregiving skills, only instead of caring for husband and children at home, they would care for patients in hospitals or clinics. Indeed, as nineteenth-century nursing pioneer Florence Nightingale declared, "Every woman is a nurse."[4]

Whatever "natural" tendencies toward caregiving women may have had, cultural and institutional pressures also steered them toward activities deemed appropriate for women. Mary Lu Brunner attended a Catholic girls' high school in Minneapolis that did little to encourage its students to pursue careers in fields such as medicine, law, or science. "I don't remember being offered a whole lot of other ideas," she recalled. "I just said, 'Well, I'm not ready to get married. Don't want to be a nun.'" Air Force veteran Bobby Smith outlined the possibilities for women in postwar America as she recalled them: "Either you got married and raised kids, or you were a secretary, a teacher, or a nurse."

Assumptions about what constituted appropriate work for women combined with a national nurse shortage to make nursing an especially viable career option for women in the years following World War II. As the hospital industry blossomed, the need for nurses was severe; in contrast to women who had taken jobs in factories during the war, nurses were encouraged to keep working at war's end. There was always a job for a nurse. Even Edy Johnson, the aspiring angel in white, realized the practical benefits of being a nurse. Johnson's father wanted her to be an artist, but she insisted that she needed a job that would allow her to help support a family. Penny Kettlewell recalled her beloved grandmother's advice: "I went to nursing school because my grandmother said 'Be a nurse. You'll always have a job. Then you can do what you want because you'll be able to make some money.'" Although becoming a nurse almost guaranteed employment, it did not guarantee a life of luxury. By 1962, the average salary for nurses was $3,900 a year, less than that for both factory workers and teachers. Nurses were not entitled to unemployment insurance, overtime pay, Social Security coverage, or collective bargaining rights.[5]

Despite these inequities, nursing was an appealing job option for many women. The first step to achieving this goal was nursing school. In the years after World War II, as the number of hospitals and demand for nurses increased, most nurses-in-training attended three-year diploma schools. Unlike the baccalaureate (BSN) programs that were housed in four-year colleges and universities and focused on classroom work, diploma schools were affiliated with hospitals and much of the training they offered was hands-on work in the hospital; upon graduation, students of both programs became registered nurses (RNs). Although supporters of four-year programs criticized diploma schools for exploiting their students as a cheap source of labor and emphasizing manual skills over intellectual capabilities, most acknowledged that diploma programs turned out competent nurses who integrated easily into staff positions in hospitals. The main reason women chose diploma programs over baccalaureate programs, however, was that they were cheaper. Even for middle-class families, financing a college education was no small task, and most parents couldn't afford (or, in Kettlewell's case, weren't willing) to pay for their daughters' educations. Former Army nurse Joan (Schlichting) Paulson was one of the few women in this sample whose parents *did* finance her nurses' training, but only on the condition that she would repay them after she found employment. Completing training in three years meant that a diploma nurse could enter the workforce a whole year earlier than those who obtained a college degree.[6]

One of the first things students learned at nursing school was the reality behind the romanticized vision of nursing. Women who grew up reading about the adventures of Cherry Ames or the romantic legacy of Florence Nightingale were often surprised at what nursing actually entailed. "My idea of being a nurse was walking around behind a doctor with an arm full of charts," recalled Bobby Smith with a chuckle. "It never occurred to me that there were things like bedpans." Mary Breed volunteered as a candy striper at the Minneapolis Veterans Administration (VA) Hospital precisely because she wanted to put to the test the idealized vision of nursing that the Cherry Ames books promoted. This proved to be an "eye-opening" experience: "It was the first time I saw a naked man," she said laughingly. "The poor little soul was wandering around without his clothes on. You're young and you learn." Still, the experience convinced her that she wanted to be a nurse.

*Like Valerie Buchan, many women who served in Vietnam knew from an early age that they wanted to be nurses.*

Once they made the commitment to continuing their education, students were put through the paces of rigorous rotations and busy daily schedules during which they learned how to nurse. Between attending classes and working in the hospital, students had limited free time. What little they did enjoy was often as regulated as their work hours. Hospital-based diploma programs required students to live in dormitories on or near the hospital grounds. Student nurses' comings and goings could thus be tracked, as could those of their male visitors. Nearly all of the women I interviewed lived in dormitories while they were completing their diploma programs. "It was all single women in a dorm. It was like a nunnery," Mary Breed recalled of her living situation. "It was separation and it was a very controlled environment." Valerie Buchan enjoyed dorm life as it offered her the chance to meet people from all around Minnesota. Whether they liked it or hated it, the regimented environment of the nursing school dormitory prepared these women well for life in a military barracks.[7]

*Fun, Travel, and Adventure: Becoming Soldiers*

Donning the starched white uniform of civilian nursing in post-war America was one thing, but trading in that outfit for the dress blues or greens of military life was quite another. It was true that Florence Nightingale and her fictional counterpart Cherry Ames had both plied their trade on the battlefield and tens of thousands of American women had served as military nurses during World War II. In fact, it was as nurses that women were first officially allowed into the ranks of the U.S. military, with the establishment of the Army Nurse Corps (ANC) in 1901 and the Navy Nurse Corps (NNC) in 1908. If women were going to be soldiers or sailors, they would do so in a capacity considered to be appropriately feminine. "Nurse" was an identity that most viewed as compatible with womanhood; "soldier" was an identity so closely associated with manhood and masculinity that military leaders and policymakers viewed it as inherently incompatible—or downright contradictory—with being female. If a woman could combine those two identities as a nurse-soldier, however, she could preserve some of her good standing as a woman even while wearing the military uniform. Even so, joining the military took women one step farther away from the stereotypical path they were expected to follow. The Minnesota nurses signed on for myriad reasons both idealistic and practical: a patriotic desire to share in the obligation of serving their country, a commitment to putting their skills to use where needed most acutely, an interest in seeing the world and having adventures, a need to find a way to pay for their final year(s) of nursing school. As Ann Rudolph recalled of her decision to join, "It was an adventure and it was a job."[8]

Women never have been technically obliged to render their services—nursing or otherwise—to the military. While men in the United States have been subjected to compulsory military service, women's civic obligations have been conceived of as duty to family, and their entry into the male-dominated world of the military was not easy. Although women had been allowed to serve as nurses at the beginning of the twentieth century, it was not until 1944 that they achieved full military status. Military policies also explicitly dictated the kinds of women who could serve: married, pregnant, or, until 1918, African American women were not allowed in the ANC. By 1947, however, the

Army and Navy Nurse Corps had become permanent staff corps of their respective service branches, and in 1949, the newly independent Air Force founded its own nurse corps. Despite their increasing acceptance and necessity in the military, nurses were often in greater demand than supply. When Valerie Buchan joined the Army Nurse Corps in 1966, the military—and the nation—was once again facing a shortage of nurses. As a result, the military nurse corps launched a two-pronged effort to attract nurses: it enhanced student nurse training programs and initiated a publicity campaign that focused on the financial and patriotic rewards of military nursing.[9]

Women in search of financial independence from their families found the military's tuition-payment program appealing. In 1965, for example, Joan Paulson was in her junior year of a three-year nursing program in Rochester, Minnesota, when a recruiter for the Army Nurse Corps paid her class a visit. The focus of his pitch was the Army Student Nurse Program. Starting in 1957, the program covered nursing students' expenses for the last year or two of schooling and paid them the salary of an enlisted soldier at the same time. In return, students made a two- or three-year commitment to the ANC and received officers' commissions after graduation. When Kay Bauer joined the Navy Nurse Corps Candidate Program while a nursing student at the College of St. Catherine in 1958, the Navy was offering such assistance only to students in baccalaureate programs. In 1968, however, the NNC expanded its student nurse program to three-year diploma schools in hopes of attracting more nurses to its ranks. Eight of the nurses I interviewed joined the military at least in part to reap the rewards of its educational financing programs. Paulson spent her final year of nursing school in the Army Student Nurse Program and began her two years of active duty in August 1966 when the ANC commissioned her as a second lieutenant.[10]

Paying for nursing school was not the only reason that nurses elected to join the military. Nurses saw in military life a chance to travel, meet interesting people, and have adventures, opportunities not often afforded women in traditionally feminine professions. The Army Nurse Corps capitalized on women's increasing desire to break free of the confinements of tradition by emphasizing that Army nurses would enjoy pay, status, training, and career opportunities superior to those of civilian nurses and on par with men. Though none of the women I met described their decision to join the military as a feminist act, they did admit that the military provided them with benefits not widely available to women. As Mary Lu Brunner explained, "I thought one way to see the world was to join the military." But for many, the reasons for joining were more than personal and pragmatic. A patriotic desire to serve their country also led them to the nurse corps. The Kennedy era had inspired many young people across the nation with its youthful vigor and optimistic faith in American ideals. President John F. Kennedy's goal of spreading American-style freedom across the globe reached into homes across the land. Even—perhaps especially—after his assassination, his call to "ask not what your country can do for you, but what you can do for your country" echoed in many young women's ears, including Penny Kettlewell's. "I was in nursing school . . . right after JFK gave his big speech," she said. "And he says 'Ask not.' Oh, what can I do? What can I do? Throw myself on the altar of the country."[11]

Kennedy's call to service resonated with many young women who grew up valuing the notion of serving others. The sacrifices the World War II generation had made to preserve the American Dream for their children were not only a national story but part of family lore. Fathers and uncles had served during the war, to be sure, but so had aunts. Mary Lu Brunner, Diane Carlson Evans, and Bobby Smith all had aunts who volunteered for military service during World War II. Many nurses who ended up in Vietnam also cared for World War II veterans at VA hospitals, as volunteers, student nurses, or new RNs. Brunner worked at a VA hospital, where she remembered seeing the veteran-patients as she walked the halls of the facility and realizing that their sacrifices were the "price we pay for our freedom." Combined with her desire to travel the world and the fact that her two brothers were already serving in the Navy Reserves, the experience during her year at the VA hospital sparked her interest in military service.

This commitment to doing good for the community beyond themselves stemmed from religious beliefs as well. Whether Catholic, Lutheran, or Baptist, religion played a major role in these women's upbringings. Their families went to church regularly, reflecting the trend toward burgeoning church membership in the postwar years. Mary O'Brien Tyrrell grew up in a Catholic family and attended

Catholic schools, and it was through her family's religious practice that she first learned about service. "I consider the service that you do at a church part of what you do for your community," she said. Her mother, in particular, demonstrated the many ways one could be of service to others by doing things such as "look[ing] out for" a disabled woman from the neighborhood. Mary Breed similarly learned about her responsibility to others through her Lutheran identity and a year spent at a Bible school in California. "Out of love, you should be helping people," she explained. But this belief "causes conflict in war," she said. "It causes a lot of conflict." For others, however, religious conviction was entirely compatible with the goals of the war in Vietnam. Edy Johnson, whose father was a Lutheran pastor, remembered that spiritual calls to service were tinged with Cold War fears of "godless communism." She recalled, "We just knew that it was atheistic and that they punished people who wanted to teach their children about God."[12]

Whether or not religious beliefs informed ideas of patriotism, being an American meant something to these women. Parents passed on ideas about what it meant to be a citizen in explicit and implicit ways to sons and daughters alike. Mary Breed's father would quiz her on the day's news each night at the dinner table. Diane Carlson Evans's mother exhorted her six children to "be good citizens." Evans said, "We knew what that was just by watching our parents' example." It meant working hard, serving one's country, and "doing something outside of ourselves." Penny Kettlewell found in her father, who made a career of the Air Force, a very explicit example of service and patriotism. "Tears still come to my eyes when I listen to 'The Star Spangled Banner,'" she said. As a child growing up on military bases, she "always stopped to salute the flag every morning. And we'd stop and salute the flag when they pull it down, and it's just like 'duty, honor, country.' I grew up with all those words."

For many young men of the Vietnam War era, it wasn't necessarily duty, honor, and country that pulled them into service; it was the Selective Service System. Women faced no such prospect, however, and some of them felt uncomfortable with the difference. They wanted to share the task of military service with their draft-age brothers, boyfriends, and cousins. When Diane Carlson Evans's brothers started getting their draft notices, she "felt some guilt, obligation, duty." "If my brothers have to go, why shouldn't I?" she asked herself. Convinced that the only answer was that she, too, should serve, she joined the Army Nurse Corps in 1966. When Mary Breed's brother returned from Vietnam to the United States in 1968, he mentioned that they needed nurses in Vietnam. With this in mind, Breed was open to the pitch of the Air Force, Navy, and Army recruiters who visited her and her classmates at Swedish Hospital. She and a friend joined the ANC in 1969.

Emphasizing nurses' duty to patients was a cornerstone of the military nurse corps' recruiting pitch as well, especially as the war progressed and popular support for it dwindled. "The world's greatest patients deserve the world's greatest nurses," proclaimed one television recruiting ad. From at least 1966 to 1970, representatives of the corps published reports from the field in Vietnam in the *American Journal of Nursing.* Running under headlines such as "Back from Vietnam" and "Mercy Mission to Saigon," these articles highlighted the romanticized drama of war and portrayed nurses as angels of mercy and emissaries of good will. The aim of such stories was to convince nurses that nursing in Vietnam was demanding, rewarding, and noble. Relatively little attention was paid to U.S. policy in Vietnam, especially in the early years of the war. It was assumed that the U.S. military—and especially its medical personnel—was engaged in a just cause.[13]

As the war dragged on, however, and the antiwar movement gained strength, it became more difficult to separate the issues of nursing and the war. Military representatives deflected attention from questions about the morality of war policy by focusing on the inherent morality of nursing: regardless of the justness of U.S. intervention, a nurse's duty was always beyond reproach. A nurse could only be chastised for failing to perform her duties. "Nurses who refuse to recognize the need for nurses in Vietnam are literally denying our American fighting men the right to professional nurse care," wrote ANC recruiter Major Betty J. Antilla in October 1969. "Why must there be such difficulty in persuading nurses to share in the defense of their country?"[14]

Other nurse corps recruiters were more attuned to the growing antiwar consciousness, even in the nursing community. By 1968—with public sentiment turning against the war after the Tet Offensive in January and the antiwar movement in full swing—it was absolutely critical for recruiters to figure out a way to attract nurses to the corps without having to resort to the moral righteousness of the war itself. Accordingly, recruiters emphasized nurses' duty to the nation as defined by caring for ill and wounded male soldiers—"brothers, cousins, fathers"—rather than to national policy or political leaders. Kay Bauer was assigned to recruiting duty for the Navy Nurse Corps in the Twin Cities area in 1968, one year after her return from Vietnam. "I think all war is wrong," she told me. "I always have." But for her, nursing was a way of combating the consequences of war, and that's how she pitched the NNC to potential recruits: "What I said was, 'OK, I don't care whether you're for or against war. It doesn't bother me at all. What I want to know is, do you have brothers, cousins, fathers over there fighting? Who's taking care of them?'" For women like Mary Breed, whose brother had served in Vietnam, this was more than just rhetoric. Breed remembered discussing her decision to join the military with a critic of the war who "told me that I would be a killer, and I would prolong the war. My answer to most people in those days was, 'Well, my brother was over there and someone took care of him.'" Just as being a nurse balanced the identities of "woman" and "soldier," it also allowed women to maintain their antiwar convictions even while wearing the uniform. Nursing in war was an apolitical act of humanity.

Still, some of the very brothers for whom military nurses were to care were less than supportive of their sisters' decisions to join the military. Diane Carlson Evans had signed on in part to share with her brothers the obligation to serve their country. Her oldest brother had quit high school to join the military, and in 1966 another brother was drafted into service. When Evans told her family that she, too, had enlisted, her brothers were displeased. "They did not want their sister in the Army," she recalled. She believed her brothers were concerned for her welfare more than anything else. Upon hearing that a third child—a daughter this time—was entering the military, Evans's father was not happy, either. He was so upset that he "couldn't speak." He pounded his fist on the table and "got up out of his chair and he walked out the door and went down to the barn." In contrast, her mother, who was a nurse herself, was very "understanding."[15]

There were reasons besides concern that family members opposed women's decision to join the military; sometimes such criticism reflected cultural stereotypes about military women. Valerie Buchan attributed the belief that military women were immoral and masculine to people who "did not want women to progress and be able to have some of the benefits of the military that were available to the men." When Kay Bauer told her family she had joined the Navy in 1958, her mother was supportive but her father was not. "Good women do not join the military. Do not darken my door again," he told her. "I said, 'Okay, I won't.' So I left." Bauer went back to her nursing school dormitory and, a week later, her father telephoned and admitted that he "shouldn't have said that." He, like many fathers of daughters in uniform, eventually became very proud of her service.

Fortunately, other women received unqualified support from friends and family, especially from those who were veterans themselves. Mary Beth Crowley's father, who by this time was nearing the end of his thirty-year career in the Army Reserves, swore her in as a second lieutenant in the ANC when she graduated from nursing school. Lynn Bower's father, who had served in World War II but never talked about his wartime experiences, was pleased to hear that his daughter had chosen to join the military. Ann Rudolph said that her parents "thought it was a great idea, especially my dad. He was a Marine, and loyalty to country was very important to him and still is to this day." Although she and her parents were excited at her decision, the full implications of it hadn't yet dawned on them. "The thought of my going in the military and possibly ending up in a war never passed my mind," she said.

### In the Line of Duty: Getting Orders for Vietnam

When Rudolph joined the ANC in 1962, Vietnam was not on most Americans' radar screens; events in Cuba and at home seemed more pressing. The situation in Vietnam did not factor into her decision to join the military at all. Nursing school was also all consuming for many students, leaving little time to contemplate—or even keep up with—events outside the hospital, much less across the globe. By the mid-sixties, however, the war was hitting home for many Americans, even busy nursing students. Donna-Marie Boulay had finished a three-year nursing program in 1963 and then went on to complete her BSN at Boston College in January 1966. By then, the United States was involved in a very hot, if undeclared, war in Vietnam. In February 1965, the Johnson administration had opened an air war against North Vietnam; a month later, on March 8, 1965, the Marines landed in Da Nang, South Vietnam. By the end of 1965, more than 180,000 American troops were stationed in Vietnam.

One of Boulay's childhood friends, Stanley, was among the first wave of Marines to arrive in Da Nang. Stanley was "a little guy," about four years younger than Boulay, who had lived near her aunt and uncle and whom she had taught to fish. Stanley had joined the Marines after graduating from high school. While Boulay was working as a nurse and attending classes at Boston College, Stanley was training for war. Boulay remembered going home to Dracut, Massachusetts, for Christmas in 1965. Stanley, not yet twenty years old, had by this time returned from Vietnam "with a plate in his head." Boulay felt she "had an obligation to people like Stanley" even though she had always been a pacifist: "I was torn between using my skills for my country that was engaged in war versus using my skills for people like Stanley. Well, the people like Stanley won in my head, so I decided I wanted to go to Vietnam." For Boulay, the war in Vietnam had become very personal, and she joined the ANC so that she could help wounded G.I.s. "I viewed it as a place to work," she told me. "I was a nurse who was in the Army." Boulay joined the Army because it was the only branch of service that could guarantee assignment to Vietnam.

All nurses who joined the military were commissioned as officers. Once they had either finished school and accepted their commission or joined the military after having worked as civilian nurses, the first stop was basic training. Basic training introduced them to the military way of life, but the women I interviewed retained their primary identification as nurses and saw their main obligation as that of caring for their patients. Army nurses attended a six-week basic training course at Fort Sam Houston in Texas; Navy nurses learned "the Navy way of doing things," as Kay Bauer described it, in Newport, Rhode Island. If nursing school had broadened the perspectives of women like Valerie Buchan by exposing them to new people and places, basic training was an even more exciting experience. As Edy Johnson said of her time at Fort Sam, "it was just a riot. It was an adventure."

Women traveled from all over the country to Texas and Rhode Island to learn about military life. They learned military terminology, hierarchy, and protocol; they learned how to march and salute; and they practiced some basic military field nursing skills, such as creating emergency airways on anesthetized goats. Those women who, like Buchan and Ann Rudolph, were comfortable with regimentation adjusted easily to military life. Others, such as Bauer and Mary O'Brien Tyrrell, challenged what Bauer called the "silly" rules and regulations and made the transition less smoothly. Still, as Buchan explained, even after surviving basic, "Nursing is your main thing."[16]

Once basic training had been completed, nurses were assigned to their first military duty station. Some of them worked at stateside military hospitals; others, like Buchan, were sent overseas, but not to Vietnam. Buchan spent two years in Japan before requesting orders for Vietnam in 1968. Others received orders for Vietnam almost immediately after basic. The women I met reacted in a variety of ways to the news that they would be going to the war zone: some had joined the military specifically so they could go to Vietnam, while others signed on only because they believed they had been assured they would not have to serve in the war zone. Still others viewed such an assignment as part of the job. Ann Rudolph had been married for only two months when she received her orders for Vietnam in fall 1965. She and her husband were unhappy that she had to go, but she viewed it as her duty. "I knew I had a responsibility to pay back my two years," she explained, "and if you had orders to Vietnam, you were going to go to Vietnam."

Mary Beth Crowley was working at Walter Reed Army Medical Center when she received her orders in January 1970. By this time, President Richard Nixon's policy of Vietnamization—withdrawing U.S. ground troops from Vietnam so that the Army of the Republic of Vietnam (ARVN) could assume responsibility for more of the fighting—had been in effect for about a year, and no other nurses at Walter Reed had received orders for Vietnam in several months. Crowley began thinking about completing her two-year obligation to the military in the Washington, D.C., area. One Friday morning, however, her supervisor delivered the news: Crowley was going to Vietnam. At this point, she said, she still believed the United States was "doing some good" in Vietnam, and so she accepted her orders with little hesitation. Joan Paulson, on the other hand, "burst into tears" when she got her orders in 1967. She had finished one year of her two-year obligation to the ANC, working in obstetrics: "I just started crying, and I said, 'I've been delivering babies. What the hell am I going to do in Vietnam?'" As was the case for Paulson, Lynn Kohl's recruiter had told her that nurses would not be assigned to Vietnam unless they volunteered; in fact, this was the condition on which Kohl had agreed to join the ANC in the first place. When she got her orders while stationed at Fort Ord, California, she was upset: "I went to my commanding officer and I explained to her the mistake. 'I didn't sign.' And she just sat there and had a grin on her face and said, 'And did you get that in writing, Lieutenant?'" Kohl arrived in Vietnam in June 1969.

Although some nurses thus greeted the news of their impending deployment to Vietnam with resignation or outrage, others were happy to receive word that they would be sent somewhere they could put their nursing skills to use. Edy Johnson, D-M Boulay, Diane Carlson Evans, Mary Breed, Mary O'Brien Tyrrell, and Valerie Buchan all wanted to go to Vietnam. Nevertheless, actually being ordered into a war zone could be chilling. When Johnson received her orders in February 1968, it hit her hard, even though she wanted to go. "This must be what it feels like to stand up in court and hear a death sentence," she remembered thinking.[17]

Some forty years after they were ordered to Vietnam, many women, now parents and grandparents themselves, wondered how the news affected their parents. At the time, they hadn't considered how worried their parents would be about sending a daughter to war. They were focused on saying their good-byes to family and friends, on packing for a one-year "adventure" in a war zone, and in some cases, on writing wills—just in case something should happen. Some parents made their concerns known. When Boulay told her mother she was going to Vietnam, "Mother was convinced she was never going to see her baby again—and she didn't. I went over a baby; I came home," Boulay paused, "a grownup." Diane Carlson Evans remembered saying good-bye to her father in August 1968: "He hugged me and he said, 'I have four sons, but I send my daughter off to war,' and he started to cry." She waited a moment before continuing. "That was all he said, but it was profound, and it never left me."

Nurses who went to Vietnam both conformed to and rebelled against the cultural, economic, and familial dictates of their generation, dictates that were themselves undergoing transformation in a society in flux. Wartime military service had long been considered a male rite of passage, comparable, some argued, to the female rite of passage of giving birth. Yet the same society that told them that their duty, as women, was to stay home and tend to family also told them that their duty, as nurses, was to put their skills to use in caring for young men battling against communism in Vietnam. While most women reconciled those two calls to service through activities in domestic settings or civilian work, the women whose stories are recounted here put them together in joining the military and going to Vietnam. There, they would use their nursing skills to care for a family of soldiers (some of whom were literal brothers) and, by extension, the American family as a whole.[18]

Valerie Buchan had been tending to her military brothers for two years by the time she arrived in Vietnam. She had joined the Army Nurse Corps after working as a civilian nurse for nine years and from 1966 to 1968 worked in a thousand-bed Army hospital in Japan, caring for soldiers who had been wounded in Vietnam and were on their way back to the United States. Her obligation to the ANC ended with her tour in Japan, but she decided to stay with the Army on "voluntary indefinite" status. When orders for her next duty station indicated she was to be assigned to Fort Sam Houston, she requested a change: "I did not want to go there. I wanted to go to Vietnam." She wanted to continue working with soldiers wounded in the war, and she still supported the fight against communism. "We were still fighting the Communists," she told me. "That was the reason that I went in and that was still what was worrying me—the communism." In February 1968, Valerie Buchan arrived in Vietnam, eight thousand miles from her hometown of Henning, Minnesota.

# 2

## *"All Day and into the Night"*
## Nursing in the War Zone

**LYNN (CALMES) KOHL** arrived in Vietnam in June 1969, one year after graduating from nursing school in Milwaukee, Wisconsin. She spent the next year working at the 71st Evacuation (Evac) Hospital, located in the dusty red clay of the U.S. base at Pleiku, in Vietnam's central highlands. When she reported for work on her first day of duty, the chief nurse assigned her to the surgical ward, where she was to spend the day observing procedures. The first patient she encountered was a young G.I. with head wounds, abdominal wounds, a missing leg, and one arm "dangling by a tendon." Several surgeons surrounded the patient, pumping blood into him as they tried to repair his broken body. One busy doctor noticed Kohl standing nearby, inexplicably doing nothing; he didn't realize it was her first day on duty and that she was there only as an observer. In the heat of the moment, it didn't matter. "He screamed at me," Kohl recalled. "'Don't just stand there—do something! He's going to lose his arm anyway—cut it off!' And he threw his scissors at me. That was my first five minutes there: I had to cut an arm off."

This incident imprinted itself on Lynn Kohl in significant ways and became a central element in her personal story of the war. That it has figured so prominently in the interviews Kohl has given—with journalists, oral historians, students—suggests not just that the war was traumatic for her but that trauma is the critical lens through which she sees and remembers her time in Vietnam. Indeed, memories of trauma—physical, psychological, political, their patients', their own—are common in nurses' war stories. But the nurses I interviewed hold such memories alongside recollections mundane, humorous, inspiring, and poignant as well. Indeed, their experiences in Vietnam are characterized by contradiction: between heartbreak and joy, hatred and humanity, loneliness and camaraderie, exhaustion and boredom.

This chapter examines some of these contradictions as it describes what it was like to be a nurse in Vietnam, from daily routines and off-duty activities to the stresses of living in a war zone and caring for traumatically injured young patients. It also shows how their time in-country changed these women. The twelve months they spent in the heat and humidity of a tropical war zone—far away from the familiar comforts of home, immersed in the destruction of war, consumed by their responsibilities as nurses—transformed these women from (sometimes) naive, often inexperienced, nurse-soldiers into extremely capable nurses and wise but weary war veterans. Although more than fifty-eight thousand Americans died in Vietnam during the war, 350,000 wounded soldiers survived; indeed, the survival rate for patients in military hospitals in Vietnam was an amazing 98 percent. Yet the same work that saved the lives of so many soldiers took an enormous emotional toll on nurses, who came home carrying the weight of having seen the human carnage of war.[1]

### Half a World Away: Arrival and Assignment

Kohl's nerves were already on edge by the time she reported to the hospital for her first day of work. The unfamiliar scents and heavy heat of southern Vietnam's rainy season enveloped her as she emerged from the plane, her Army nurse dress uniform rumpled from the twenty-four-hour journey from California to Vietnam. Within seconds, before she had descended all the stairs from the plane to the tarmac, she heard a popping sound. "All of a sudden people were running around and screaming and hollering and people were pushing us down and telling us to run over to this building," she said. "We had no idea, but we were under attack, small arms fire."

Having survived her first war experience, Kohl spent the night at the 90th Replacement Center. The next morning, she was assigned to the 71st Evac in Pleiku. Reminders that she was in a war zone were unrelenting. During her helicopter flight to Pleiku, enemy fire downed a second helicopter that was heading to the same destination. When she finally arrived at the hospital, it was too late for her to meet with the chief nurse, and so she made her way to her "hooch"— her living quarters for the next year—where she met her hoochmate, Lynda. "We're sitting there talking one minute," Kohl recalled, "and I hear a whistle and the next thing I know nobody's there and I hear a thud. And I had no clue what was going on. And then Lynda came and she grabbed me and she's pulling me in. She says, 'Get under your bed! Get under your bed! We're under a rocket attack!'" Within the first forty-eight hours of her arrival in Vietnam, then, and before her traumatic experience with her first patient, Lynn Kohl had experienced at least three frightening and disorienting events.[2]

The chaos that Kohl remembered about her initial days in Vietnam would eventually become commonplace, but the transition was not easy. No matter how well trained the soldier—male or female, nurse or combat grunt—nothing truly prepared him or her for the shock of entering a war zone. Nurses learned early on that working in Vietnam would be something entirely different from civilian—or even stateside military—nursing. And all around them were reminders that they were far away from home.

Nurses' memories of their transition from stateside to combat zone nursing began with the long flight from the United States to Vietnam. Most Army nurses boarded a commercial airliner on the West Coast in full dress uniform, which consisted of skirt, jacket, pumps, hat, gloves, and purse. Their formal attire contrasted with the Army green fatigues that the male soldiers wore during the flight. It wasn't just their dress that set them apart from their fellow travelers, however; nurses were often one of only a few women (including the civilian flight attendants) in the sea of anxious faces of young people heading to war. Still, for the next twenty-four hours—and for the next twelve months—these many men and few women would share life-altering experiences. Some would not make the return flight home; others would come home wounded, physically and/or mentally; most would return significantly different people than they were on that first long flight.[3]

The gravity of what loomed ahead of them was evident in the relative quiet on board the plane. As Diane Evans said of the flight she shared with one other Army nurse and more than two hundred

G.I.s in summer 1968, "We're two women in a planeload full of men ages eighteen to twenty-two. You'd think there'd be all this—like college students—laughing and partying and having fun. No, it was very quiet. It was very silent." Even flights that were more lively for much of the trip across the Pacific turned somber as the descent into Vietnam began, as Mary Breed recalled: "The next thing we heard on the airplane was, 'To your left is the coast of Vietnam.' That airplane became silent. People had been chitchatting. It became silent because now reality was here. We were going to land."

Breed landed at the air base in Bien Hoa, about twenty miles northeast of Saigon, near the U.S. Army headquarters in Long Binh. The first thing she noticed when she stepped off the plane was the heat. "It just kind of took your breath away," she said. The next thing to capture her attention was "the faces of the people leaving" Vietnam to return to the United States. "There was something different," she recalled. "I didn't know if it was age. I didn't know if it was the trauma look. I didn't know if it was the thank-God-I'm-leaving-here look. But you did notice there was something different." Eight months later, it would be Breed passing the new arrivals as she made her way to her "freedom bird," the airplane that would carry her home. Even if, like Breed, most nurses landed in Vietnam without incident, evidence of the war surrounded them as soon as they emerged from the plane. Diane Evans and Valerie Buchan both remembered the sobering sight of American troops with rifles and bandoliers of ammunition lining the walkway from the airplane to the airport to offer protection against possible enemy attack.[4]

The first stop for most Army nurses (as well as scores of male soldiers) was either the 90th Replacement Battalion at the U.S. complex at Long Binh, just outside of Bien Hoa, or the 178th Replacement Company at Camp Alpha in Saigon. It was at the replacement centers that incoming soldiers received their assignments to units throughout South Vietnam. Several of the women in this study remembered the bus ride from the airfield to the replacement center as a shocking experience. The heat, the dust, the smells, the bus windows covered with protective grills, the poverty outside those windows—everything seemed foreign. As she peered out the windows of the bus on her way to the 90th in September 1965, Ann Rudolph saw "all these little children, naked, squatting in the little Vietnamese squat position. Some of them defecating, some of them peeing, many just running around in and out of the streets." She said that it was "pretty devastating to see that this is indeed the way they were living." When she arrived in Vietnam in February 1967, D-M Boulay was similarly taken aback by her new surroundings. In addition to the unfamiliar clothing that the Vietnamese wore, she was struck by the poverty she saw. "I'd looked at poverty of that extent only in *National Geographic* pictures," she explained, "and here it was in real time. I was just flabbergasted that people lived like this."[5]

Once they arrived at the replacement center, however, nurses entered the more familiar territory of a U.S. military base. They spent a few days there, awaiting assignment to a specific hospital elsewhere in Vietnam. At the 90th, they had time to adjust to the new time zone, acclimate to the tropical weather (and bugs) of Vietnam, and relax at the officers' club if they so chose. Although some nurses arrived with essentially their whole hospital unit intact and so knew where they would be assigned and with whom they would be working, most nurses, like most soldiers in general, arrived and departed Vietnam as individuals. On occasion, nurses traveled on the "buddy system" with one or two other nurses and tried—sometimes successfully, sometimes not—to get orders for the same hospital.

As was the case with receiving orders for Vietnam in the first place, there was some confusion over whether or not nurses had any say in their assignments once they arrived in-country. Mary Breed remembered being told that she could request a specific hospital assignment but said that it turned out to be another of "those little lies they tell." Rather than being asked where she would like to spend her year in Vietnam, she was told she would be going to the 95th Evacuation Hospital in Da Nang. Fortunately, the friend with whom she had traveled to Vietnam was also assigned to the 95th. When Mary Lu Brunner arrived in Vietnam in June 1968, the head nurse at the 90th showed her and her friend a map of Army hospitals in need of operating room (OR) nurses and asked them where they would like to go. Her friend wanted to be near the ocean, but Brunner wanted to see the mountains. The Army honored Brunner's request and sent her to the 71st Evacuation Hospital in Pleiku.

The Army operated several different kinds of hospitals in Vietnam. Surgical hospitals were the smallest, generally holding between sixty and one hundred beds. They were located close to the field and were often the first stop after a dust-off (helicopter ambulance) had picked up a soldier in need of immediate trauma surgery. Field hospitals could accommodate three hundred to four hundred patients, while evacuation hospitals were larger still, housing up to five hundred patients and offering general and specialized medical and surgical care. All twelve Army nurses I interviewed worked in an evacuation hospital for at least part (and, in most cases, for all) of their tours. Navy nurses served aboard one of two ships, the USS *Repose* or the USS *Sanctuary;* at the naval station hospitals in Saigon (until 1966) or Da Nang (from 1967 to 1970); or, as Kay Bauer did, as part of an advisory and training team stationed at the Vietnamese provincial hospital in Rach Gia in the southern Mekong Delta region of Vietnam. Navy nurse Mary O'Brien Tyrrell worked at the U.S. Naval Hospital on Guam, where wounded Marines in need of more significant care were sent before returning either to Vietnam or the United States. Air Force nurse Bobby Smith worked in both kinds of Air Force medical units that operated during the war: the stationary hospital at Cam Ranh Bay and medical air evacuation (medevac) flights that provided medical care to wounded patients en route to hospitals within or outside Vietnam.[6]

Once linked to a hospital, nurses were then assigned to a specific unit within the hospital (emergency room [ER], operating room [OR], intensive care [ICU], medical, orthopedics, etc.) and to their living quarters. Military hospitals were part of the larger base complexes. In addition to the hospitals and living quarters, bases also contained living quarters for the combat and support units assigned to that base, mess tents, post exchanges, chapels, officers' and enlisted clubs, and recreation areas. Sometimes there was more than one hospital on a single base, as in Pleiku, which was home for a time to both the 71st Evac and 18th Surgical Hospitals. Mary Lu Brunner worked in the OR at the 71st and described the base as "a big dust bowl with concertina wire wrapped all the way around." She estimated the base to be the size of "a few city blocks each way," with paved roads and hooches akin to "little cabins in northern Minnesota, lining the sidewalk." Ditches ran alongside the sidewalk to manage runoff from the heavy rains of monsoon season. Covered walkways led to the hospital, where sandbags lined its out-

*Nurses and other enlistees enjoyed occasional down time, including USO (United Service Organization) tours that brought stars such as actor Dean Jones, shown here with Ann Rudolph, to the war zone.*

side walls to guard against incoming rounds. Army hospitals were often Quonset huts—dome-shaped corrugated metal structures— arranged in an "X" or "H" shape with the nurses' station at the juncture of the arms of the unit. Dust-off choppers would land on a helipad near the hospital to deliver their human cargo to the care of the doctors and nurses on duty.

Nurses' living quarters varied from tents and Quonset huts to air-conditioned trailers and two-story cement buildings. The physical amenities of both hospitals and living quarters depended to some extent on the size and location of the base. Whatever the situation, the nurses I met reported that they tried to make their hooches as comfortable as possible. Edy Johnson sought to brighten her "dreary" quarters by putting contact paper on the walls and ordering a vacuum cleaner from the Sears catalog to keep the dust under control. Mary

Breed decorated the walls of her hooch with a Minnesota Vikings poster, items she purchased at the post exchange (PX, the base store), and other mementos she received from family back home.

Nurses assigned to hospitals on larger bases typically had access to relatively modern, if shared, bathroom facilities. Joan Paulson remembered G.I.s teasing her about the comparative luxury she and other nurses at the 67th Evacuation Hospital in Qui Nhon enjoyed with the running water and flush toilets in the nurses' quarters. Soldiers teased Ann Rudolph in another way: when she and other nurses showered in the roofless stalls near the 93rd Evac in Long Binh, helicopters would "buzz" by overhead to take a quick look. She took it in stride, laughing as she recalled the incidents. Mary Beth Crowley described the outdoor toilets at the 17th Field Hospital in An Khe as "just a hole over a big fuel can." Although the nurses' quarters had sinks, toilets, and showers, she described the latter as "sort of creepy" because they were often populated by large bugs. For Crowley, using these rudimentary facilities was one of the hardest adjustments she faced in Vietnam because "it was just so foreign."

Transitioning from life in the relative safety and comfortable context of American culture to the scarcities and unfamiliar customs of the war zone in Vietnam proved challenging in many ways. If adjusting to the bugs, heat, and toilet facilities was difficult, however, nursing in a war zone tested these women on another level entirely.

*The Daily Grind:*
*The Physical and Emotional Work of Nursing in Vietnam*

The average age of the combat soldier in Vietnam was nineteen. At an average age of twenty-four, nurses seemed like elders in comparison. Still, nearly two-thirds of Army nurses who served in Vietnam were novices in their profession, with two years or less of nursing experience under their belts. For those who had gone straight from nursing school to Fort Sam Houston for basic training, what little nursing experience they had was obtained under the auspices of the military hospital system, whether they were working in operating rooms or delivering babies for officers' wives. These young women were just developing their professional nursing competency when they were sent to care for American soldiers in Vietnam, and the transition was jarring. Even nurses who had worked for many years before going to Vietnam and had highly developed skills found it challenging to translate their knowledge to battlefield nursing. Not only did they care for bodies torn apart by land mines, booby traps, mortars, gunshots, or shrapnel but they also treated a vast array of diseases—such as malaria, skin diseases, and fevers of unknown origin—that thrived in a tropical war zone. Nevertheless, nurses adapted quickly and, along with the doctors and corpsmen with whom they worked, provided excellent medical care for their patients.[7]

Nurses were busy. They routinely worked twelve-hour shifts, six days a week. When the hospital received mass casualties (mass-cals), their work days extended for as long as they were needed. Like Lynn Kohl, several of the nurses I met recalled the shock of their first day on duty. On her first day in the ER at the 24th Evac in Long Binh in 1971, Lynn Bower struggled to get an IV started on an injured G.I., a "real Minnesota-looking" kid. As she wrestled with the IV, the first sergeant came over and told her that she wouldn't be able to get it in. Bower kept trying until the sergeant lifted the patient up to show Bower that the G.I.'s "whole back side was gone." "I just felt the room spin," she said. Later that same day, she lost her treasured gold bandage scissors—a graduation gift from her mother—when the patient whose uniform she was trying to cut off literally came apart in her hands. "I had taken his boots off and his feet were floppy. Then I went to grab his belt at the waist and when I pulled . . . he came apart at the waist" she said softly. "He just opened up and the *blood* just started coming out." She left her scissors on the litter with the patient, too shaken to contemplate reaching in to retrieve them.[8]

Although her first encounter with war casualties was less bloody than Bower's, Air Force nurse Bobby Smith remembered it with just as much emotion. Smith was the medical crew director on a flight that was transporting combat casualties from Vietnam to a hospital on the East Coast of the United States. After she boarded the plane for the last domestic leg of the flight, she recalled seeing "all these kids laying in litters and blue pajamas, and I looked at them and they looked like they were fourteen years old, like they were little kids. And I was kind of choked up, and I started crying." Smith left the plane while she regained her composure and then returned and went to work putting her patients at ease.

Smith's memory of this incident is revealing. Unlike Lynn Kohl and Lynn Bower, whose recall of their first days centered on the physical trauma of dismembered bodies (and, indeed, on their role in that dismemberment), Smith faced patients in a relatively calm, sanitary, and ordered environment. Their wounds were not fresh; they were clean; their pain was being controlled as much as possible; they were alive. Yet she remembered this comparatively benign meeting of her first casualties with as much distress as Kohl and Bower had described theirs. It wasn't only the physical trauma of war wounds that unsettled so many nurses, then; it was the emotional stress of having to care for young men whose lives had been altered so profoundly by their service to their country.

No matter how experienced or capable they may have been, nurses often were unprepared to deal with this element of the job. Smith had graduated from nursing school in 1955 and joined the Air Force in 1958, six years before she boarded that flight across the United States. She was an experienced military nurse, and yet, seeing those young G.I.s affected her deeply. Lynn Bower had joined the ANC while she was still in nursing school and so was new to the field when she arrived in Vietnam. She believed that her nurses' training had prepared her for the physical work of nursing but not for the emotional elements of the job. A great deal of her frustration stemmed from the fact that her patients were so young: "These guys aren't even adults! They can't vote at home. They can't vote! . . . But they're dead. That's the stuff that made me crazy."

But duty called, and nurses had to figure out a way to deal with their emotions so they could care for their patients. A few of the nurses I interviewed said they released their emotions by crying, though never in front of their patients. Others took refuge in music or books or drink or prayer. Most of them said that they stifled their emotions, burying them deep inside so they could perform their day-to-day duties. Every time she boarded a medevac flight, for example, Bobby Smith "shut everything down." Doing so became such a habit, she said, that "after a while, I didn't have to shut it down. I *was* shut down." This was, after all, what nurses had been trained to do. Patients came first. "Part of the nurses' training," Smith explained, "was 'Well, you can't cry because you won't be any good. That's not helping the patients. . . . Turn it off.'" This was a functional necessity of nursing, she agreed, especially during wartime, "because if you stop and think about it, you'd become so devastated you [couldn't] function." The long-term consequences of this shutting down could be severe, but in the meantime, there were soldiers to heal.

And heal they did. They healed soldiers with gunshot and mortar wounds, with injuries from land mines and booby traps. They treated G.I.s with broken limbs and fractured skulls. They cleaned mud and dirt and shrapnel out of holes blown into bodies, treated disarticulations of the hip, saw people burning from white phosphorous. They tended to patients with wounds from fragmentation grenades and traumatic injuries from head to toe. They cared for people suffering the effects of dysentery, malaria, mysterious fevers, even the bubonic plague. They helped preserve the lives of Vietnamese prisoners of war who had tried to take the lives of Americans and Vietnamese allies who had risked their lives alongside Americans. They delivered babies for local civilians, treated tumors in young children, eased the pain of innocents caught in the crossfire of war. They administered medications, changed bandages, cleaned infected wounds, cut off or helped save limbs in surgery. They scavenged for supplies when inventories ran low and devised creative ways to make do with what they had. They learned to jump at the sound of choppers that brought new patients for them to heal. They became familiar with the smell of blood and decaying, infected flesh. They adjusted to the sight of strong young bodies torn apart by war. They made life-and-death decisions doing triage and shouldered more responsibility than they ever would have in civilian nursing.[9]

They healed their patients' bodies but also cared for their psyches. They helped write letters to family and girlfriends at home; they served hamburgers, fries, and Cokes to soldiers who had spent the last weeks or months living on C rations or mess hall food; they played the latest music and decorated the hospitals for the holidays. They joked, they listened, they held hands. They made their patients as comfortable as possible in every way they could and tried not to think too much about the lives that awaited those who would return home without legs or arms, or with ruined faces, or with sexual dysfunction, or about the dangers that awaited the soldiers they healed enough to send back into the field. They wished they didn't know what they knew, what "multiple frag wounds" or "distartic of the hip" looked like, what burning flesh smelled like, what a dismembered body felt like, what the fear and desperation of a nineteen-year-old soldier sounded like. They wished they could separate themselves from their senses, where the experience of nursing in Vietnam lodged so deeply in their bodies. But yet, through it all, they kept on, in the name of their patients.

### The Number-One Priority: The Patients

At the heart of the war stories I heard from these nurses were the patients they served. The patients were the reason they were in Vietnam to begin with. These women were nurses before they were soldiers, and they were more committed to their patients than they were to the military, the war, or their country. Their patients were primarily wounded American military personnel, young men who often came from working-class backgrounds and were more racially diverse as a group than the nurses who cared for them. Mary O'Brien Tyrrell described the patients she treated in the Navy hospital on Guam: "The average age was nineteen. They were young boys. They were scared." Some nurses worked in units where they had a chance to get to know their patients, while others saw patients only in the operating room, one after another, anonymous and unspeaking. Some nurses welcomed a personal relationship with those under their care; others kept their patients at arm's length to guard against any further pain associated with caring for wounded men.[10]

The nature of nurses' relationships with their patients depended at least in part on the hospital unit in which the nurses worked. Those who worked in the emergency room, operating room, or intensive care unit often had little chance to get to know their patients. The soldiers were either under anesthesia for surgery or heavily medicated for pain management in the ICU. Moreover, these patients did not spend much time in such units. Those who came into the ER were triaged and sent to the next most appropriate unit (surgery, medical ward for infections or diseases, etc.), depending on their needs. If a patient had had surgery, his next stop was the recovery room. From recovery, he was sent to another ward where he would spend his time either recuperating before returning to the field or in the ICU where the goal was to stabilize him enough to medevac him to another hospital for further treatment. D-M Boulay's patients in the ICU units at the 36th and 93rd Evacuation Hospitals were therefore with her for only twenty-four to forty-eight hours before they were transferred elsewhere, and they spent much of that time unconscious or heavily medicated.

Thus the nature of the work in these units precluded nurses from getting to know their patients on a more personal level. Nevertheless, patients often made lasting impressions on the nurses. Lynn Kohl and Lynn Bower certainly had vivid recall of the patients they encountered in the OR and ER, respectively, even if they never knew those men's names. During her time in the ER at the 12th Evac, Valerie Buchan didn't get to know many of her patients well, either, but more than thirty-five years later was still "bothered" by the burn victims she encountered there. "They were hurting so badly, and they were very conscious," she said. She recalled one particular patient, a "tall, well-built" African American man who had been burned in a helicopter crash: "I can still remember his eyes. He looked to me, 'Help me.' I could see in his eyes, 'Help me. Help me. Help me.'" He was alive when he left Buchan's hospital for a stateside military hospital, but she never learned what ultimately became of him.

Sometimes nurses made conscious decisions not to know too much about their patients. Although patients who came into the OR sometimes were cognizant and able to talk, Mary Lu Brunner found it easier if they remained anonymous: "When I first got there, it was easy to call the individual by his name, find out where he was from. You'd read the chart, and you'd say, 'So-and-so is from Wisconsin,'" she explained, "but then that got pretty tough. As I realized how awful and devastating those wounds were, it was harder for me to know that John was from Wisconsin. I'd rather think that he didn't have a name and I didn't know where he was from." Nurses (and doctors and corpsmen) also relied on dark humor to insulate themselves from the trauma that surrounded them. Those who didn't have to deal with conscious patients on a personal level depersonalized them by referring to them as "crispy critters" (for burn patients), "horrendoplasties" (for patients with multiple disfiguring wounds), "train wrecks," or "whistles" (for those who were really "blown away"). Though it may have seemed harsh to outsiders, using this language was a matter of survival for nurses. "Somehow it made it easier," Lynn

Kohl explained. "We had to do those things in order to be able to do [our job]."

Some nurses did get to know their patients, if only fleetingly. When D-M Boulay moved from the ICU to Ward 3 at the 36th Evac, she became more familiar with her patients, who were recovering from minor surgery before returning to their home units. When I asked her if she remembered any particular patients from Ward 3, Boulay told me about a "thin and tiny" young man who would venture into nearby towns to spend time with prostitutes and would return with "the most god-awful venereal disease infections." She also met a "Tennessee plowboy" who rotated through Ward 3 two or three times with minor injuries, only to be sent back to the fighting. She met him again later, when she was at the 93rd Evac during the 1968 Tet Offensive. He had been "exceedingly badly wounded" this time. "I was on duty the night that he died," she said softly, "and I held him in my arms as he died." This possibility—that she would heal a soldier who would be sent back to the field and killed in the fighting—made the work on Ward 3 "traumatizing" for Boulay, so much so that she requested a transfer to another unit, even if that meant leaving the 36th Evac; she was sent to the ICU at the 93rd.

Many of the nurses I interviewed described feeling an enormous sense of responsibility for their patients, and with this sense of responsibility came fear. They were scared that their skills would not be enough to save young men who looked at them with pleading in their eyes. "I'd go to work every night scared to death. What am I going to see tonight that I might not know?" recalled Mary O'Brien Tyrrell. "It was a huge responsibility." They did their best to save their patients but then worried about what they were saving them for and what kind of dangers or lives they were returning them to. They also feared the helplessness that came when they had exhausted all of their medical expertise and knew a patient still would suffer and die. As Diane Evans explained it when describing a night she spent talking to an "expectant" patient who was covered in field dressings from head to toe, "I think my biggest fear was watching somebody die who was young. Now, in nurse's training, I'd seen old people die and [victims of] car accidents, but I hadn't seen a soldier die. I was really afraid, because I thought 'He's going to die. I'm the only one here and what am I going to do? There's nothing I can do. I can't do anything.'" She stayed with him all night, administering morphine to lessen his pain and talking to him so he would know he was not alone. Still, he died. And when a patient died, nurses suffered. "I think every time somebody died, part of me died, too, with them," said Mary Beth Crowley.[11]

Like Boulay and Evans, many nurses discussed one or two particularly memorable patients, but the memories were not always or only traumatic. In fact, nurses didn't often hold dying patients in · their arms, given the high survival rate of G.I.s who made it to the hospital from the field. They recalled severely wounded patients, to be sure, but they also remembered patients who made an impact on them for their humor or kindness or unique circumstances. Ann Rudolph, for instance, said that some of her patients repaid the kindness she had shown them at the 93rd Evac by writing poems for her. One of Edy Johnson's patients on the orthopedics ward at the 93rd— a skinny nineteen-year-old with blond hair and a southern drawl whose jaws were wired shut—proposed to her. She discouraged him by pointing out that she was almost old enough to be his mother (she was twenty-eight at the time). Mary Beth Crowley described a couple of G.I.s who had been struck by lightning. One man had had a cross hanging around his neck, and its likeness had been burned onto his chest. The other man's zipper had been fused together, and he lost his foot as a result of the lightning burn: "I remember I told him, 'Yes, you lost your foot. But you get to go home. You had to lose something, but you get to go home.'" Diane Evans even took something positive from the otherwise frightening night she spent with the dying soldier. "I think I felt it that night I was with that young man," she said, "just feeling the grace."

Although wounded G.I.s were nurses' primary focus, almost all of the nurses I talked to also had clear memories of treating Vietnamese children. Civilians who otherwise had scant access to western medical care sought help from American military hospitals, and most hospitals had entire wards dedicated to Vietnamese patients. They arrived at the hospital with wounds they had acquired from living in the middle of a war zone as well as with medical problems that local facilities were not prepared to handle, such as cleft lips and palates, birth defects, and tumors. Kay Bauer routinely cared for Vietnamese children at the provincial hospital in Rach Gia, but this part of the job came as a surprise to some nurses. "I went over there thinking, 'I'm going to help care for soldiers,'" Mary Beth Crowley said. "I never thought about caring for children."

The experience was both rewarding and difficult. Crowley cared for a young girl who had severe burns as a result of an accident in her home. She remembered the girl crying in pain as Crowley removed her bandages. When she learned the girl had died, Crowley felt an odd mixture of relief and despair—relief that the girl would no longer have to suffer such excruciating pain; despair at the loss of such a young life. Mary Breed's first patients in Vietnam were two children who had white phosphorous burns and died as a result of their injuries. She also had fond memories of "Joey," a young boy who had a large tumor that made it difficult for him to breathe. She described him as "the happiest child you would ever want to see" and "one of my cuties." The medical staff at Breed's hospital attempted to remove the tumor surgically, and Breed assisted with his surgery. Although he survived the surgery, Joey died in recovery. This was one of the few times Breed could remember crying while in Vietnam. "It's too bad that he couldn't have had a life," she said as she showed me a picture of her "cutie."[12]

Language, cultural, and political differences sometimes made caring for Vietnamese patients challenging. The nurses I interviewed had different opinions as to whether the military had sufficiently prepared them for living in a different culture before they arrived in Vietnam. During basic training at Fort Sam Houston, Army nurses visited a mock Vietnamese village that had been set up at Camp Bullis, but most of them didn't recall learning anything particularly useful or significant about Vietnamese history, culture, language, or people. At least one nurse, D-M Boulay, faulted the military for not teaching her about Vietnam. "No history. No understanding of the language," she recalled ruefully. Such cultural ignorance affected nurses and their Vietnamese patients. Valerie Buchan cared for a young boy who required an IV drip. She regulated the IV fluid very carefully, in order not to overwhelm his small body, but would often find the line opened all the way. She wondered how that kept happening, until one day she noticed the boy's mother adjusting the IV flow: "She thought if a little was good, a lot was better, and that I was being stingy, I suppose, with the IV fluid." Buchan had no way to tell the mother what was happening because Buchan didn't speak Vietnamese and the mother didn't speak English.

Although most nurses I met had no qualms treating children or civilian casualties, the situation was a bit more complex when the patient was a prisoner of war (POW). Their training emphasized that a nurse's first obligation was to care for the patient in front of her, regardless of who that patient was. Mary Lu Brunner and D-M Boulay remember caring for POWs, and both said they didn't have any difficulties in doing so. Valerie Buchan performed her necessary duty when treating enemy wounded but admitted that her "attitude was not the same." An injured North Vietnamese female patient spit at Joan Paulson, which made the already difficult situation of tending to an "enemy" even more tense.

Political differences that defined some patients as allies and others as enemies thus affected nurses' attitudes toward their Vietnamese wards, but outright racism sometimes did, too. The Vietnamese were widely referred to as "gooks" by Americans and were thought by some to be an inscrutable and backwards people who had little regard for human life. American nurses who served in Vietnam were not always immune to such racist stereotyping. Some came to Vietnam with racist images of its people, while others who considered themselves to be liberal and open minded before going to Vietnam were disturbed to find themselves "learning" to hate the Vietnamese after a few months in-country.[13]

None of the nurses I interviewed described themselves as having had overtly racist attitudes toward the Vietnamese, nor did they say they used the term "gook." Still, Mary Breed hinted at some degree of American arrogance when she said that she and her colleagues were "not mature enough" to "handle the diversity" and so, rather than learning the names of the Vietnamese children whom they treated, bestowed American names—such as "Joey"—on them instead. D-M Boulay described an incident in which another nurse's racism and frustration with the war became deadly. A Vietnamese baby was brought to their hospital after the Tet Offensive, and the nurse turned his IV up too fast and effectively killed him. Boulay was convinced she did it intentionally, "all because he was Vietnamese." Though we may never be able to confirm that this nurse killed this baby on purpose for racist reasons—no formal allegations were lodged against her, Boulay explained, because the hospital staff was too busy in the aftermath of the Tet Offensive to do anything but work and sleep— the story is suggestive of the degree to which nurses, like soldiers in the field, felt their moral foundation begin to crumble in the face of war. Perhaps they, too, succumbed to the temptation to see all Vietnamese as the enemy, especially in the aftermath of a brutal battle such as the Tet Offensive was. And, despite all the fond rhetoric, surely not all nurses were angels all the time. "It wasn't a slip," Boulay assured me. "That was her signature."

Still, many of the nurses in this study left Vietnam with great respect for its people, customs, and culture. They spoke highly of Vietnamese people's hard-working nature and ability to remain "upbeat," as Edy Johnson put it, in the middle of a war zone. Navy nurse Kay Bauer had the opportunity to experience Vietnamese culture more than most. The goal of her work at the Vietnamese provincial hospital in Rach Gia was to help prepare the hospital and train its staff to perform surgery. Thus, 90 percent of her time in-country was spent with Vietnamese people, both as patients and as colleagues. The hospital lacked typical American medical amenities, even things as basic as running water, electricity, and screens for the windows. On the rare occasion that they received wounded American soldiers, they simply triaged them and prepared them for transport to another, better-equipped facility. Although their first priority was to assist injured Americans, most of their patients came from the surrounding countryside.

Cultural differences that played a relatively insignificant role for most American military nurses were a daily part of Bauer's life in Rach Gia. From learning not to interfere with a family's decision to let a critically ill baby die to adapting to the Vietnamese fish- and vegetable-based diet to figuring out from her Vietnamese counterparts how to treat dengue fever and tetany, Bauer learned as much from the Vietnamese as she taught to them. Like other nurses, she was struck by the ways in which Vietnamese families rallied around their ill or injured; entire families would camp out in the tight quarters of the hospital while their ailing family member was recovering. Bauer also remembered treating a boy who had shrapnel embedded in his back. She needed to get an X-ray to determine how deeply and widely the shrapnel had penetrated the boy's back, but neither she

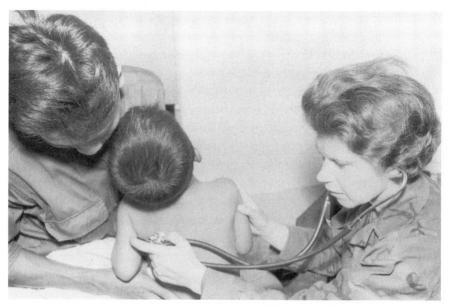

*Kay Bauer routinely cared for Vietnamese children at the provincial hospital in Rach Gia.*

nor her corpsman could figure out how to use the "antiquated" X-ray machine in the hospital. A Vietnamese maintenance man knew how to operate it, however. "We promoted him. He's no longer in maintenance. He was now our X-ray tech," she said with a laugh. They found and removed the shrapnel, with the little boy talking and laughing all the while.

Bauer also had more sober memories of the war's effects on the people of Vietnam. For instance, she recalled that a Vietnamese woman arrived at the hospital after traveling by bicycle for three days, pulling her injured soldier son in a cart behind her in hopes that the American surgical team could save him. By the time she reached the hospital, however, he had already died.

Although American military nurses thus had considerable contact with Vietnamese patients of one sort or another, American G.I.s were still their first priority, and they described the men with respect and affection. As Valerie Buchan said of the soldiers she treated, "They were fine people. They were not baby killers. They were not people who went over there and lost their moral way. They were people who went over there and did what they could. They were our finest, finest young men." Buchan's passionate defense of American soldiers says as much about contemporary and postwar controversies over who was to blame for the war as it does about soldiers' actual behavior. War and memories of it function through contradiction; it is possible that even fine young men (and women) faced moral challenges for which they were not prepared, sometimes staying true to their sense of right and wrong, sometimes giving in to the lesser passions that war inflames. So it is that D-M Boulay can describe a nurse killing a Vietnamese baby and Buchan can insist on the moral behavior of American troops, and both stories can, in some meaningful way, be true. In any case, none of the nurses I interviewed spoke ill of the men for whom they cared.

Instead, for nurses whose own war stories are so often arranged around memories of their patients, those patients became emblems of the war's forgotten heroes. And in return for the sacrifices those soldiers had made, nurses had given their patients everything they had. "We worked," Buchan said. "We worked. We worked. We worked all day and into the night." As busy and overwhelming as this work could be, however, not every moment in Vietnam was consumed by work or tragedy.

### Madcaps, Medcaps, and R&R: The Lighter Side of War

Nurses spent a good part of their time in Vietnam working under difficult circumstances trying to save horrifically wounded patients. But there could also be long stretches of slow days and down time. As Mary Lu Brunner explained, there were days "that were just as long and boring as there were the ones that were ultimately busy." Thus, nurses' stories about their year in-country weren't only about the traumas of war; they also were about young people trying to have fun and feel at home halfway across the world. Nurses passed their off-duty time in the company of their friends and colleagues, finding things to do on or near the base, volunteering their services to help local civilians, or traveling outside of Vietnam on their R&R (rest and recuperation). The military had promised nurse-recruits fun, travel, and adventure, and in many ways, it delivered.

One of these nurses' fondest memories of their time in Vietnam was of the close camaraderie they established with each other and their colleagues in the hospital. Although the nurses, doctors, and corpsmen may have come from very different backgrounds in their previous lives at home, such differences were put aside in the extreme circumstances of Vietnam, especially while they were on duty. Male and female hospital staff worked together as a team to care for their patients and to support each other in the trying circumstances in which they labored. "Nobody had a family over there. Nobody had any place to go," Valerie Buchan said of herself and her colleagues. "It was like a little club where we were taking care of each other." Like so many other war veterans, Buchan was hard pressed to find that same kind of camaraderie once she returned home. Mary Lu Brunner credits her colleagues for helping to keep her sane during her tour. "Your lives are intertwined," she explained. "I think I could have been really crackers if it hadn't been for that group of people leaning on each other."

Corpsmen held a special place in nurses' hearts. When asked about the working relationships among hospital personnel, the nurses I interviewed rarely mentioned the doctors but almost always talked about the corpsmen. Corpsmen were enlisted men, often conscientious objectors, who were trained as medical technicians. They usually had no medical experience prior to their military service and arrived in Vietnam with only a six-week military medical training course under their belts. Some of them went out in the field with combat units as medics, while others worked in hospitals with doctors and nurses. Oftentimes, nurses were responsible for training the corpsmen at stateside hospitals before they were sent to Vietnam. As Mary O'Brien Tyrrell recalled about her time at Camp Pendleton in California, before she left for Guam, "I taught the corpsmen to do everything that I knew how to do." Nurses like Tyrrell felt a great sense of responsibility for their corpsmen, knowing that they would be the first point of contact for soldiers wounded in the field and that the corpsmen themselves would be in danger of being wounded as well. They also had great respect and admiration for what the corpsmen did, with so little training, in the hospitals alongside the doctors and nurses. "The corpsmen were just wonderful human beings," said D-M Boulay. "They were almost all conscientious objectors, both at the 36th and the 93rd. Many of them were college grads; many were married people. All were male. All were saints."

Although nurses were technically corpsmen's supervisors and superiors (all nurses were officers, while corpsmen were enlisted men), nurses felt a great loyalty toward their corpsmen. "I have wonderful memories of my corpsmen. They were just amazing," said Diane Evans. "They all knew that I really cared about them. And I was always backing them up." As long as they could perform their job, Evans would let minor infractions of hospital rules pass. According to several nurses, however, corpsmen sometimes found it difficult to perform their medical tasks because they were exhausted from having stood guard duty prior to their shift in the hospital. As enlisted personnel, Edy Johnson explained, these men "were both corpsmen and soldiers" and so had to fulfill the obligations of both: tending to the wounded and guarding the base from enemy attack. Lynn Kohl recalled the toll these double shifts took on her corpsmen, when they would work twelve hours in the hospital and then have to stand guard immediately thereafter or after only a couple hours of rest. She attributed increasing drug use among enlisted men working in the hospital to this exhausting regimen, as they resorted to "uppers" to keep them awake on guard duty.

Nurses and corpsmen socialized on their off-duty hours as well, despite military policies prohibiting fraternization between officers and enlisted personnel. The larger bases had separate clubs for officers and enlisted personnel, but not all after-hours interaction took place in the confines of those clubs; sometimes the nurses I interviewed said they would venture into the enlisted men's club in civilian attire to hide their officer status. Although the differences in rank between nurses and corpsmen reflected slight variations in age, class (officers had some postsecondary education), and race (most doctors and nurses were white, while corpsmen were more racially diverse), these were young men and women who were trying to make the best of a stressful situation far away from home. They took comfort in each other and engaged in the same kinds of activities young people at home enjoyed: they listened to music, partied, played games, and went dancing, sometimes as platonic friends, sometimes as romantic partners. They threw birthday parties and "Hail and Farewell" get-togethers for those who had just arrived and those who were about to leave. They played checkers and cribbage and volleyball, and when Mary Beth Crowley's father sent her a package full of bubble gum, they had a bubble-blowing contest. They would watch movies on outdoor screens, trying to make sense of the plot as the reels were shown out of order. Some drank alcohol to pass the time and numb the pain; some opted not to drink at all. They sang along with the Fifth Dimension and Jethro Tull and Vicki Carr as they listened to music on reel-to-reel tapes. They saw USO shows, Bob Hope shows, Martha Raye shows, and shows by Filipino bands covering popular American music. They played practical jokes on each other and bent military rules in search of a little fun. Mary Breed ordered a pair of roller skates from the Sears-Roebuck catalog and skated down Highway 1 near Quang Tri. Air Force nurse Bobby Smith and a fellow nurse stole an Army jeep so they could drive to a beach and go snorkeling. They talked, they read, they attended church, they wrote letters. The difference was that they did all of this in the middle of a war zone.

The war zone's location in Vietnam afforded some interesting opportunities to learn about another culture on off-duty hours. Although most of their time was spent at work or on the base, nurses reported that they would occasionally venture out into the local community to do some sightseeing, shopping, or, as D-M Boulay and her friends did, eating "on the economy" to avoid the "terrible" Army food. Although many nurses traveled outside of Vietnam on R&R— to Bangkok, Hong Kong, and even Australia—they also had a chance to see parts of Vietnam beyond the confines of American military bases on two- or three-day in-country R&R passes. Valerie Buchan spent a couple of days at Vung Tau, a beautiful beach area about eighty miles from Saigon. She and a friend stayed in an old French resort and enjoyed the beach and a good restaurant on their much-needed break from the work at the 12th Evac in Cu Chi.

The politics of the war complicated the relationship between nurses and Vietnamese people, however. Guerrilla warfare meant that it was very difficult to distinguish friend from foe, and civilians were often caught between the communist and anticommunist Vietnamese forces who were trying to win their hearts and minds. Mary Lu Brunner described the confusion she felt: "You didn't know who was who anyway. There was the Vietnamese and then there was the Viet Cong and then there was the North Vietnamese and then there were the people that were helping them. You're just saying, 'Wait a minute. This doesn't make a lot of sense.'" Other nurses recalled hearing stories that supposedly trustworthy Vietnamese who worked on the American military base by day turned into Viet Cong enemy by night. As a result, Ann Rudolph viewed the Vietnamese who worked on her base as "shifty" and Valerie Buchan became impatient with their "mixed loyalties."[14]

Buchan liked and respected the Vietnamese workers she met but wished they could definitively align themselves with one side or the other. It wasn't until some years after the war that she began to understand how difficult it was for poor, rural Vietnamese whose main concern was survival to balance the competing pressures placed on them by the North Vietnamese and National Liberation Front (NLF) on one side and the ARVN and Americans on the other. Lynn Kohl had a conflicted relationship with the "mama-sans"—the Vietnamese women who worked as maids for American personnel—and other Vietnamese workers on her base in Pleiku. On the one hand, she "thought that they were really nice," hard working and intelligent. On the other hand, she was suspicious of them, especially after some women who worked on the base were caught "setting up rockets aimed at our hospital" one night. Her distrust turned to fury when, just before she was due to return to the United States, a mama-san stole all the money Kohl had saved during her year of work. "So not only did I go through all that," she said of the stresses of working in Vietnam, "but I didn't even have any pay for doing it."[15]

It's hardly surprising that such conflicts between Americans and Vietnamese developed, given the underlying context of war, racial and cultural differences, and economic imbalances. Still, one of the goals of U.S. policy in Vietnam was to win the hearts and minds of the Vietnamese people, a task made difficult by just these kinds of challenges. One way the U.S. military sought to ease some of these tensions was through its Medical Civic Action Program (MEDCAP). Nurses, doctors, and corpsmen went to local hamlets and villages, where they helped establish medical clinics, visited schools to provide immunizations, taught civilians about the benefits of hygiene and simple wound care, brought children with correctable birth defects to military hospitals for surgical repair, and provided medical care and loving attention to children in orphanages and residents of leprosariums. Bobby Smith's hospital at Cam Ranh Bay "supported four villages and an orphanage," even though the French-speaking nuns who ran the orphanage warned the Americans that any supplies they left at the orphanage would be commandeered by the Viet Cong. Smith and her colleagues understood that they thus were indirectly treating the Viet Cong. "But what could you do?" she asked. "They're sick, they're injured, they've been shot, something. You help them. They're people."[16]

These relationships often benefited the Americans as much as they did the Vietnamese. G.I.s who worked in Army nurse Penny Kettlewell's hospital discovered that a nearby orphanage had run out of oxygen for the children who needed it, and so they "swiped" things from the ward at the hospital, traded them in for oxygen tanks, and delivered the tanks to the orphanage. Rather than upbraid these men for their actions—she was a captain and outranked them—she remembered thinking, "I should put them in for medals. Because they found a way to take this anger at the country and use it for something that was immediately constructive." Mary Breed regularly visited an orphanage in Da Nang. One day, a young G.I. from Iowa joined her on the deuce-and-a-half (military truck) that was transporting her to the orphanage. He told her he was worried about going home after the war, about how he'd react to his younger brothers and sisters after having learned to suspect even the youngest of children as potential enemies in Vietnam. He spent the day with Breed at the orphanage, fishing with the kids. On the way back, Breed remembered, the G.I. said to her, "I want to thank you. You helped me. Now I can look at the Vietnamese as people."

Mixed in with exhausting days of work and the tragedy of caring for wounded G.I.s, then, were moments of tranquility, laughter, and even boredom. When things were quiet, nurses could almost forget they were in a war zone, even if they couldn't quite forget they were half a world away from home. They found peace in the calm, solace in each other, and, sometimes, a newfound sense of themselves and their place in the world as they experienced life in a culture so different from their own. If, for a time, it seemed the military's promise of fun, travel, and adventure had been fulfilled, however, the war always came back.

*A Year of Living Dangerously: Life in the War Zone*

Most women remembered the moment they truly realized they were living and working in the middle of a war zone and that the danger applied to them, too, not just to soldiers in the field. For Lynn Kohl, this moment occurred as she landed in the middle of a firefight. For Diane Evans, the seriousness of the situation was brought home not just by the armed guards surrounding her as she exited the airplane but also by the silent, watchful door gunner on the helicopter that transported her from the 90th Replacement Center to the 36th Evac in Vung Tau. "He sat there, both hands on the weapon, looking down at the ground," she remembered. He didn't speak to her until she disembarked: "He said, 'Good luck, ma'am, and keep your head down.' Those were his only words." For Mary Beth Crowley, it was one night at the 90th Replacement when she and another nurse made a trip to the bathroom and flares went off overhead. A flare "lights up the sky but it sounds like gunfire. I remember the two of us just starting screaming," she recalled with a laugh. "'We're going to die the first day we're even here!' So we made it through that. They weren't shooting at us."

Nurses were not, in general, targets of enemy fire in Vietnam. In a guerrilla war without traditional front lines, however, danger loomed everywhere, even in hospital compounds. Eight American military women and sixty American civilian women died in Vietnam during the war. Of the military dead, Army nurse Sharon Lane was the only to be killed by enemy fire, the result of a rocket attack at the 312th Evac Hospital in Chu Lai on June 8, 1969. The others died from illness or accidents. Although none of the women I met were wounded in Vietnam, the war intruded in their lives in dangerous and disruptive ways.[17]

American military hospitals typically had a large red cross on the roof or tarmac. This symbol helped dust-off pilots locate the landing pad where they unloaded the wounded, but it also supposedly safeguarded the facility from enemy attack. Hospitals were just one part of larger bases, however, which were not presumed to be immune from such threats. Some hospitals were on bases located in areas known to be particularly dangerous, such as the 12th Evac in Cu Chi. Approximately thirty-five miles northwest of Saigon, Cu Chi was a strategically important area that was home to a network of under-ground tunnels built, operated, and populated by NLF forces and lo-cal civilians. The multilayer tunnels provided shelter from American and ARVN weapons and served as a staging ground for NLF offen-sives, but they also contained more general living, dining, and hos-pital quarters. The 12th Evac, along with the rest of the American base at Cu Chi, was situated directly above these tunnels. When her patients told her that the Viet Cong were living underneath the hos-pital, Valerie Buchan recalled, she thought it was just "crazy talk." She never feared getting hurt while in Vietnam but remembered being cautious after an explosive rigged to a mess hall tray detonated while G.I.s stood in line for lunch. An enemy squad also penetrated the base defenses on one occasion and blew up a number of Chinook helicopters. "I remember running from my hooch over to the emer-gency room and over on one side was this red fire. I remember think-ing about 'the rockets' red glare' that it talks about in our National Anthem," she said. "It was just this huge, red, awful-looking fire, all that gasoline burning down there."

Buchan's base wasn't the only one to be penetrated by the enemy. Mary Beth Crowley was at the 17th Field Hospital in An Khe in April 1970 when the red-alert alarm sounded to warn everyone that the enemy was on base. Shortly after midnight, Crowley awoke to the air-raid siren and a military policeman (MP) pounding on her door, telling everyone to get out and go to the hospital. Crowley—in night-gown, helmet, flak jacket, and "flip-flop shoes"—made her way to the hospital, where she helped evacuate patients into a nearby bunker. "My legs were shaking so hard I could hardly walk," she remembered of making her way through the noise and commotion of enemy at-tacks on a nearby helicopter squadron. She spent the night in a bun-ker with fellow nurses, doctors, and corpsmen. Lynn Kohl's sense of security, already fragile, took another decline when she discovered a dead NVA soldier outside of her hooch one morning after the previ-ous night's enemy attack.[18]

Even if the enemy hadn't infiltrated the confines of the base, rock-et and mortar attacks made life precarious for nurses in Vietnam. Diane Evans said there were "many times" when she feared for her safety in Vietnam, and she had particularly vivid memories of a rock-et attack at the 71st Evac in Pleiku that blew the hooch next to her "off the face of the map." She said the hit was "so excruciatingly loud that it was like a jolt," and there was no time to run to a bunker. Instead, she crawled under her bed. The vibration from the rocket shook her mirror off the wall and to the floor, where it exploded into tiny shards of glass. A fellow nurse was under her bed nearby, and she called Evans over so that they could endure the attack together. Evans crawled through the glass in her helmet and nightgown and joined her friend underneath her bed. "Edie has rollers in her hair and she can't get her helmet on," Evans said with good humor. "She's also eating crackers with peanut butter and jelly. I said, 'Edie, are you eating?' She said, 'Yes. If I'm going to die, I'm not going to die hungry.'" Fortunately, neither of them suffered anything more serious than puncture wounds from the broken mirror; they slept under the bed until the next morning.

After the first few weeks in-country and the first few rocket or mortar attacks, the nurses I met said they learned to adapt to the contingencies of war while continuing to provide patient care. For Kay Bauer the war was a distraction, an obstacle to the smooth functioning of the provincial hospital to which she was assigned. Located as they were in a remote, rural area of southern South Vietnam, surrounded by Viet Cong, the dangers were ever present. Bauer recalled one instance in which she and a fellow nurse visited an ARVN compound to watch a movie. They left before the movie was over, just in time to avoid being caught in the explosion of mines that the Viet Cong had set up while everyone was enjoying the show. She also remembered seeing helicopters crash into the water near the hospital. "It was a constant thing," she said. "You couldn't just have a daily life. There was always this war interrupting it."

Mary Beth Crowley, having survived her first red alert in flip-flops and flak jacket, acknowledged that after a while, "you become pretty blasé about it." The red alerts became a nuisance, a hindrance to getting a good night's sleep, so much so that she and her colleagues would take Ritalin to help them stay awake while on duty the next day. Lynn Kohl, too, became inured to the threats that so unsettled her on her first days in Vietnam. "As the year progressed," she explained, "it was not unnatural to wake up in the morning under my bed and going, 'Oh, must have had a rocket attack last night because

I'm under here.' It's so automatic; you're so tired and exhausted, so it just was an automatic thing."

The events of early 1968 jarred many nurses out of such automatic responses, however, as the scale and intensity of enemy attacks increased dramatically. In late January, the NVA and NLF launched a series of surprise attacks on major population centers throughout South Vietnam during what had traditionally been an unofficial truce marking the Lunar New Year, or Tet, holiday. Although the Tet Offensive did not achieve the goals the Vietnamese communists had set and was repelled effectively by American and ARVN forces, it unsettled Americans' confidence in the progress of the war.

For Americans who were in-country at the time, the Tet Offensive was more than unsettling; it was overwhelming. Three of the nurses I interviewed were in Vietnam during the offensive. D-M Boulay was at the 93rd Evac in Long Binh when, at 3:00 a.m. on January 31, 1968, she was directed to a bunker to wait out the attack. She was on duty later that morning when the ammunition dump, a mile away from the hospital, blew up and collapsed one wall of the ICU. She and another nurse hauled a "great big, heavy guy in his great big, heavy cast and put him under the bed on the cement floor." She worked twelve-hour night shifts for the next several weeks, describing the period as "exceedingly busy." Indeed it was: the 93rd admitted more than six hundred new patients during the first week of the month-long siege. "You wanted the time to be scared or for your heart to slow down," Boulay explained, "but you didn't have time, because it was nonstop."[19]

Penny Kettlewell and Joan Paulson, working at the 67th Evac in Qui Nhon during Tet, also recalled the shock of a nearby ammunition dump exploding. Paulson remembered the noise—the air sirens, the mortar fire, the explosions. She was off duty that night, and so she and her roommates took cover underneath their beds until they were called to the hospital: "We stayed in the hospital and got our patients under the beds and got them to safety. We had blackouts for three days. We were there. We were working in darkness. You could see tracers going by our high windows." Kettlewell, too, helped patients to safety once the red alert was issued. She and her colleagues saw an American soldier get shot down from a guard tower:

"Another guy grabbed a jeep and ran out there and got him, threw him on the top and brought him back." Elements of the surreal colored her recall as she noted that doctors from the hospital stood on the nearby runway taking pictures of the "chaos" and the illuminated sky. "It was a very bizarre place," she said.

The effects of Tet reached beyond the borders of Vietnam. Although she was stationed on Guam and thus safely removed from the dangers of the offensive, Mary O'Brien Tyrrell worked the same kinds of long hours that in-country nurses did. The naval hospital expanded its capacity to accommodate the influx of new patients, and nurses had to work extra shifts in surgery. "During Tet," she recalled, "we would line up two surgery tables in a 'V' so that one anesthesiologist or anesthetist could handle two patients while the surgeons did their thing. We just worked all the time."

The Tet Offensive lasted for about a month. "In the grand scheme of things," Boulay recalled, "Tet was brief but awful." Joan Paulson agreed. "It was startling, and then scary, and then you thought, oh, my god, what's going to happen?" she said. "Then, it stopped and we carried on." Many nurses worked themselves to exhaustion tending to casualties of the fighting while remaining on high alert themselves. It was their work that kept them going even through these times of extreme danger. Years after the war, however, many nurses still have nightmares, flashbacks, and disturbing memories about their war experiences, as do many war veterans. The sound of a helicopter flying overhead is especially evocative for nurses, as Diane Evans explained: "Nurses react the most strongly to that because that's when we know the mass casualties are coming in. We know we have to respond. We have the adrenaline rush. We have to get ready. We have to get prepared, pull on our flak jacket, pull on our helmet, get the boots on, get to the hospital, get things done." Part of nurses' war-related anxiety thus stemmed from the conflicting desire to save themselves and to save their patients. But nurses were taught that patients came first. This commitment to their patients came at a cost to themselves, however, as Evans pointed out: "When the red-alert siren went on or there were mass casualties, we weren't running *away* from the situation. We were always running *to* the situation that was urgent and terrifying and frightful. . . . We were never running away to protect ourselves."

Fear, joy, anger, compassion, doubt, pride, excitement, boredom, frustration, love, hate—the nurses I met experienced all of these during their year in-country. They agreed that war is terrible and should be avoided at all costs; they saw the horrible consequences of war every day. But they also acknowledged that some good came of their time in Vietnam. They made good friends; they learned about another culture; they discovered new strength in themselves; they found fun, travel, and adventure. Perhaps most importantly, they honed their nursing skills and they saved lives. Although nurses arrived in Vietnam with varying levels of experience, they all came home as seasoned, extremely capable professionals. Yet this very professionalism came with a cost. The more committed they were to their patients, the more they sacrificed of themselves. Their commitment may have served them and their patients well while they were in Vietnam, but it would have lifelong consequences for many nurses once they returned home.

Lynn Kohl survived her year in-country. She learned how to adapt to living and nursing in a war zone. She survived the rocket attacks, the trauma of tending to severely injured soldiers, the challenges of living in a foreign country. Despite the many difficulties she encountered in Vietnam, Kohl valued the friendships she made while there and acknowledged that her tour "made me stronger." But she was a different person in June 1970 than she had been in June 1969. The war followed Kohl home, holding her in its grips for years afterward. War affects many veterans this way, to be sure. But for the nurses who served in Vietnam, the legacy of the war in their lives had something to do with their experiences as women in a war zone. Many American soldiers in Vietnam confronted the contradictions of war—the terror and the joy, the brutality and the humanity, the hate and the love. Women who served in Vietnam faced another contradiction, however: that between their identities as women and as soldiers. Men were "natural" soldiers, expected to go to war; women were not.

# 3

## *"You Just Did What You Had to Do"*
### Women at War

**WHAT WAS IT LIKE** to be a woman at war? For Mary Breed, it meant living in a world of extremes. On one end of the spectrum, she faced the insinuations (and sometimes outright accusations) that she had joined the military for the same reason every nurse supposedly had: sexual adventure. On the other end, she encountered the gallantry of male G.I.s who would have done anything to protect her from the dangers of the war zone. "The people that knew you were good to you," she said. "They looked out for you. The guys protected you, really protected you." She recalled only one instance in which she felt she was in particular danger because she was a woman—a long trip from Da Nang back to her hospital in Quang Tri, during which she had to rely on a number of unfamiliar men to transport her through dangerous territory by jeep, truck, and helicopter. Mostly, though, she had fond memories of her relationships with the men she encountered in Vietnam, especially the corpsmen who affectionately referred to her as "Mom Breed" after she covered them with blankets while they slept during one long night shift.

Not all interactions with men in Vietnam were so easy or friendly, however. As Mom Breed herself admitted, "Some people think it's wonderful to be the only woman around so many men. It can be just the opposite. It can be frightening. It can be not so wonderful." The nurses I interviewed told stories about the difficulties of being a woman at war, difficulties that ranged from the mundane (trying to find makeup at the post exchange) to the commonplace (dealing with the attention, however respectful, of so many men) to the dan-

*Mary Breed, center, and other nurses adapted with humor and ingenuity to the masculine environment of a wartime military.*

gerous (fending off unwanted sexual advances). Whereas chapter two focused on nurses' adjustment to life in the war zone as nurses, this chapter concentrates on their experiences as women.

### Soldiers in Skirts: Military Policy and Practices

It didn't take Navy nurse Kay Bauer long to be outfitted for life in a war zone when she reached Saigon in January 1966. The morning after her arrival, the military issued her and the rest of her surgical team uniforms, t-shirts, helmets, and boots. "Everything except our underwear was camouflage," she recalled. When the supply officer gave her a rifle and some ammunition, she said, "'I'm a nurse. What do I do with this?' They draped it over my shoulder, piling all this stuff up. At that point, I weighed 102 pounds, and I fell over with all this equipment." Although Bauer recalled this incident with a laugh some forty years later, at the time she was concerned. As a nurse, she had received no weapons instruction of any kind during basic training. She was reassured by the fact that some of her colleagues on the team had served in London during World War II and were experienced with rifles and pistols.

Being posted at a remote Vietnamese provincial hospital meant that every two or three months, one member of Bauer's team would take three days off to fly to Saigon for supplies and to pick up a paycheck. When it was Bauer's turn to claim her check from the Navy post in Saigon, she encountered some difficulty. The male sailor who was distributing the checks directed her to the Army post instead, telling her with all due respect, "Ma'am, we don't have any Navy women in-country." Advised against traveling in uniform, Bauer wore civilian clothes during these trips to Saigon, and so she had to produce her Navy ID card as proof that she was, in fact, a member of the Navy: "I'd hand him my ID card and say, 'I'll tell you what. You go back in your records and if you find a record that matches this ID card, you pay me. If you don't, you don't pay me. How's that for a deal?' Every time, he'd come back with his eyes very wide and say, 'You *are* here in-country!' 'Yes.' Then they'd pay me."

Bauer's experiences, while somewhat unique due to her station at a Vietnamese hospital in the countryside, reflect occurrences that were common to many nurses who served in Vietnam. Military policy and practices alternated between emphasizing and downplaying women's differences from men. Sometimes these gender-based differences were troubling to nurses; other times they were simply nuisances to be endured. As Joan Paulson put it, "This is the Army. It's made for men, so you just did what you had to do as a woman." For the most part, however, the nurses I interviewed felt that the military treated them fairly as women, even when it treated them differently than their male counterparts in policies regarding nursing assignments, combat duty, and family status.

The Vietnam War was the first war during which the question of whether to assign male or female nurses to the combat zone was an issue. For more than fifty years, military nursing had been the exclusive domain of women; both the Army and Navy Nurse Corps excluded men from their ranks from their beginning in 1901 and 1908,

respectively. In 1955, however, Congress passed legislation authorizing reserve commissions for male nurses. The Army Nurse Corps extended regular commissions to male nurses in 1966, as did the Navy
Nurse Corps in 1968.[1]

In general, the ANC believed it best to avoid gender-specific nursing assignments, but policy hinged on a cost-benefit analysis: grant-
ing requests for male nurses could permanently establish those positions as men's and so discriminate against female officers, while
honoring requests for female nurses meant constructing separate latrines and living quarters. Although for a while some Army hospitals
in Vietnam—especially in forward combat medical units—employed
only male nurses to avoid the costs associated with accommodat-
ing females, they soon integrated women into their staffs because
the benefits of doing so outweighed such costs. Not only did female
nurses provide patients a "healthy psychological lift" but they also
better maintained standards of care that tended to deteriorate in
units where the male nursing staff began to identify more closely
with their male doctor counterparts and neglected some of the traditional duties of nursing. Once female nurses joined the unit, wrote
the Army's chief nurse in Vietnam in 1969, "personal hygiene, patient
care and . . . morale" improved noticeably.[2]

Assigning female nurses to duty in Vietnam was also a simple
matter of numbers: women outnumbered men in both the civilian
and military nursing fields and therefore outnumbered men among
the ranks of military nurses in Vietnam as well. The nurses I interviewed worked with, at most, a handful of male nurses in Vietnam.
Edy Johnson, Kay Bauer, Mary O'Brien Tyrrell, and Penny Kettlewell
described their male counterparts as dedicated, skilled professionals
who provided excellent care for their patients. When Johnson arrived
at the 93rd Evac in spring 1968, her head nurse was a male captain.
She described him as "a wonderful role model of nurse and caring
human being" who "seemed like a fatherly figure to our young patients, providing great consolation just by his presence." Johnson did
not notice that doctors or patients treated male nurses any differently than they did female nurses.[3]

Occasionally, a male nurse would attempt to elevate his status,
as one of Kay Bauer's male nurse colleagues did when he asked his
patients to call him "Doctor." Bauer and another female nurse re-

sponded by telling him that "if he was not happy and proud to be a nurse, to leave the profession and try another that suited him." Male nurses developed "easy relations" with doctors, according to Kettlewell, because officers' living quarters were segregated by sex; thus, male doctors and nurses, all of whom were officers, bunked together, separate from the female nurses. Mary O'Brien Tyrrell said that a couple of male nurses with whom she worked always got the "best assignments" because they knew how to "kiss up" to the female nurse administrators. She also pointed out, however, that some female nurses were equally willing to curry favor with male doctors. Overall, women's relationships with and memories of male nurses were very cordial and respectful.[4]

If the military sought to preserve gender distinctions through its fifty-five-year policy of excluding men from nursing, it continues to do so through its combat exclusion policy. Men can now be military nurses, but women still technically cannot be—though in reality they often are—warriors. Although excluding women from combat has become murky business with the twenty-first-century wars in Afghanistan and Iraq, it was quite clear during the Vietnam War. For the nurses in this study, this situation did not present much of a problem. For one thing, they viewed themselves as nurses more than as soldiers; their role was to heal the wounds of war, not to inflict them, and so they had no desire to participate in combat. Even if they had taken offense at the gender distinction in the military's combat policy, they still would have been unable to participate in combat because the 1949 Geneva Convention defined all permanent medical (and religious) personnel as noncombatants.[5]

Because both U.S. military policy and the Geneva Convention defined nurses as noncombatants, then, weapons generally were not a significant part of their military experience. Like Kay Bauer, most nurses said that they received little or no weapons instruction during basic training. Army nurses Joan Paulson and Penny Kettlewell remembered taking a few shots with a .45-caliber handgun during basic, but most other nurses only vaguely recalled some kind of weapons-effects training, designed to give them a chance to imagine the kinds of wounds they would be treating in Vietnam. Mary Beth Crowley said she "never touched [a weapon] in basic" but "did see what an M16 can do to a large can of sauerkraut." None of the nurses in this study besides Kay Bauer possessed a weapon in Vietnam.[6]

Although nurses were noncombatants and did not carry weapons, they were serving in a combat zone. In a guerrilla war that lacked clearly identified combatants and clearly marked front lines, even nurses in the supposedly safe rear area where most hospitals were located faced some degree of danger. In recognition of this fact, the military provided nurses with combat pay, a small amount added to their regular salaries for their service in a war zone. Sometimes this gender equity provoked comment from men. Joan Paulson remembers male combat grunts good-naturedly teasing her and the other nurses at the 67th Evac about receiving combat pay: "They'd say, 'Oh, you're getting combat pay and you have running water and flush toilets? You shouldn't be getting combat pay.'"[7]

If the military thus acknowledged the potential dangers nurses faced by issuing them combat pay, its record of providing nurses with practical defenses against such danger was less consistent, according to the women I interviewed. Lynn Kohl recalled that there were no bunkers for the nurses at the 71st Evacuation hospital in Pleiku. "They had bunkers for the male officers and the enlisted men, and none for the nurses," she said. Some of the enlisted men "felt sorry" for Kohl and the other nurses, and so they put some sandbags up to form a "little abutment" for them. "But that's all we had," she explained. There was a bunker near Mary Beth Crowley's quarters in An Khe, but it often had water in it, and so she and her fellow nurses waited out red alerts with their patients in the bunkers near the hospital. During the 1968 Tet Offensive, Penny Kettlewell remembered, there were not enough flak jackets to go around, and so she and the other nurses at the 67th Evac in Qui Nhon went without. Still, in most cases, nurses had access to protected spaces and protective gear when necessary.[8]

The military highlighted differences between men and women in areas other than combat regulations. Women's status in the military had long been circumscribed on the basis of their status as wives, mothers-to-be, and mothers. From their inception, the Army and Navy Nurse Corps defined their ideal nurses as educated, young, white, single women. Until the World War II era, the ANC and NNC discharged any woman who married while in uniform; married women and women with children under age fourteen were not allowed to join the corps even after the 1947 Army-Navy Nurse Act established the corps as permanent fixtures and permitted officers who married while on duty to remain active in the Reserves. Married women were finally allowed to join the regular Army—not just the Reserves—in late 1964. The Army Nurse Corps made pregnancy, regardless of marital status, grounds for discharge until 1970 and considered it a disability until 1975. The idea was that women could not do justice to both family and corps and that family had to come first. Moreover, the military was not willing to provide special accommodations for the needs of wives, pregnant women, and mothers. Military policymakers also assumed that child rearing was primarily a mother's responsibility and men were the main breadwinners in the family, regardless of whether their wives worked outside the home. Accordingly, married male soldiers were entitled to dependent benefits for their families, but married female soldiers were not.[9]

These discriminatory family policies had a limited impact on the women I interviewed because most of them were single and childless. For Ann Rudolph and Lynn Bower, however, the policies were much more than words in a handbook. Rudolph was married before she went to Vietnam but was denied separation pay—a special allowance given to servicemen and their families during periods of physical separation due to deployment. She and her husband even wrote to their U.S. senator in protest, "to no avail. He responded but said that husbands are able to work and don't need support." Rudolph never did receive any separation pay.[10]

Bower was twenty-two and unmarried in 1971 when her long-term boyfriend suggested that her vomiting might be a sign of pregnancy. The medical clinic at Fort Bragg, where both she and her partner were stationed, had refused her request for birth control, and so she went without and ended up pregnant. When she was home on leave before deploying to Vietnam, her mother noticed that she was pregnant and told her, "You can't go like that." Bower said she placed several calls to military officials to inform them of her pregnancy, but "nobody called me back." So she went to Vietnam. "All my uniforms fit," she said, "so I got on a plane." Describing herself as naive, alone, and confused, Bower said she assumed she would just have the baby and keep working. Her chief nurse at the 24th Evac only found out about her pregnancy when Bower inquired about the possibility of getting married in Vietnam (her boyfriend was serving his third tour in-country at the same time) and mentioned that she was pregnant. When the chief nurse reacted with indignation, Bower told her that she had tried informing the Army of her pregnancy before leaving the United States and that a record of her physical exam was on file; she hadn't been trying to hide it. Bower refused the chief nurse's suggestion that she fly to Okinawa for an abortion, and so the Army began processing paperwork to send her back to the United States. "I didn't get all those rules," she recalled, but "it was a big thing to get me gone before I had the baby." Six weeks into her tour, Bower was sent home.

For years, Bower felt guilty for going home early, referring to herself as one of "the others"—those whose stories lack a "typically successful ending." She said, "I come from a family that pays their debts, and I owed, and I expected to do my work." It was Army policy, however, that prevented her from doing so. She spent her last few weeks in uniform at Fitzsimmons General Hospital in Denver, where everyone was "very, very nice" about her situation. She and her boyfriend married during this time, and so when she was finally discharged from active duty herself, she became a military dependent. She gave birth to a baby boy in February 1972.[11]

From deployment decisions to dependent benefits, from combat status to family status, military policy made gender a relevant difference among its soldiers, often discriminating against women in the process. Still, most of the nurses I interviewed were content with their treatment by the military. Valerie Buchan said she was treated fairly and equitably by the military during her time on active duty; it wasn't until she was in the Reserves in the 1980s and the paperwork for her promotion to lieutenant colonel got "lost" for over a year that she felt she encountered any sex discrimination. If gender-specific military policy had a relatively insignificant effect on most nurses in Vietnam, however, being one of only a handful of women in a sea of men had a far greater impact on their daily lives.

*Women in Uniform: Being Female in a War Zone*

American military women were a relative rarity in Vietnam. Approximately three million American men served in Vietnam, but fewer than ten thousand women donned the uniform and went to war. When overall troop strength was at its peak in early 1969, approximately 550,000 Americans were serving in Vietnam; of those, only 916 were Army nurses. American women in uniform—nurses or otherwise—were vastly outnumbered in Vietnam, and as such, were a treasured commodity. Male military officers valued women's presence as a morale boost for male troops. "There is nowhere else in the world where the American woman is such a great morale booster," said Major Henry Voegele, a head nurse at the 3rd Field Hospital in Saigon. Such attitudes also came from the pinnacle of military leadership in Vietnam, when General William Westmoreland said, "When my soldiers come into the hospital I want them to see a woman in a white uniform, with lipstick and her hair done up." ANC recruiting advertisements emphasized the healing effect of nurses' femininity as well. "In the Army, you're . . . needed for your skills and training," proclaimed one ANC ad from 1970. "You're needed, too, for your woman's touch. Your cheerfulness. Your reassuring smile in the middle of a long night." Being cared for by an Army nurse would soothe a soldier's soul as much as it would heal his wounds.[12]

Women boosted men's morale because they were women. It didn't matter what kind of uniform from which branch of service they wore, it didn't matter if they were "pretty" according to the conventional standards of the day, it didn't matter what their jobs were. It mattered that they were women, that they provided a feminine counterpoint to the masculinity amassed in the hundreds of thousands of American G.I.s sent to Vietnam to defeat communism. Men who had been "humping the boonies" for days on end, through mud and jungle; fighting insects and disease as well as the Viet Cong; eating out of tin cans and washing in streams and rivers; battling their fear of unseen enemies, of booby traps and land mines, of dying—these men welcomed the sight of a woman. Women, even those in uniform in the middle of a war zone, seemed to represent something other than war, an arena of relative safety, a touch of the home for which soldiers were fighting and to which they longed to return.

The femininity nurses represented was thus a decidedly American, and usually white, femininity. Soldiers called American women in Vietnam "round-eyes" to distinguish them from the "slant-eyed" Vietnamese women they encountered as hard-working field laborers, dangerous potential enemies, or alluring yet manipulative prostitutes. A 1966 book of cartoons and limericks published for G.I.s to capture "the lighter side of the war" was rife with these images of Vietnamese women:

> *A bar girl wore 38-D's*
> *Rather much for a Vietnamese.*
> *So they searched her, with pleasure,*
> *And discovered this treasure:*
> *One grenade, one plastique, two punjis.*

The more common image of Vietnamese women was as scheming bar girls or prostitutes who would get G.I.s drunk and steal their money before or after providing them with their sexual services:

> *He made up his mind he would ball it*
> *With some cute little whatchamacallit.*
> *Ah, she gave such delight—*
> *Till she left in the night*
> *With his shirt and his watch and his wallet.*[13]

In this context of racist sexism—as well as an alienation that stems from living in a foreign culture in a dangerous situation—American G.I.s placed a high value on American femininity. Ann Rudolph was a young, pretty blonde who had spent some of her earlier time in the military modeling for the Army. When she was in Vietnam in 1965 and 1966, she found a warm reception from G.I.s for her attractive, all-American looks. "I remember them always being happy to see round eyes," she recalled, and offered a simple explanation for G.I.s' interest: "Obviously, the majority of people in that country do not have round eyes. So seeing a blonde round-eye was refreshing for them." G.I.s would ask to take pictures of Mary Beth Crowley because they were so excited to see an American woman: "They'd say, 'I haven't seen a woman in six months. Could

I just take your picture and tell them when I get back that I saw a woman?'"[14]

Racial and national identity merged smoothly for white nurses in Vietnam; the only reason they stood out among the troops in Vietnam was that they were female. But they were in the racial majority—at home, in the field of nursing, and in the military. As such, they were able to take their own race for granted as the norm from which the relatively few nonwhite nurses deviated. Although there are no hard and fast statistics on African American and other nonwhite women in the military nurse corps during the Vietnam era, the numbers were small. The women I interviewed for this project, all of whom were white, remembered working with only a few nonwhite nurses at their military hospitals in Vietnam. Mary Breed remembered one of her colleagues being deluged with attention because she was the only African American female on the base in Da Nang. "*Every* African American guy would visit her," Breed recalled. "She used to sit outside . . . because she didn't want everyone coming into her hooch. She wanted her privacy. But yet, there was an identification thing. She wanted to be nice to people." Mary O'Brien Tyrrell recalled a similar situation facing her only African American nurse colleague on Guam.[15]

Whatever their race, nurses indicated that they were aware of the uplifting effect they had on men, especially those who had returned from the field. Edy Johnson explained that G.I.s associated women with the safer atmosphere of the rear: "The fact that there were round-eyed women around, American women" made them feel safe because they believed the military "certainly wouldn't put women where it was dangerous." Even when high morale turned on sexual attraction, nurses were sympathetic toward their young patients. Lynn Bower remembered that a group of women from the Miss America pageant toured one of her wards at the 24th Evac, visiting with young male patients who were too sick to leave their beds. "Then [the women] left and you had these little tents under the blankets," she said. "They were in physical agony, and missing home." As understanding as she was, she admitted that the situation was difficult for her, too. "Who had to deal with them? I'm only twenty-two myself. The boys did *not* make rude comments. They did not. I'm not saying that," she explained. But she bore the effects of stifled sexual desire in her patients nonetheless. "I spent a couple night shifts on the wards. I got so many marriage proposals. It was, 'I just don't want to die without having been married. I don't want to . . .'" She paused. "It was just so sad. Just so, so sad."[16]

It wasn't only generals and G.I.s who appreciated femininity in the war zone. The nurses I interviewed understood that soldiers valued feminine women, and in many ways, they tried to live up to those expectations. Before Mary Beth Crowley left for Vietnam, a nurse who had already served in-country advised her to "just keep wearing makeup. The guys like that. Wear mascara and lipstick and you'll look good, and wear perfume." But many nurses valued such things for themselves as well and were as invested in maintaining their feminine identity as were the men around them. The second part of the nurse's advice to Crowley reflected this. "Buy real fancy underwear before you go over there," she advised, "and, even though you're wearing fatigues, you'll still feel nice in your underwear." "You'll still feel nice" meant "you'll still feel like a woman."

This was no small task in Vietnam. Even though the military emphasized the differences between men and women and wanted women to be as feminine as possible for the male troops, the realities of living in a war zone operated by a masculine institution made it difficult or impractical to find the accoutrements of femininity. Nurses' uniforms became the subject of much debate. In its recruiting ads, the Army Nurse Corps typically featured women in the traditional white uniform of nursing despite the fact that, in most hospitals, nurses wore fatigues and boots. White uniforms were simply not a viable option for nurses working in the hot and dusty or muddy conditions of Vietnam. Navy nurse Kay Bauer was supposed to wear a starched white uniform with white shoes, nylons, and cap but found it difficult to do so in a setting that lacked electricity, running water, and starch and that regularly recorded temperatures in the mid-nineties. Instead, she and a female nurse colleague had a local Vietnamese woman sew a more casual, lightweight white shift dress that they wore without nylons or cap; they saved the more formal summer blue uniform for the occasional visit from military or civilian dignitaries. When Bobby Smith arrived at the Air Force hospital in Cam Ranh Bay, "they told us we had to wear whites," a directive that the nurses laughed off as impractical and silly. Instead, they found some Army fatigues that they adjusted for use in their hospital.[17]

Although lightweight fatigues were a much more practical option than either white duty uniforms or the herringbone twill fatigues originally intended for Army nurses in Vietnam, they often didn't fit women's smaller stature. Footwear was also an issue. White shoes may have been more traditional and feminine, but boots were the footwear of choice. Initially, however, they were not designed for women's smaller feet. "For the longest time," D-M Boulay recalled, "everybody had to wear men's boots, and they didn't exactly fit well." Whether or not military officials or male patients wanted pretty, made-up, coiffed nurses at bedside, Ann Rudolph said that practical concerns far outweighed any pressure or inclination to be feminine: "It would have been totally impractical to wear white anything."[18]

Practical considerations aside, however, nurses were young women who still wanted to feel like young women. As Joan Paulson put it, "We did pay attention to our makeup and our hair just simply because that was the only part that was us. I mean, we wore fatigues, we wore boots, we wore baseball caps." Getting products to enhance feminine appearance was a challenge in Vietnam, however. Post exchanges on base sold tampons and perfume, but Mary Beth Crowley's mother had to send her the mascara, blue eyeliner, and Clairol #9 lipstick that she wore. On rare occasions, Ann Rudolph wore a civilian dress for a trip into town, but otherwise she spent her workdays in fatigues and her off-duty hours in shorts. Mary O'Brien Tyrrell brought a mini-skirt from home and became known as "Guamanian Twiggy" for introducing the style to the island. Kay Bauer regularly went "downtown" near her hospital in Rach Gia to have her hair and nails done by local Vietnamese women. If military women were—or wanted to be—feminine, then they would have to find ways of being so on their own. They were caught in a double bind, told to be different from male soldiers but also expected to fit in and adjust to the male norm. So it was that Westmoreland both insisted on nurses wearing white uniforms and makeup *and* "admired the nurses in Vietnam, living in mud-surrounded tents, using outdoor latrines, eating from mess kits in rain or under blistering sun, seldom finding opportunity for a bath."[19]

The fine line that nurses had to walk—between being too femi-

nine and not feminine enough—was especially evident in their social interactions with men. Sometimes, men equated femininity
with sexual availability. Long-standing stereotypes of both female
nurses and female soldiers centered on sexual deviance as their detractors accused them of being "loose" women who enjoyed serving
men sexually. One man suggested to Mary Breed that nurses went
to Vietnam "to get laid. Some people thought that's what nurses did
all the time." Popular media images of hypersexual military nurses
didn't help. Some guys "thought you were—I hate to say it—like
[the nurses on] *M*A*S*H*," Breed recalled. After she got back from
Vietnam, Joan Paulson spoke publicly about her experiences during
the war. She said that some interviewers would ask, "'Are nurses like
they say nurses are?' My dad always worried about that, too. I guess
we kind of had a reputation. And there was 'Hot Lips' Houlihan [to
stoke the fires of such stereotyping]." While being feminine boosted
men's morale by softening the masculine environs of war and holding out the prospect of intimate contact with a woman, if taken too far
and turned into promiscuity, it turned back on itself. Being properly
feminine and available was one thing; being sexually wanton was
another. Sexual aggression, even assertiveness, was presumed to be
the domain of men. As Valerie Buchan explained, people thought
military women were "sexually loose and probably didn't use good
language. I think they thought that you lost your femininity, became
more masculine."[20]

In the eyes of many midcentury Americans, the most masculine,
sexually deviant women of all were lesbians. Indeed, the other pre-
vailing stereotype of military women was that they were coarse, man-
hating homosexuals who joined the military to satiate their sexual
appetite for other women. The nurses I interviewed did not say they
were hampered by such accusations, nor did they have much to
say about the presence of actual lesbians in their units in Vietnam.
Lesbians weren't telling, and straight women weren't asking. "It wasn't
open," Army nurse Joan Paulson said. "If there were people who were
seeing one another of the same sex, they could have done it easily
and I wouldn't have even known it." In contrast, D-M Boulay was surprised to learn about the military's antigay policy after she had been
discharged. She had "no idea" that homosexuals were not allowed to
serve in the military, she said, because she and her colleagues knew

of "several" openly identified lesbians and gay men. She said no one hassled them because "they pulled their weight at their job and that was highly valued." She also attributed the easy acceptance of various sexual identities to a general attitude among medical professionals: "We tend to be understanding of human beings in all their configurations, so when you're at war, there's no difference." Still, her experience seems to be the exception rather than the rule.[21]

If nurses were largely immune to probing questions about their sexual orientation, they certainly were not safeguarded from unwanted sexual attention from men. High-ranking male officers sometimes "requested" the company of nurses to liven the atmosphere at their after-hours social gatherings. Air Force nurse Bobby Smith said that nurses were "detailed sometimes to go to parties for visiting so-and-so." Although occasionally Penny Kettlewell happily would accept an invitation to visit officers and enjoy the amenities they provided—especially the Australians, who had a hospital in the beach area of Vung Tau and were "a classy bunch"—she resented having to socialize with "groping generals." She said, "You came up with anything you could come up with to avoid going there." Mary Lu Brunner always made sure to attend such parties in the company of a married couple with whom she was friendly. "They'd see to it that I got home," she explained. Even outside of such formal get-togethers, Kettlewell grew tired of having to fend off advances from officers, often older and married, who were "acting like absolute jerks." Lynn Bower encountered such behavior on her first day in-country, at the 90th Replacement, when a "full-bird colonel" who "had had a few drinks" propositioned her. Luckily, two male captains overheard this exchange and intervened on Bower's behalf. Male soldiers also stepped in another time when a G.I. attacked a fellow nurse in Bower's living quarters and "wanted to rape her." The friendly soldiers prevented the attack from going any further; afterwards, the nurses had a guard on permanent duty outside their hooch.

Although frustrating and frightening, such extreme examples of sexual predation by men in Vietnam were the exception to the rule among the women whose stories are recounted here. More often, they shared memories of good times, told with good humor . . . such as when Mary Breed went to see Bob Hope with another nurse and some of the corpsmen from her hospital. When they arrived, one of the corpsmen suggested that Breed use her feminine wiles to get the group closer to the front. She and another female nurse agreed to lead the charge, so to speak, toward the stage. "We started to inch our way down the hill . . . and came to this fence, this huge fence. People were taking a lot of pictures of Chris, because she's so darling. All I know is that we were going to climb over this fence, and as my rear end is going over the fence, people are taking pictures. Thank God I was thinner then," she joked. Once she found her seat, Breed noticed a "cute" guy from New York and decided to take *his* picture. When he asked her why she was photographing him, Breed responded, "'I haven't seen a round-eyed man for so long.' . . . The whole group around me laughed. It was *so* funny."[22]

These kinds of recollections outnumbered stories of inappropriate behavior by men. Most of these women said they did not experience sexual harassment, and none had themselves been assaulted. Even if men's interest in them was more benign, however, it was ever present, and women had to decide how to respond. Nurses worked long hours and often wanted to spend their leisure time relaxing out of sight of inquisitive male eyes. Nevertheless, romantic, and sometimes sexual, relationships did occasionally develop in Vietnam. Youth, hormones, danger, distance from home, and a severely imbalanced ratio of men to women combined to make liaisons with the opposite sex available (at least for women) and appealing. "Everybody had a boyfriend over there," recalled Mary Beth Crowley. "They were very easy to come by." Even women who were relatively inexperienced in relations with men found they were highly sought after. "You could have been an unattractive woman and you would still get hit on," Joan Paulson said with a laugh. "Which was very flattering and kind of fun."

Still, most of the women I interviewed said that if they dated at all, they did so within certain limits. Military fraternization policies forbade social relationships between officers and enlisted personnel, but doctors were more likely to be older and already married by the time they went to Vietnam. Mary Beth Crowley and Ann Rudolph both noted that this didn't always stop single (or married) nurses from forming relationships with these "geographic bachelors"—as Mary O'Brien Tyrrell called married men who put away their wedding rings (and vows) while in Vietnam. "There were affairs going on right and left," said Rudolph, who was herself married. "That was part of being away from home, [but] that's not a piece of my world then or now." Some nurses chose to socialize with married men for the safe companionship it provided. D-M Boulay spent some of her leisure time with married men in a "platonic, I-need-a-social-companion" way, where "the closest physical contact you had was someone to hold your elbow to guide you up the stairs or something like that."

For many of these nurses, however, enlisted men—whether corpsmen, troops stationed on base, sometimes even patients—were the social partners of choice, despite the military antifraternization policy. They spent most of their working hours with enlisted men and were closest in age to them. Edy Johnson once went on a date with a sergeant (a noncommissioned officer) to the enlisted men's club, during which she made sure to wear civilian clothes so that her officer rank would not be evident. Relationships between nurses and G.I.s ranged from close but platonic friendships to intimate romantic relationships. Mary Breed was known as "Mom Breed" not only because she treated her corpsmen with maternal concern but also because she refused to engage in any kind of romantic relationships with soldiers. From the outset, Breed made it clear that she "believed in the sanctity of marriage." If she agreed to have dinner with a married colleague, "that was all there was going to be, because he had a wife at home." Mary Beth Crowley "went out a lot" but said that she had decided before she even arrived in Vietnam not to get into "the sex business" because she understood that life in Vietnam "wasn't real life." She formed a close relationship with someone near the end of her time in An Khe, but it fizzled when she moved to the hospital in Qui Nhon. "It didn't really break my heart at all," she said. "He never heard from me and I never heard from him, and I'm not going to search him out at this point."

Some nurses were in committed relationships while they were in Vietnam, either with civilian men left behind at home or with G.I.s they met in-country. Ann Rudolph married before she went to Vietnam, and Joan Paulson was engaged when she got her orders; neither of their partners served in Vietnam. The separation was hard on both couples. Rudolph remained faithful to her husband while she was in the service but believes her experiences in Vietnam contributed to some of her postwar marital difficulties. She and her husband divorced in 1978. Although Paulson was engaged while in Vietnam, she dated a Mexican American corpsman for the last half of her tour in-country. "Six months [away] and the heart grows fonder. Another six to eight months and the heart wanders," she explained. She recalled "just spending time" with the corpsman and that they had a "pretty good time." When she returned home, she and her fiancé broke up for a while before recommitting to each other and marrying. The subject of Vietnam is not an easy one for Paulson and her husband. "We've had a very happy marriage," she said. "But we never talk about Vietnam much."[23]

Other nurses became seriously involved with men they met while serving overseas. Lynn Kohl, Mary O'Brien Tyrrell, D-M Boulay, and Mary Lu Brunner all either married or were engaged to military men they met abroad. Lynn Kohl met her first husband in Vietnam, as Tyrrell did hers in Guam. Boulay's future husband was an obstetrician-gynecologist stationed at the 24th Evacuation hospital in Long Binh when Boulay was at the 93rd Evac, also in Long Binh. They met at a party at an officers' club but remained platonic friends because he was married to someone else at the time. They kept in touch after they returned from Vietnam, however, and married after he and his first wife divorced. Brunner came home from Vietnam engaged to a Green Beret, but they never married. He had six months left in his tour when she came home, and he wanted her to stay with him in Vietnam until his tour was complete. "I said, 'I'm out of here. Thanks, anyway. I'm gone,'" Brunner recalled. She returned to the United States in July 1969 and was "disengaged" by February 1970. She and her former fiancé remained friendly, however, and she described his wife as "a really nice gal." Brunner married her husband in fall 1971.

Overall, then, these women recalled safe, fun, social relationships with men in Vietnam. When asked if they had ever experienced anything bordering on sexual harassment, many responded with a quick and firm "no." For D-M Boulay and the women with whom she worked, sexual harassment was not a problem. "No," she said. "Absolutely not. Not during my time." In fact, women more often spoke of the gallantry of their male peers than they did any kind of intrusive attention. "I know there are scandals about rape and those kinds of things," Mary O'Brien Tyrrell commented. "I never felt threatened with that. Never." That the women I met were lucky enough to have such positive contact with men does not mean that every woman in uniform had similar experiences; harassment, even assault, did occur. But for the women in this study, being female was grounds for especially courteous treatment from the men around them, especially their patients. "I'd not been in that kind of environment where men were quite so gallant," explained Boulay. "So, in a sense, it was quaint and helpful." Being a nurse also helped. They were angels, after all.[24]

### Angels in Fatigues: Nurses in Vietnam

"The Marines treated us like queens," Mary O'Brien Tyrrell said of her experiences with men in Guam. "The sergeant would come up and he would say, 'Now, are you having any trouble with anybody, Miss O'Brien? I'll take them out to the back porch and take care of it.' There was no monkeying around with the nurses." Many of the women I met echoed Tyrrell's sentiments. It seemed that every tale of unwanted advances by one G.I. ended with two or more G.I.s intervening on the nurse's behalf, and it was the latter part of the story that the nurses emphasized. Edy Johnson said a "skinny little second lieutenant" firmly told a warrant officer who had been pestering her to dance, "Sir, the lady doesn't want to dance." Another time, two men physically removed one of their drunken friends who had been making "inappropriate" comments to Johnson, apologizing to her on the way out. Lynn Bower said that when G.I.s found out she was pregnant, they were especially chivalrous, offering to step in if her boyfriend was not a "stand-up guy." Valerie Buchan spoke highly of the patients she treated: "I just can't say enough for how they treated us. They were so grateful for anything that you could do for them. They were so respectful. They were just a joy to [care for]. I didn't run into a single one that I don't feel that way about."

These stories of respectful, even gallant, behavior of military men—whether patients, peers, or subordinates—speak to the special status nurses enjoyed in Vietnam. Women who joined the military broke a long-standing gender boundary, but those who signed on as nurses inhabited a space somewhere between the supposed extremes that gender stereotyping promoted. In instances in which the supposedly contradictory statuses of "woman" and "soldier" clashed, "nurse" became the mediating identity, one that allowed women to be both woman and soldier but neither one fully. "Nurse" granted the soldier an exemption from the dirty business of killing in war while also providing the woman a legitimate reason for being in the war zone. That all nurses were officers also afforded them the privileges of rank that commanded respect from anyone, male or female, below them in the military hierarchy. That they were engaged in a traditionally feminine, nurturing occupation exempted them from some of the hostility that men who felt threatened by women in uniform may otherwise have displayed. As Lynn Kohl explained, men had "better feelings toward you as a nurse than as an officer."

Male veterans' own accounts seem to parallel these nurses' recollections. Though most men probably didn't have occasion to interact with American women during the war, many of those who were unlucky enough to be wounded and sent to a hospital took special solace in the care they received from female nurses. In 1966, Staff Sergeant Barry Sadler, best known for his hit "The Ballad of the Green Berets," captured this warm regard in the song "Salute to the Nurses": "Many a wounded soldier's pain is eased for a while," he sang, "by opening his eyes to see a nurse's smile."[25]

Years later, grateful appreciation filled men's memories of these encounters. From mementos left at the Vietnam Women's Memorial thanking the nurses for their efforts to web pages and YouTube video tributes, from personal stories shared in combat veteran support groups to letters written to their long-ago caregivers, male Vietnam veterans routinely expressed a sense of camaraderie with the nurses. Most of these admiring references to nurses come from men's postwar accounts (as do nurses' equally fond descriptions of their patients) and thus could be attributed to the bond Vietnam veterans formed as they sought support, companionship, and redemption after such a controversial war or even to the evolution of "politically correct" perspectives on women's capabilities and wartime service. Memories and the language through which they are expressed often reflect the current political and personal landscape as much as they do the actual past. Still, both nurses and male veterans have consistently and widely described their relationship as amicable, suggesting that such recollections are more than postwar creations. And it was the special gendered relationship that characterized nurses' interactions with their patients that made such wartime camaraderie likely. Men thanked and praised nurses not just for their medical competency but also for being "American wild flowers" and, most frequently, "angels."[26]

Traditional images of angels center on ethereal beings sent to deliver God's message to the masses, bestow mercy on the down-trodden, and intercede between God and man. Although religious use of the term "angel" included militant male angels who waged war on behalf of a higher power, the secularized use of the term generally applied to females thought to be especially selfless and benevolent, who reside above the ugly fray of passionate emotion and heated conflict. "Angel" had long been used to describe nurses, a reference to their patient and self-sacrificing care of the ill and wounded. Angelic nurses were pure and chaste as well, in contrast to the "naughty nurse" image that lay at the other end of the sexualized stereotyping scale.[27]

For nurses who served in Vietnam, the angel image provided some degree of protection against the stereotypes of both nurses and military women as promiscuous, hypersexualized women. In the context of war, the term took on added significance. Not only were they tender caregivers; they were also somehow separate from the military and the war it was waging. If soldiers got dirty in the muck of the war and women were mired in men's carnal desires, nurses—angels—rose above it all. Being a nurse exempted women from having to participate in war, even as they attempted to piece together the broken bodies that were war's casualties. It sheltered them from having to make moral or political decisions about the righteousness of U.S. involvement in Vietnam—although many would come to do so anyway. But, as Kay Bauer said, nurses were there to heal, not to harm. Even if the enemy shot at her, she said, "My job is not to shoot at them. Whereas, the guys had to do that. That was their job; it wasn't mine."

Men's view of nurses as angels thus tapped into a wellspring of sentiment and symbolism. But nurses' special status was also grounded in laws and policies that defined medical personnel and women as noncombatants as well as in the realities of war wherein nurses' professional skills became the difference between life and death for injured G.I.s. "It was more of an occupational way of regarding people," according to D-M Boulay. "We were noncombatants, and because of our skills, we were highly prized human beings. We were safe places. We lived in a safe place. We worked in a safe place. And what we did was valued." Diane Evans also pointed to her status as a nurse in explaining the "tremendous respect" men had for her and her colleagues in Vietnam: "I felt that people were watching out for me. I knew that right from the beginning."

The vaunted status nurses enjoyed was reserved for them specifically. While all American women were valued as "round-eyes," only the nurses were "angels." Women who enlisted in other branches of the military also often enjoyed cordial relationships with their male peers but did not, as a group, command the same kind of attention as the nurses. Their numbers were smaller, their work different, their relationships with men less intimate. While a nurse's job was certainly to care for the physical needs of her patients, it also involved comforting them emotionally as well.[28]

One of the most frequent themes in nurses' stories about their time in Vietnam is that they often acted as surrogate wives, sisters, mothers, or girlfriends for their patients. They held their patients' hands, listened to their worries, and eased their fears. They stood in for all the women the soldiers had left behind, and they did so willingly and without complaint. Army nurse Ann Rudolph considered this part of the job. She loved nursing because she wanted to "make a difference in people's lives." In a war zone, she saw it as her duty to "bring a little home to them, smile at them, pay attention to them, give them time." Mary O'Brien Tyrrell viewed her responsibilities to her patients in much the same way. "I talked with them," she explained, and gave them "the kind of comfort that I think their sister or mother or wife would have wanted to provide for them." Sometimes nurses played roles for dying patients who confused them with their actual sisters. "This one young man was off to the side and I was standing by the litter," Lynn Bower recalled. "He said something about [me] being his sister or something. I just said, 'Yes,' because I knew he was expectant. . . . I stood there, and I was just whoever he wanted me to be until he passed. He was the first, but he wasn't the last by any means."[29]

Assuming a sisterly role for their patients "seemed rather natural" to Joan Paulson: "We were really peers." The same was true for

Edy Johnson, who had five younger brothers of whom her patients reminded her. "I was like a big sister looking after them," she remembered. The only time that proved difficult was when a patient developed a "crush" on her and demanded more of her attention than he actually needed. In an attempt to discourage his affection, she tried to be "very matter of fact and businesslike about it." More often than not, Mary Beth Crowley's patients would see her "as a pal, or like a sister," roles she assumed easily and with humor. Her corpsmen good-naturedly referred to her as "Gracie Slick" (a reference to the lead singer of Jefferson Airplane). She remembered going swimming in the ocean one day, and a G.I. asking to take her picture when she got out of the water. "I'd kind of gotten stuck in this undertow, so I came out and I had my hair in pigtails and I think one of them was here and one was here," she said, pointing to the front and back of her head. "I had a two-piece suit on. I had so much sand in this suit, I could barely walk. And this G.I. runs up and says, 'Can we take your picture?'" she recalled laughingly. "Are you crazy?"

If nurses filled in as sisters for their patients, G.I.s—whether patients or corpsmen—often acted as brothers for the nurses. Indeed, there was a reciprocal relationship of caring between G.I.s and nurses. D-M Boulay discovered that she had "more brothers than I ever knew." Patients appreciated both the professional skill and emotional support nurses provided, as did the corpsmen who witnessed nurses' attentiveness to injured soldiers. The corpsmen who worked with Mary Breed gave her a cassette tape of rock music for Christmas 1970, accompanied by a note: "'To our Mom Breed. Take care and best wishes to you. P.S. Sweet thoughts for those who care.' They knew I cared about them and they knew I cared about the soldiers we took care of," she explained. As head nurse of the air evacuation unit in the Navy hospital on Guam, Mary O'Brien Tyrrell made sure her patients received the best medical care, to be sure. But she also paid attention to the details that would make their stay as comfortable as possible, right down to the hamburgers, fries, and Cokes she made sure were available to them. In return, they treated her and the other nurses "like queens." Corpsmen also appreciated the fact that nurses rarely "pulled rank" on them. "I should have been an authority figure, I suppose," Mary Lu Brunner said, "but I wasn't. I was more on the same level and playing field." As a woman and a

*Mary Lu Brunner commented, "I thought one way to see the world was to join the military."*

nurse, she also "felt protected by my little group of corpsmen and the NCOs—noncommissioned officers—that were in charge of them. It was like a little family."

The bonds that nurses formed with G.I.s were strong and lasting. Mary O'Brien Tyrrell got choked up when she spoke about the love and respect she felt for—and from—the Marines she encountered at the Navy hospital in Guam: "I love Marines. I will *always* love Marines." Although she admitted that shouldering the responsibility for caring for such badly wounded young men was "traumatic," she was humbled by the enormous sacrifices her patients had made: "What was my trauma compared to their trauma?" Diane Evans had high regard for the men with whom she worked in Vietnam, fondly recalling the "tremendous respect which the men had for us as nurses." Being a nurse was critical to this positive relationship with male

G.I.s. Joan Paulson reflected on the situation: "I mean, look at us: nurses. We're going to care for them. We're going to nurture them," she said. "We were the same age. We were officers so they had to respect us. And yet, we were kind of maybe even like the fruit, the untouchable fruit. Maybe it made us more alluring. We were there; we were the angels. We were the angels."

Mom Breed. Gracie Slick. Guamanian Twiggy. These monikers reflect the various ways women who served in the war theater fit in with the men around them, from maternal mentor to fun-loving peer to fashion-conscious icon. Each was an officer, a woman, and a nurse, and each of them had to figure out what these things meant against the backdrop of war. With great commitment and honor, the nurses I met fulfilled the obligations of both nursing and military service; they put their nursing skills to the best possible use in tending to those who had sacrificed so much for their country, and this was their way of serving their country. As women, they adapted with humor and ingenuity to the masculine environment of a wartime military. That they were round-eyed angels helped in this task immeasurably.

Mary Breed had arrived in Vietnam on September 5, 1970. Nine months and three days later, in June 1971, she returned to the United States to attend her father's funeral. She had been roller-skating down Highway 1 in Quang Tri when a military jeep pulled up behind her and took her back to her colonel's office. She thought she was in trouble for her extracurricular activity and was confused when she found Colonel Johnson crying and a Red Cross worker waiting for her. "Your father is dead," the man from the Red Cross told her. "Do you want to go home?" "I thought, 'Well, what a stupid thing to say. Of course I want to go home.'" Word traveled fast across the base that Mom Breed had lost her father and would be returning to the United States. Although she received many kindnesses from her friends and fellow nurses, she was especially moved by the response of men who worked in the Graves Registration unit on base: "Colonel Johnson handed me an envelope just before I was taking off from Quang Tri, and she said that the guys [from Graves] had started collecting money for me." Although Breed didn't know anyone from Graves, the colonel told her that the men "remembered me from working with casualties and they respected me." She paused. "I could cry to this day, because maybe I was young and foolish, but you never thank people enough. You never thank them . . ." With money in her pocket and sadness in her heart, Mom Breed was on her way home.

# 4

## *"Home to a Foreign Country"*

### From War in Vietnam
### to War at Home

**CAPTAIN BARBARA "BOBBY" SMITH** returned to the United States in August 1967 after having spent one year at an Air Force hospital in Cam Ranh Bay, Vietnam. For the two years prior to her tour in-country, Smith had worked with the ill and injured on air evacuation flights from Southeast Asia; she would spend the two years after her time in Vietnam doing the same. For five years, then, Smith tended to Americans wounded in Vietnam. When she left for Vietnam in August 1966, controversy about the war "wasn't a really big thing," she said. "We were going to do all good things." By the time she came home a year later, however, things had changed: "It was like I came home to a foreign country. Because it wasn't the country I left."

Many returning veterans felt the same sense of alienation that Smith did. One day they were toiling in the dust and heat of a poverty-stricken, war-torn Vietnam; the next day they were back in a shiny, wealthy United States that seemed to be at war with itself. They were disillusioned to find that the world to which they had so longed to return no longer held a place for them and that what they viewed as honorable service to their country brought so much dishonor. These kinds of homecoming experiences have become a central component in the overall story of the war, but usually the focus is on the male combat veteran. This chapter places the returning nurse at the center of the story. Like their male counterparts, many of the women I met swept their service under the rug and descended into a long silence about their experiences in Vietnam. Their gender provided women who wished to hide their veteran status a ready disguise; they simply put away their uniforms and resumed lives as wives, mothers, and nurses. Although they may have seemed to be just like the civilian women around them, the year they spent in a war zone changed them in important ways.

### *Sinking into the Quagmire: Questioning the War in Vietnam*

When Bobby Smith was at the Air Force hospital in Cam Ranh Bay, a young Marine patient asked her if she thought the United States should be in Vietnam: "I thought, 'Wow. I don't think so.' But I didn't say that. I said, 'Well, I don't know. I don't know enough about it. People smarter than me are running this. If they think so, then yes, I guess so.' That's about all I could tell him. If I had said no, he probably would have curled up his toes and died." Smith's view of the war changed during her time in-country, but she "didn't want to deal with it" and instead focused all of her attention on her patients.

One of the most profound and unsettling changes that many of these women underwent began while they were still in the war zone as they started to question the war and, by extension, their country. Declining morale among troops was one of the most obvious signs of discontent with the war. The later in the war the nurses in this study served, the more they noticed low morale in their patients, their colleagues, and themselves. Ann Rudolph was in Vietnam from September 1965 to July 1966 and doesn't remember low morale being a problem. When she was in-country from February 1967 to March 1968, D-M Boulay thought the spirit among her patients was "pretty good." Mostly, she said, they kept themselves busy to avoid thinking about the wounds they had just sustained. By the time Diane Evans left Vietnam in August 1969, however, "the morale was terrible." She attributed this decline in attitude, at least in part, to the chaos that was occurring at home. "The war protests were at their height," she explained. "The morale definitely was going down. I think it was noticeable amongst everybody. The other nurses that I served with, we were all tired. We were exhausted. Some of us were sick."

It wasn't just the home front that was chaotic, though. Lynn Bower described her brief time in Vietnam—six weeks in late summer 1971—as "craziness." During one red alert signifying that Viet Cong were on the compound, the officer of the day came to her desk, put down his .45 pistol, and told her there were two bullets in it—one for her and the other nurse on duty. He would shoot the nurses before he would let the VC capture them, he told her. Penny Kettlewell heard about such directives, too, accompanied by the idea that such a fate would be preferable to being "raped by the 'gooks.'" Thus, even if this was not official military policy and no such shooting incidents have been documented, the story reflected widespread belief about the special sexual peril American women faced at the hands of the Vietnamese enemy and that it was American men's difficult duty to protect them from it. From Bower's perspective, however, such logic made the world seem upside down and out of control. "It was just Looney Tunes," she said.[1]

Declining morale was especially evident to Kettlewell, who served two tours in-country, the first in 1967–68 and the second in 1970–71. Although she was in Vietnam for the 1968 Tet Offensive and stationed at a hospital with a troubling lack of effective leaders, Kettlewell said that the situation was even more disheartening during her second tour. By that time, President Richard Nixon's strategy of Vietnamizing the war was in full swing. Drug use and racial tension had increased markedly, while military discipline "was shot, gone." "By the last six months I was there," she said, "absolutely no one wanted to be there. They were pulling a number of units out of the country. They were closing hospitals. No one wanted to be there." She described soldiers coming in from the field "wired" on the stimulant Dexedrine that the military had supplied to its medics for use in the field. She would refer these G.I.s to the social workers on base, who administered sleep aids to the exhausted, strung-out soldiers.[2]

Low morale often coincided with drug use among troops. Although a number of nurses said that drug use was not common among troops or medical personnel while they were in-country, others described it as pervasive. Valerie Buchan said that she did not see needle tracks (indicating heroin use) on any of her patients at the 12th Evac in Cu Chi in 1968–69, "not even a single time." "As far as I was concerned," she stated, "there was no drug problem at the 25th" Infantry Division at Cu Chi. Mary Breed and D-M Boulay both remembered soldiers and medical personnel using alcohol—sometimes quite extensively during their off-duty hours—but nothing else. "Drugs were not prevalent," Boulay said. "It was not a problem. It was just on the verge of being a problem."[3]

Taken at face value, coverage of the issue in the *New York Times* corroborates Boulay's account. From 1965 to 1967, the only articles about drugs in Vietnam centered on new antimalaria medications for soldiers. By February 1968, however, the *Times* was reporting on the Pentagon's "fight on drug use in Vietnam," with marijuana being the specific target of such efforts. Two and a half years later, heroin use by G.I.s in Vietnam had become cause for alarm, and in May 1971 the newspaper proclaimed that "G.I. heroin addiction is epidemic in Vietnam." President Nixon and Congress made fighting drug use by soldiers a national priority the next month. At least one scholar has argued that such accounts must not be taken at face value, however, because the media, the Nixon administration, and the Democratic Party all significantly exaggerated the extent of the drug problem for commercial or ideological reasons. Instead, drug use among troops in Vietnam reflected patterns similar to those among civilians at home, experimentation more than addiction, and increasing frustration with the war. According to this argument, low morale prompted soldiers to experiment with drugs as a means of escape; drug use did not cause the decline in morale.[4]

Mary Beth Crowley (1970–71) and Lynn Bower (1971) were in-country when both hard drugs and bad morale were more common. "Starting in August of 1970," Crowley said, "we saw more drug usage among our own corpsmen." She recalled one corpsman who sought treatment for what he thought might be drug-related hepatitis. When she was unable to find a vein in his arm from which to draw blood, he did it himself. "He knew where to go," she explained. She remembered another corpsman who was reluctant to leave Vietnam because he feared it would be more difficult to obtain drugs in the United States. Lynn Bower described walking across base and stepping on plastic capsules that held illicit drugs: "When you walked in between the Quonset huts, you flipped them with your feet. They crackled. There were so many." Bower had sympathy for the G.I.s with drug problems, however. Years after her return from Vietnam, she would dream about a young man who had come into the ER at the 24th Evac and gotten "down on his hands and knees, begged me to give him some drugs, because he was jonesing," or going through with-drawal. "I just thought, here's this young man from home who never in his life woke up, went to the mirror, and thought, 'I wish I could be a raving addict.'" She counts him among the war's casualties.

Nurses who witnessed this kind of drug abuse attributed it to growing disillusionment with the war. G.I.s expressed that sinking morale and rising disillusionment in ways besides tuning in, turn-ing on, and dropping out, however. Respect for military discipline and hierarchy waned as soldiers listened to the antiestablishment anthems of their generation, insisted on growing their hair, sported peace symbols on their helmets, read underground G.I. newspapers, formed race-based power groups, went on "search and avoid" (in-stead of "search and destroy") missions—or blatantly refused to en-gage in combat. Penny Kettlewell said she had "card-carrying mem-bers of Vietnam Veterans Against the War" among her corpsmen and fellow nurses during her second tour. One of the most pernicious forms such dissent took was fraggings—the intentional killing or wounding of inexperienced or unpopular officers by soldiers under their command.[5]

Several of the nurses in this study said they had heard about fraggings from their patients. Joan Paulson, who was in Qui Nhon from 1967 to 1968, said that there was "a price on officers' heads," especially on "green" lieutenants whom troops feared would lead them into dangerous situations. Army nurses Mary Breed and Penny Kettlewell, both of whom served 1970–71, recalled treating fragging victims in their respective hospitals. Breed remembered one particu-lar "frag a friend" incident in which a group of guys "hated this one lieutenant because he made them go back to an area where they had been before and lost people." One of the men in this unit put a gre-nade in the lieutenant's hooch, the explosion of which sent several casualties to the OR: "I went to this ward and somebody asked me about this lieutenant. I said, 'Well, he's in intensive care, but he'll be dead shortly.' They said, 'Good!' This is how I heard about fragging." By the time she was at the 24th Evac in Long Binh during her sec-ond tour, Kettlewell was seeing more and more casualties who were victims of violence by other Americans. "About halfway through my tour is when, all of a sudden, all the fraggings were happening," she said. "It no longer was the honest war wounds. There were people that had shot themselves or each other." She attributed this behavior to the "desperation" G.I.s felt at being pawns in the political game the war had become. "Nobody had any idea what they were over there for at that point," she explained.

It wasn't just combat troops who were becoming increasingly confused about the war's purpose and prosecution; some nurses were, too. As was the case for many G.I.s, nurses' primary focus was on getting their work done and surviving the day. "It was just a day-by-day life," Valerie Buchan said. "You just plodded along and did what you could." Even so, in the course of treating G.I.s who had come in from the field, nurses said they heard things that started to chip away at their understanding of what the United States was doing in Vietnam. G.I.s complained about politicians interfering with the military's ability to wage an effective war; about being used as bait to lure the Viet Cong or North Vietnamese Army into a firefight; about not being able to shoot back at the enemy; about military officers dining on steak and lobster while combat grunts were slogging it out in the muddy fields and living on C rations. Soldiers described seeing friends die in a battle over a particular piece of ground and then abandoning that hard-won territory to the enemy the next day. A few nurses said they began to question the morality of American conduct during the war as well when they heard stories about American soldiers pushing captured VC out of airborne helicopters during interrogations or about high-ranking military officials keeping a coterie of Vietnamese prostitutes healthy and available for G.I.s. The nurses who recalled such things were careful not to place undue blame on G.I.s, instead attributing such behavior to the "reality of war." Indeed, as nurses came to identify more closely with their patients—the injured young men who placed their confidences and vulnerabilities in the hands of the women who cared for them—they were loathe to criticize them and instead often adopted the G.I.s' perspectives as their own.

Many of the nurses I met questioned the war in their own right and based on their own experiences as well, and the target of their increasing anger was American political leaders. If many Americans at home sensed a significant gap between what politicians said was happening in Vietnam and what was actually happening in Vietnam, nurses saw it up close. Bobby Smith remembered reading about the war in the *New York Times* "Week in Review" section while she was in Vietnam. "It was nothing like what was really happening," she said. For one thing, the casualty figures were off. In a war where success was measured by the "kill ratio"—the relative number of enemy dead to American dead—there was a concurrent pressure to exaggerate the numbers of enemy killed and underreport the number of Americans killed. Smith and Lynn Kohl both found American casualty figures to be misleading. "I saw the body bags stacked," Kohl explained, "so I knew how many casualties there were." The figures the newspaper reported were considerably smaller: "It wasn't even as much as we had at our base alone, and that was just ours."

Valerie Buchan, Diane Evans, and Lynn Bower took exception to President Nixon's claims that the United States was not moving beyond the borders of Vietnam. Buchan knew that the United States was bombing Cambodia well before the publicized ground "incursion" of April 1970. "Anybody that was there at the time [in 1969] will tell you that it was going on," she said. Evans also knew that U.S. troops were involved in activities in Cambodia because many of her patients were wounded across the border, a mere thirteen kilometers from her hospital in Pleiku. Bower recalled hearing Nixon assure Americans that the United States was not involved in operations in Laos in 1971. "And just that day in the ER, we had taken fellows that were flown in from Laos," she said. "But because we weren't supposed to be there, we were supposed to cut off their uniforms and put them in a bag" to be disposed of, lest the telltale red dust of Laos be discovered on their fatigues.[6]

Other nurses questioned the validity of the war once they understood that not all Vietnamese welcomed—or benefited from—the American presence. Mary Beth Crowley had supported the war when she first arrived in Vietnam in February 1970, but her attitude soon changed. "Probably after six weeks in Vietnam, I kind of had a change of heart," she said. "I thought, 'I wonder what we are doing and why we are here, because it sure seems to me that the people really don't want us here.'" Nurses also saw the toll American firepower took on innocent civilians. While she was working at the 24th Evac during her second tour, Penny Kettlewell treated many burn patients, most of whom were Vietnamese children. She remembered one Vietnamese mother trying to smother a burned child in a desperate attempt to spare him the painful life that would follow. "It was just bizarre," Kettlewell said. "You just think what are we doing here? We're only creating more havoc. I think by my first tour, I had figured out that if I were Vietnamese, I would have been a VC. First the French invade and run their country for how many decades and then we take over? All these people ever wanted was to be left alone to raise their rice, take care of their families, worship their ancestors, and be happy."

D-M Boulay said she and the "vast majority" of the nurses and doctors with whom she worked became "more and more opposed to war in general and that war specifically because of the carnage, not only to G.I.s, to U.S. citizens, but to the civilian population." She described the war as "racist," based on what she learned about Vietnamese history while in-country, and said she did not buy into the "domino theory"—the idea that if Vietnam fell to communism, so would the rest of the countries in Southeast Asia, and then "the Communists would soon be knocking on San Francisco's door." She said, "I always thought it would be laughable and silly if it weren't so horribly tragic."

Not every nurse viewed U.S. involvement in Vietnam with a critical eye, of course. But even those who had been "gung-ho" or in a "military mindset" when they first arrived found it difficult to maintain their faith in the U.S. mission. Edy Johnson "had very mixed feelings." On one hand, she thought there "probably was a purpose" for the war and that the media's coverage of it skewed against Nixon and those who were "willing to lay their lives on the line." On the other hand, she felt there had been missed opportunities to resolve the situation without so much bloodshed. Valerie Buchan believed in the domino theory and the validity of fighting communism throughout her tour. Still, she wondered, "Why is it someone can't figure out a way to get this ended? By the time I came home, I had a lot of thoughts like that. I couldn't understand what was going on that it went on and on and on and on like that."

By the time she came home in 1969, Diane Evans had undergone a significant transformation. "My political conscience was born in Vietnam," she said. After treating the Vietnamese victims of napalm and white phosphorous and seeing "the horrific wounds and the suffering and the kids who were orphaned by the thousands," she began questioning the logic of the war: "That's when I started asking 'Why?' . . . and I wasn't getting any answers." When she realized that President Nixon was not being truthful in his public statements about the war, she began to "really feel the betrayal. I can't tell you the terrible feeling you have when you're serving in a war zone and you feel betrayed. You feel betrayed by your government." But she also felt betrayed by the American people who blamed soldiers for all of the war's ills.

### From DEROS Day to the World: Coming Home

Valerie Buchan, who had joined the Army Nurse Corps in 1966 because she knew she had something to contribute—to her country, to her patients, to the fight against communism—left Vietnam on September 10, 1969. She had spent a year caring for wounded soldiers in the dangerous Cu Chi area of Vietnam, working first in a surgical unit and then as head nurse in the emergency room. More patients went through the ER at the 12th Evacuation hospital that year than in any other Army hospital in Vietnam. By the time she was scheduled to depart, then, Buchan was tired: "I remember sitting on my suitcase when I was waiting for the plane and thinking to myself, 'Well, this is a place I won't ever come back to.' I looked around before the plane came and I thought, 'It's goodbye, Vietnam. I'll never come back here.' I had done what I could and that was it."[7]

When Buchan got home, she was distressed by all the venom directed at those who had served in Vietnam. She resented it when ignorant protesters called G.I.s "baby-killers" when she had known them to be caring young men who went to extra lengths to assist Vietnamese civilians. But it wasn't just the antiwar contingent who failed Vietnam veterans, in Buchan's eyes. It was also older veterans, who blamed Vietnam veterans for bringing shame on the United States by losing the war. It was the U.S. government, who sent soldiers into an impossible situation and then failed to help them transition to life as a civilian again. It was those who accused Vietnam veterans suffering from post-traumatic stress disorder of faking it in order to secure (scanty) government benefits. The whole system, the whole country, failed the sons and daughters it had sent to Vietnam, who longed for nothing more than to return home once again.

Every American soldier who served in Vietnam knew his or her DEROS: Date Eligible for Return from Overseas. Except for the Marines who served thirteen months, the standard tour of duty for military personnel in Vietnam was twelve months. Before they even set foot on the soil of Vietnam, soldiers—including nurses—knew the exact day they would board their "freedom bird" and return to "the world," or life in the United States. Although thoughts of the world and all that awaited them there had sustained them during their long year in Vietnam, several of the fifteen nurses in this study had mixed emotions when their DEROS actually arrived.

Edy Johnson left Vietnam on April 2, 1969. Excited to return home and reunite with friends and family, she was also sad to leave the friends she had made during her time in Vietnam. "It was kind of hard saying goodbye to the people that you'd worked with," she explained. "You felt like the work wasn't done, and you were leaving people behind that you were concerned about." Diane Evans also felt a sense of responsibility to the newly arrived nurses who came to relieve her when she left Vietnam in August 1969: "Just when we were getting really good at what we were doing, our tour of duty was over and we went back home. Then the new people came in and then that whole learning curve had to start over again. . . . It was like you *knew* what they were in for, and you just didn't want them to have to go through what you just went through."

Other nurses, however, had fewer reservations about leaving Vietnam. Like Buchan, they felt they had exhausted their skills and energy in Vietnam and were eager to get back to life as they had known it. D-M Boulay's departure had been delayed several days because of the 1968 Tet Offensive, and so when she finally boarded the airplane bound for home, she was ready. "I think I'd use the word 'relieved,'" she said when describing her feelings that day. "I didn't have enough energy to be excited." Ann Rudolph was thrilled to be leaving Vietnam in July 1966, anxious to return to the man she had married just prior to her deployment overseas.

Rudolph was one of the lucky ones: she didn't encounter any particular animosity upon her return. To the contrary, she found considerable support—from the passengers and crew on her flights home to the "seminary family" she joined with her husband, just in time for their one-year anniversary. Mary Lu Brunner, Mary Beth

Crowley, D-M Boulay, Edy Johnson, and Joan Paulson also had no particular difficulties upon their return to the United States. Kay Bauer had quite a positive experience. When she boarded a Northwest Airlines flight from San Francisco to Minneapolis in January 1967, the crew somehow guessed that she had just arrived from Vietnam, despite the fact that she was in civilian clothes. Instead of vilifying her for her participation in the war, however, they rolled out the red carpet: "They said, 'Oh, welcome back. Now we know you haven't had any ice cream. How would you like some? We know you haven't had a steak in a long time. Would you like one? Are you tired? Do you want to stretch out? We'll fix one of the seats in back for you.' Can you imagine? Now how many people had that kind of a welcome back?"

Not many, according to numerous women I interviewed. Rather than solicitous flight crews and welcoming crowds, they recalled homecomings fraught with tension between veterans and the antiwar movement. Much of this tension preceded any actual contact with antiwar activists, however. So hostile were the protesters, nurses were told, that any obvious signs of military allegiance would make them instant targets of abuse. So military officials told nurses to remove their uniforms before leaving the insular environment of the military base. Even Bauer remembered such instructions. "Don't talk to people about the fact that you've been in Vietnam," she was told. "Just forget about where you've been and what you've done." Lynn Bower, Penny Kettlewell, Lynn Kohl, and Joan Paulson also remembered being advised to trade in their uniforms for "civvies." Kettlewell took off her uniform after she returned from her first tour in 1968 to avoid the "peaceniks running around" the Seattle area; when she flew into Travis Air Force Base in San Francisco in 1971, after her second tour, she was told, "Take your name tags off. Take your rank off. Take anything off that signifies you've been in Vietnam." That was as much advice as the military gave them about how to adjust to life back in the United States. "We got no debriefing," Kohl said. "They just sent us home. The only thing that they told us was 'take your uniform off and throw it away.'"[8]

Some women did not discard their uniforms when they got home, certainly not if they were still committed to the military. Valerie Buchan remained on active duty for two years after she returned to the United States. She spent those years at Fort Devens, Massachusetts, where she was surrounded by others who had served in Vietnam, including nurses who understood the specific stresses she had encountered and with whom she could "work out a lot of things." Working at a stateside base allowed Buchan and other active-duty Vietnam veterans to slowly adjust to life outside the war zone. "We gradually could feel our freedom again," she said. Kay Bauer also stayed in the military after her return from Vietnam. Following a short leave at home in Minnesota, she went to Quantico, Virginia, where she had the chance to digest her wartime experiences with Marines who had also been in-country. She soon returned to Minnesota, where she was responsible for Navy Nurse Corps recruiting in the Upper Midwest. Surrounded by military personnel, other war veterans, and supportive friends and family, Bauer said she was "always treated like I was a hero."

At least until 1970. Three and a half years after Bauer returned from Rach Gia, Vietnam, she found herself once again in a war zone, this time in Minneapolis. On August 17, 1970, Navy officials called Bauer and told her not to come to work that day. The Federal Office Building in Minneapolis (where her recruiting office was located) had been blown up at three o'clock that morning. The building housed military induction offices for the metropolitan area, but the bomb had been placed just outside of Bauer's office near a basement entryway. The next day's *New York Times* reported that damages to the building totaled half a million dollars. "That was scary," she remembered. "Here I am, I have survived the war. They blew up some places [I'd] been over there, but I'm here in Minneapolis."[9]

A couple of months later, on October 4, the danger became more personal when the house next door to hers was, as the *St. Paul Pioneer Press* put it, "blown to bits," killing its two occupants. Investigators initially thought that a gas leak may have caused the explosion but later determined that plastic explosives were responsible for the blast that flattened the house. At one point, Bauer said, Navy investigators considered the possibility that her home may have been the intended target; her house was almost identical to her neighbors', she frequently drove a Navy car home at night, and the same kind of explosives had been used in both the bombing of the federal building and the explosion next door. Bauer herself may not have been the specific target of such violence, in either case, but tensions surrounding the war and the military were high at this volatile time. Although it was never clearly determined that the Bauer home was the actual target and no one was arrested for the crime, the combination of the previous bombing incident, suggestive possibilities about mistaken identification, and a generally heated antiwar climate made for an alarming situation for Bauer.[10]

The three and a half years between Bauer's return in early 1967 and the bombing incidents in late 1970 made a difference. Opposition to the war was growing by 1967, to be sure. Three months after Bauer returned to the United States, for instance, the National Mobilization Committee to End the War in Vietnam held antiwar rallies on both coasts. In October, Stop the Draft Week drew thousands of young people to antiwar actions across the country. Some of Bauer's military compatriots were getting into the act as well, with the formation of Vietnam Veterans Against the War (VVAW) in spring 1967 and rioting at Fort Hood, Texas, in October by soldiers about to be deployed to Vietnam.

In 1968, it seemed to many Americans that they saw as much homegrown violence on television as they did violence from the battlefront in Vietnam. From the assassinations of Martin Luther King Jr. and Robert Kennedy in April and June, respectively, to the melee at the Democratic National Convention in August, it seemed to many Americans that the war had come home. Although Richard Nixon won the election that fall by promising to end the war abroad and to restore law and order at home, a year later the war was still raging and antiwar sentiment had spread from the outer edges of youth, college, and countercultures to mainstream America.

Nixon sandwiched his "silent majority" speech between two massive national antiwar demonstrations in fall 1969, which together attracted nearly 1.5 million Americans. Six months later, campuses across the country exploded in outrage over the U.S. "incursion" into Cambodia and subsequent killings of four students at Kent State University in Ohio. Sentiment against the war was becoming both more militant and widespread. In 1970, members of the radical SDS-splinter group the Weathermen went underground after the accidental detonation of a bomb they were making killed three of their own and drew the attention of the FBI; that summer, the Weathermen took responsibility for bombing a New York City police building and a bank. In August that year, one week after the bombing of Bauer's office building in Minneapolis, radical antiwar protesters bombed the Army Math Research Center at the University of Wisconsin–Madison, killing a university researcher. It was the fringe of the antiwar movement that committed such extreme acts and tarnished the image of the generally peaceful, if increasingly frustrated, movement. Still, antiwar sentiment, if not activism, was pervasive. By 1971, 71 percent of Americans believed U.S. intervention in Vietnam was wrong and 58 percent went so far as to call the war "immoral."[11]

By the time Bauer's office and neighboring house exploded in 1970, then, passions about the war were running high. Those who supported the war—or at least did not support the antiwar movement—were angered by the antiwar movement's willingness to resort to violence and offended by its critique of traditional American values. Those who opposed the war were frustrated by the failure of peaceful protests to make any measurable difference in policy and became increasingly desperate in their attacks against the war and those who represented it. The irony, of course, is that many veterans came home with the same kinds of criticisms of the war that the antiwar movement espoused.

Whether they returned with a vague uneasiness about the war or a firm opposition to it, however, the nurses I interviewed, like so many Vietnam veterans, were taken aback by the antiwar movement. They were not prepared for the vitriol they felt was directed at returning troops. After her return, Bobby Smith found herself surrounded by vocal opponents of the war—including a professor at the University of Colorado where she was an art student. He was a "draft dodger," she said, who "picked on" her and other veterans "constantly." Even though she may have shared some of the protesters' concerns about the war, she took great offense at their tendency to level their criticisms at soldiers. "Why pick on the people that went there out of a sense of duty, that had no choice of being over there?" she asked more than twenty years later. "The country sent them to defend assholes like this guy. So why pick on the troops? If you're going to make a fuss, go to your senators or something. They're the ones that are responsible for that. Not the G.I.s." Valerie Buchan had a similar view of war protesters. Regardless of her own discomfort with the war, she found demonstrations against the war alienating. "I sort of looked at those people as enemies at that time," she explained. "I thought, 'They're supposed to be supporting the troops, and here they are doing all this crazy stuff.'"

Even nurses who returned with a clear opposition to the war often were reluctant to ally themselves with the antiwar movement. Although she didn't "see any sense in the war" by the time she came home in July 1969, Mary Lu Brunner couldn't bring herself to participate in any antiwar activities because she thought it would be too "devastating" to the troops she had left behind. Penny Kettlewell, who would have declared herself for the Viet Cong if she'd been Vietnamese herself, had no allegiance to the antiwar movement when she returned home in 1971. "People, literally, were calling you every name in the book," she said. "They were spitting at you. They were just being vile." Even though she was very critical of the war—and "with more to base it on" than civilian protesters—there was no way Kettlewell was going to join forces with a group that seemed so hostile to those in uniform.

Two of the nurses I met took their antiwar stances in dramatically different directions. Kay Bauer saw no contradiction between her belief that "all war is wrong" and her position as a recruiter for the NNC. Like Smith, she felt that war opponents should seek the ears of politicians, not military personnel. "Don't give me a hard time. I'm doing a job. My job is to take care of these people who are hurt," she told those who criticized her. D-M Boulay, on the other hand, cast her lot with the antiwar movement when she became active with VVAW in Minneapolis. She went to meetings and a couple of events. She wore a black antiwar armband to work at Hennepin County General Hospital, for which she received a lot of "flak" until she identified herself as a veteran and explained her reasons for opposing the war. Her tenure as an antiwar activist ended when she attended a demonstration at the University of Minnesota during which students and police had an encounter that involved tear gas. "It's as close as I ever got to any kind of activism against the war," she explained. "I couldn't take the violence."

Boulay's association with VVAW raises the question of the exact nature of the relationship between the antiwar movement and returning veterans. The most common understanding is that the relationship was hostile and that, as some of the nurses in this study reported, antiwar activists abused returning soldiers, blaming them for the war's failings. Indeed, this has become a parable for how not to treat our current generation of veterans. Yet Boulay's experience with VVAW suggests another possibility—that there were also instances of alliance between the two groups. At least one scholar has argued that the very existence of a group like VVAW suggests a friendly repartee between veterans and protesters and that the iconic image of protesters spitting on veterans exists in myth and (errant) memory more than in actual fact.[12]

None of the women veterans I interviewed said that they had been spat on, but they insisted that it had happened to others. When Penny Kettlewell arrived at the civilian airport in San Francisco in 1971, protesters were lined up at the gate, hurling verbal insults, if not spit, in her direction. "What they called me, and the things they said, were just unbelievable," she said. Joan Paulson was immune to attacks because she had removed her uniform before leaving military ground, but "people did spit," she assured me. "If you [had] a uniform on, they would spit at you." Although Lynn Kohl did not encounter any hostility from war protesters when she arrived in California in 1970, her hoochmate and friend Lynda Van Devanter did. "People spit at her and hollered things, obscenities, to her," Kohl said. In any case, most of the nurses I met remembered feeling dishonored by the antiwar movement, whether or not they had had any personal encounters with it.[13]

No wonder, then, that so many Vietnam veterans opted to hide their wartime past from view. But it wasn't just the antiwar movement that made them do so. Even well-meaning friends and family contributed, however inadvertently, to veterans' sense that they should not talk about their time in Vietnam. Lynn Kohl met her parents in Hawaii on her way from Vietnam to the United States in June 1970, though the vacation wasn't quite what she had planned since her "mama-san" had stolen the money Kohl had saved for the occasion. Still, she was happy to be reunited with her loved ones—even if they never asked her anything about the year she had just spent in a war zone. "I was waiting for them to ask me questions," she said, "but they never did. I thought, 'Well, maybe they don't want to hear anything,' so *I* didn't say anything." Only many years later did Kohl discover that her parents were waiting for her to broach the topic, afraid that asking about it would be too upsetting to her.

Kohl was not alone in feeling stifled by the response she received when she returned to the world. Veterans' sense of displacement was making national headlines by 1970, when the *New York Times* described them as "silent, perplexed, unnoticed." Nurses could be counted among the confused mass of Vietnam veterans. Although the worst she encountered upon her return was an uncomfortable silence when she mentioned her wartime service on Guam, Mary O'Brien Tyrrell was sensitive to the implied accusation of wrongdoing. But, she noted, it wasn't personal. Nobody "had hostile feelings towards *me*," she explained. "It was a cultural thing. There was no understanding." Even nurses who were welcomed home by friends and family felt the sting of a wider cultural ambivalence toward the war and its veterans. Being told to take off their uniforms and not talk about what they had done for the past year, Joan Paulson believes, turned veterans into the country's "dirty secret," the victim blamed for the crime. Made to feel responsible for all of the war's political and moral ambiguities, veterans learned to simply "shut up," in Paulson's words.[14]

### Silent, Perplexed, Unnoticed:
### Adjusting to Life in the United States

Once the initial shock and disappointment of their return to the world wore off, women Vietnam veterans faced the daunting task of carving out a new life at home. Some of the women I met stayed on active duty after their return; some joined the Reserves; some severed their ties with the military once and for all. Many of them remained in the nursing profession, while others pursued new ventures, too worn out by their wartime experiences to return to bedside nursing. Some made Minnesota their permanent home; some moved from state to state, even overseas, as they followed personal or professional life developments. Some married and had children; some didn't. Regardless of where postwar life took them, however, many nurses shared a reluctance, even refusal, to talk about their experiences in Vietnam. Those who did share their story did so only with trusted friends, often fellow veterans. But even that was a rarity among the women I met. Most women simply put their wartime lives behind them. And for women, this seemed easy to do. "Nobody wondered" if she was a veteran, explained Mary O'Brien Tyrrell: "I was a woman, so why would they suspect?"

Being beyond suspicion allowed those who wanted to do so to keep their wartime experiences a secret. It was a secret closely guarded, shared only with others who had survived the war. Army nurses Mary Breed and Mary Beth Crowley met briefly in Da Nang during their 1970–71 tours. Once back in Minnesota, they both ended up working in the surgical intensive care unit at the Minneapolis VA hospital. There, in the safety of each other's company, the two of them talked about Vietnam. Doing so helped Breed work through some of her anger. As she put it, "We became our own post-traumatic stress group, just from talking, just natural talking together." Their friendship was significant to Crowley, too, who had otherwise put Vietnam behind her. In the early 1970s, she wasn't talking about the war to other friends or family because it was "over and done with." And she certainly didn't mention such a "taboo subject" to any of the men she dated out of fear that they would think there was "something wrong" with her if they'd known she was a veteran.

Remaining in the military shielded some women from such social discomfort and provided them with positive relationships. Edy Johnson's tenure in the Reserves ensured that her time in Vietnam stayed a "high point" in her life: "There was so much groundwork that was already laid that you could start a conversation because you had the same understanding, basically, and the whole rest of the world could kind of drop away." So comfortingly familiar was the military environment—and so confusing life at home—that Diane Evans and Penny Kettlewell actually rejoined the Army Nurse Corps after having been discharged. In her second stint with the ANC, Evans worked at a stateside Army hospital, where she cared for wounded Vietnam veterans. "It was a healthy thing for me to do at the time," she said. "I'd put myself back into the military, taking care of Vietnam vets where I felt like I could use my skills. I had empathy for these guys because I had witnessed what they had gone through in Vietnam." Kettlewell joined the ANC again specifically so she could go back to Vietnam. She had been working at a civilian hospital in New Jersey, but it wasn't going well. "The whole country

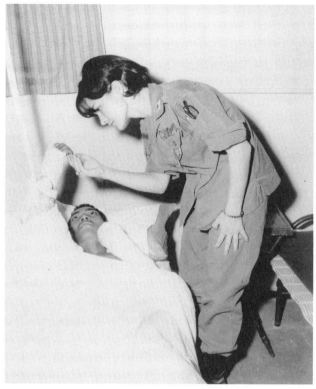

*Edy Johnson's tenure in the Reserves ensured that her time in Vietnam stayed a "high point" in her life.*

was crazy," she explained. "I couldn't adjust. And I felt like Vietnam was home. America wasn't home. I had to go back to where things were more sane."[15]

A military environment alone wasn't a guarantee that women would have an easy time claiming their status as Vietnam veterans. When Lynn Bower returned to the United States so she could be discharged from the military and have her baby, she lived with her active-duty husband on a base in Kentucky. In taking off the uniform, however, Bower erased her own military life. No one on base knew she had been in the military. She wasn't discussing Vietnam with her husband, who had also served in-country. She didn't mention it to a Vietnamese neighbor who had fled the war. After she divorced and moved to Minnesota, she still wasn't talking about Vietnam, not even with a colleague who had been a nurse in World War II. Bower explained that even if she had been inclined to talk about her time in Vietnam, "nobody wanted to hear about it." Things began to change a bit when she met Valerie Buchan and Edy Johnson in the Reserves. Although their experiences in Vietnam 1968–69 were dramatically different from her own in 1971, Bower said that being around them helped "save my sanity."

Mary Lu Brunner returned from Vietnam in July 1969 and joined the Reserves shortly thereafter. She also worked at the VA hospital in Minneapolis. Although both environments were veteran-friendly territory, she did not speak about Vietnam. "I just fell right back into life," she said, "and I didn't tell people I was there." She recoiled when her husband told people at social gatherings that she was a Vietnam veteran: "I said, 'Don't do that. I don't want to talk about it.' It's not something you can just say a few words about, you know. And nobody wants me to describe what it was really like anyway, to be honest."

This sense that the war was too big and awkward a subject to broach in casual conversation kept Mary O'Brien Tyrrell quiet on the matter as well. She did her best to blend in with the women around her once she returned to Minnesota after the war. She was married, raising children, working part time. She bore no markers of her eighteen months in Guam, called no attention to her status as a veteran. But when conversation turned to the subject of how she'd met her husband and she mentioned that it had been while they both were on active duty in Guam, "the whole room would get quiet. Well, then I didn't talk anymore." Like Tyrrell, many women indicated that they took cover in their positions as wives and mothers, spared intrusive questions about what they did during the war by cultural assumptions that women were not veterans.

After her final separation from the military in 1972, Diane Evans embraced her domestic civilian role. "I was raising babies and working and doing the things many women do, getting on with their careers and their families and their husbands," she explained. "During this time, Vietnam was not a part of my life. I did not talk about it. I did not keep in touch with any of my friends from Vietnam, colleagues I had worked with, and I was not talking about Vietnam even with my husband." Former Army nurse Joan Paulson didn't talk about Vietnam with her husband, either. It wasn't that she was uncomfortable with the subject itself; in fact, she was one of the few nurse-veterans who said she spoke rather freely about her time in Vietnam to friends and family who were interested in hearing about it. But her wartime service carried a slightly different weight in her relationship with her husband, whom she married after she returned to the United States. Although war separates many couples, usually it is the woman left behind at home, waiting for her boyfriend's or husband's safe return. Paulson's husband-to-be was exempted from service due to a congenital back problem, however, and so it was he who waited for her. "I think he may feel odd," Paulson speculated. "He said, 'I have nobody that I have anything in common with. Who's got their girlfriend over there? Not a lot.' He [knew] a lot of girls who had their boyfriends over there. It's just something that we didn't share."[16]

The burgeoning women's movement didn't have much to offer women veterans in their adjustment to life as civilian wives, mothers, workers, and citizens. The second wave of American feminism had been gaining speed since the 1963 publication of Betty Friedan's *The Feminine Mystique.* From equal pay to personal politics, feminists confronted the many ways in which women suffered sexist injustice. In an event that would come to seal the image of all feminists as bra-burning radicals, young activists staged a protest at the 1968 Miss America pageant in Atlantic City, New Jersey, during which they threw the trappings of female oppression—bras, girdles, cosmetics—into a "freedom trash can." Though no bras were actually burned that day, this became the iconic image of American feminism. Feminists of all varieties spoke against the war in Vietnam as well. Some based their opposition on women's "natural" abhorrence of violence and their maternal instincts, while others levied political critiques of American racism and imperialism in Vietnam. But they had little, if anything, to say to women who had voluntarily joined the male-dominated military, gone to war, and come home to find themselves overlooked as veterans and in awkward relationships with nonveteran husbands.

For their part, whether they disagreed with its goals and methods or simply found it irrelevant to their postwar lives, most nurses I interviewed had little to do with the women's movement. Edy Johnson had read Friedan's book in the mid-1960s and later heard about the "protest marches and bra burnings and wondered what all the fuss was about." Once the movement made legalized abortion one of its primary goals, Johnson's previous disinterest turned to disagreement and she became active, instead, with the prolife group Minnesota Citizens Concerned for Life.[17]

Other women veterans had been traumatized by the war and stung by the stigma attached to anything associated with it and so simply wanted to come home and blend in. They did not seek any activity that would expose them to further condemnation, whether that was speaking against the war or against sexism. And to the extent that feminism had been branded as a radical rejection of marriage, makeup, and men, many women veterans I met weren't interested. In an attempt to create some semblance of a normal life upon their return from Vietnam, many women sought just the things that feminists seemed to ridicule. "When I came home after my military discharge, I was all wrapped up in preparing for my wedding that occurred nine months later," Mary O'Brien Tyrrell explained. "We soon had two children, who were five and three years old when we divorced. So I was just trying to keep my head on straight and earn a living while raising two kids by myself. It was all consuming and I have no recollection of anything constructive offered by the women's movement." So all consuming was her life as a single mother that Tyrrell also submerged most of her memories from Vietnam.[18]

Busy lives, controversial politics, public indifference or hostility, and the trauma of war were all factors in nurse-veterans' decisions not to speak about their time in Vietnam. The women I spoke to described another layer of invisibility, however, that stemmed from assumptions that women were not war veterans. "Who would suspect?" asked Mary O'Brien Tyrrell. Not the flight attendant who noticed the Army boots that Mary Breed carried on her way home from Vietnam: "Isn't that cute?" the stewardess said. "She's carrying her husband's combat boots." Not the Veterans of Foreign Wars post that directed Kay Bauer to the Ladies Auxiliary, where "all of our nurses and all of our females are." Not the women at the neighborhood coffee klatch, or the coworkers at civilian hospitals, or even the soldiers at a husband's military base. Without the uniform on, nurse-veterans were "just" women. And many of them took advantage of the cloak of invisibility that being female provided. They took refuge in their gender.[19]

Nurses came home from Vietnam as changed people, wiser but wearier for their year in-country. "It was the most defining year of my life," said Diane Evans. Though it awakened her political conscience to the ways in which power was used and abused by political leaders, it also had a "profound impact . . . in many positive ways." She had "practiced a lifetime of nursing in one year," and the lessons in perseverance she learned in Vietnam helped her in pursuing hard-won goals in later years. Ann Rudolph "came back stronger," she said, "less naive, more worldly." She also came back with her "heart and soul and conscience" intact, her faith having held strong during the war.

If Rudolph's spiritual foundation kept her afloat in Vietnam, others' faltered in the midst of war. Mary Lu Brunner was horrified to find herself wishing that President Lyndon Johnson would "bomb the heck out of" North Vietnam to bring the war to a halt: "You're not thinking about what the bombs are doing to the land and to the people. You think, 'How could that come out of your mouth? Aren't you supposed to be Christian and loving of all and lay down your life?'" Her anger wasn't directed only at the North Vietnamese, however. "I wouldn't have believed that I could have ever hated anybody as much as I hated the people that made us go to that war," she said. Mary Breed also harbored an anger toward the U.S. government "that lasted for a good ten years." Lynn Kohl came home with a deep-seated distrust of American leadership as well, but her year in Vietnam also took a more personal toll on her: "Before I got there, I was always happy-go-lucky, laughing a lot. Life was joyful. Afterwards, I could not find the joy in life."

Still, life went on. There were husbands and babies to care for, jobs to maintain, lives to reinvent. Women who chose to pursue a nursing career in midcentury America, who volunteered for military service, who survived a year in a war zone were strong women. They knew how to keep moving, how to set and achieve goals, how to survive. And so they did. And for a while, things seemed fine. Occasionally they might notice an odd reaction to a mundane circumstance, such as when Valerie Buchan was walking across the base at Fort Devens one "blustery fall evening." The wind had blown a string across the steps she was ascending: "I can remember that my foot stopped in midair. I . . . stood there like a statue, because that's one of the things that we were taught to look for, strings and wires that were not in a place where they should be. . . . Soon I realized where I was and that this was not a booby trap."

For many women veterans who quietly tried to resume lives as nurses, wives, or mothers, the gender-based invisibility that was once a refuge became a trap. Even some who retained their ties to the military found that women war veterans were invisible. Bobby Smith had planned to make a career of the Air Force. But after her return from Vietnam, she had trouble boarding an airplane "without thinking it was going to fall out of the air and I was going to die," so she "got out" and joined the Reserves. She lived in rural California for a while because she "couldn't stand being around people." Then she moved to Colorado, where she encountered the antiwar art professor. She quit her job in a civilian hospital there because she "had an attitude" and resented having to get a doctor's permission to give a patient aspirin when she had been responsible for so much more in Vietnam. She moved to Minnesota to continue her art education and found that she "could not walk in a hospital without getting the shakes." This was in the early eighties, "when post-traumatic stress was first becoming known." She thought maybe she was suffering from post-traumatic stress, and so she sought help from the VA, but her claim was denied.

Shortly thereafter, Smith contracted bilateral pneumonia while on active duty with the Reserves. She was sent to the VA hospital in Minneapolis, which had trouble finding a bed for her because "they didn't take care of women." While she was in the hospital, she heard about an upcoming television program about nurses who had served in Vietnam. She watched the program at home and "fell apart. I cried for the first time in I don't know how many years," she said. A day later, she talked to Diane Evans on the phone. Then she met Mary Beth Crowley. And Kay Bauer. "Suddenly I realized I wasn't the only one that felt the way I had been feeling. And one thing led to another . . . and we started this support group." If neither the military nor the VA would take sufficient care of women veterans, the women would do it themselves.

# 5

## *"From 'Nam Back to Sanity"*
## Nurses, PTSD, and the VA

**WHEN ARMY NURSE PENNY KETTLEWELL** returned to the United States after completing her first tour in Vietnam in 1968, she had trouble adapting to her new life. She was distressed by the constant firing of guns—"the big ones, the little ones"—at her next duty station at Fort Sill, Oklahoma. She cried upon seeing head-injury patients while she was working at Fort Dix in New Jersey and fought with her colleagues at the civilian hospital where she worked after her discharge. "I couldn't adjust from 'Nam back to sanity," she said. So she rejoined the ANC and went back to Vietnam from 1970 to 1971. Life after her second tour was no easier than after her first, however. She went to anesthesia school in Ohio and then moved to a 240-acre farm in Sandstone, Minnesota, where she lived for fifteen years. But by 1985, she was "crashing and burning." She said, "I couldn't even remember what hospital I'd been stationed at in 'Nam. I couldn't remember when I was there. I could remember Heddy [a friend and fellow Army nurse killed in a helicopter crash in Vietnam]. She haunted me." She suffered from nightmares and panic attacks. She could muster up enough energy to go to work at St. Luke's Hospital in Duluth but then came home and would "just sit," unable to eat or do much of anything else. "I felt like I wasn't even existing," she said. "I contemplated suicide a hundred different ways."

Had Kettlewell served during the U.S. Civil War, her postwar difficulties would have been attributed to either "soldier's heart" or "nostalgia." If she'd returned from service in World War I, she would have been thought to be suffering from "shell shock." "Battle fatigue" would have explained such troubles after World War II, for even the Greatest Generation suffered for its victory. By 1985, however, Kettlewell's symptoms had been officially recognized by the psychiatric community as indicators of post-traumatic stress disorder (PTSD). Whatever the term, the malaise was generally thought to be a man's issue, the consequence of being sent into battle and fighting to the death. But nurses who went to war to save lives suffered from their experiences as well. This chapter examines women Vietnam veterans' experiences with PTSD. Although not all Vietnam veterans experienced PTSD after their wartime service, many did, and nurses were no exception. Conditioned to take care of others rather than themselves, however, many nurses had a hard time acknowledging that they needed help. "Nurses were just supposed to suffer," Kettlewell explained, "bite your lip, and buck up and just do it. That's your job. You shouldn't get medals for it." But, as Diane Evans put it, "Who takes care of the caretaker?"[1]

### *Flashbacks, Forgetting, and Fighting: Nurses and PTSD*

All of the nurses I met described some degree of hardship and tragedy during their time in Vietnam, but not all of them returned home carrying the same burden from the war. Army nurse Joan Paulson "came out of that war fairly intact," she said, "because I did view a lot of it as rather pragmatic." Fellow ANC veteran Edy Johnson believed that her training had prepared her so well for what she saw in Vietnam that she "had nothing to resolve" when she came home. Even those who admitted the war had affected their postwar lives in significant ways were reluctant to give too much weight to their own suffering. Ann Rudolph came home with "uncomfortable" reactions to the sound of helicopters flying overhead and was convinced that the stresses of her wartime experiences contributed to the demise of her marriage, but she was careful to point out that others had it worse than she did. "I'm not going to negate my experiences," she said, "but compared to some of the other stories I've heard, I think I came out pretty lucky, almost unscathed." Still, Penny Kettlewell was not the only nurse who had difficulty finding her bearings once she returned from war.

Most of the women I interviewed came home with some long-term psychological effects of their time in Vietnam. Veterans of all wars have been known to suffer from adjustment difficulties after their return from the battlefield. But it wasn't until 1980—seven years after U.S. troops officially withdrew from Vietnam—that the mental health community recognized such problems as a condition in its own right. That year, for the first time, the *Diagnostic and Statistical Manual of Mental Disorders, Third Edition* (*DSM-III*), listed post-traumatic stress disorder among its diagnostic categories for mental illness. Since then, the definition of the disorder has been scruti-nized and debated by the psychiatric profession, but the generally accepted understanding of PTSD is that it is "an anxiety disorder that can occur following the experience or witnessing of a traumatic event." PTSD in veterans is most often associated with stress related to combat, though it can affect female (and male) war veterans who served in noncombat capacities as well.[2]

A major national study of Vietnam veterans' postwar readjust-ment found that 53.4 percent of men and 48.1 percent of women who served in the Vietnam theater had, as of 1988, "experienced clinically significant stress-reaction symptoms." Other studies have shown that nurses' job of caring for war-ravaged bodies and bearing the responsibility for saving young lives on a daily basis was sufficiently stressful to induce PTSD; they needn't have felt their own lives to be at risk (though they may have) or have participated in the act of tak-ing a life to be traumatized by their wartime experiences. In general, women are more likely than men to experience long-lasting PTSD and to display symptoms of emotional numbing and depression rather than anger and substance abuse. Many of the fifteen women in this study reported experiencing one or more symptoms associ-ated with PTSD.[3]

One of the most frightening elements of PTSD is that it takes its victim back to the scene of the traumatic event, whether through relentless, upsetting memories or visceral reliving of the original ex-perience. Sometimes images of the war or a patient or a particularly distressing episode in the hospital ran like a film through a nurse's mind; other times, the memory resided just below the surface of consciousness, rearing up with a vengeance after some similar situa-tion, image, or smell triggered it. Air Force veteran Bobby Smith, for example, was visiting her mother in Long Island, New York, when an airplane crashed just a few miles away. She watched news coverage of the crash and subsequent rescue, but instead of seeing a civilian airliner, the plane became an air evacuation flight from Vietnam. As she drove back to Minnesota from New York, she kept "playing this over. I couldn't get it out of my mind, that it's an air evac plane and these are all my patients and I can't do anything."

Flashbacks are memories so vivid that they seem not to be memories at all, but a magical transporting across space and time such that the sufferer feels as though she is literally reliving the prior event. Penny Kettlewell was working at St. Luke's Hospital in Duluth in the mid-1980s, ten years after she returned from Vietnam for good, when she treated two Native American victims of a particularly horrific car accident: "I looked down and for all the life of me, they looked Vietnamese. And then the smell of all that blood and vomit and everything . . ." She struggled to find the words to describe the moment. "I did the appropriate things. No one knew this was happening to me but me. But I could hear gunshots in the background." Kay Bauer felt like she was back in Vietnam, too, as she sat in church for Good Friday services long after her return: "They turned off all the lights and started having the sounds of lightning and thunder," she said. "Well, to me, it was not lightning and thunder. Here I am, right back in Vietnam again with the helicopters and the people coming in injured."

Nurses also relived some of their most traumatic war experiences in their sleep as patients and events from their past came back to them in nightmares. Lynn Bower started having three recurring nightmares just after she took a nursing job at St. Mary's Hospital in 1980, each of them about patients she had treated in Vietnam: the young G.I. whose lower body came apart in her hands, the soldier who begged her for drugs because he was going through withdrawal, and a major who had overdosed on an antidepressant to relieve the despair he felt at having to lead young men to their deaths. These dreams disturbed her so much that she could hardly sleep at night and could barely function at work during the day. The war intruded on D-M Boulay's nighttime peace as well. After her return from Vietnam, she worked at Peter Bent Brigham Hospital in Boston and lived with five other nurses in a nearby house. One night, one of her roommates returned home late after a date. Boulay's room was near the front door, and when she heard the noise of her roommate returning, she had the first of what she called her "wake-me-up-screaming" nightmares. Her room in the house was small, as was her hooch in Vietnam where she spent the 1968 Tet Offensive huddled in fear, "absolutely certain I was going to be killed." When the noise of her roommate's return startled her awake, Boulay wasn't in a house in Boston: she was trapped in a hooch in Vietnam, awaiting her own death.

If sounds triggered disturbing memories for nurses, so too did sights and smells. Thirty years after she completed her tour overseas, Diane Evans attended an out-of-town wedding. She stayed with one of the bride's relatives, a chef who was making the wedding meal of beef tenderloin. It was a hot summer day, and when Evans walked into the house where the chef was preparing the meat, "it was Vietnam," she said. "There was this big slab of meat with blood all over the place, and she was cutting it. Now, I saw the limbs. That was a body. It wasn't a slab of meat. I was viscerally sick. I was so disturbed. I didn't say a thing to anybody. I just went out of the house." Penny Kettlewell was haunted by the smell of blood, a serious liability for a nurse who worked at a trauma hospital. She remembered being covered in blood one day as she tried to put a breathing tube in a patient in Duluth. "The worst thing for me is the smell of blood," she said. "When I was in 'Nam, I would have blood literally stuck to my skin. My fatigues wouldn't move on my legs because they were just glued there with this blood." When she smelled the blood that day in Duluth, she "actually dissociated": "I felt like I was standing over in the corner, watching this other person who looked like me doing all of this."

PTSD is a roller-coaster ride of both excessive and disappearing memories, however. Although people with PTSD relive the past in flashbacks and nightmares, they also have trouble intentionally calling up specific details from the past. So it was that the memory of her friend Heddy haunted Kettlewell, yet she couldn't remember the hospital at which they both had served. In addition, trauma survivors often don't want to talk about their experience or engage in any behaviors that might prompt recall of the trauma. The nurses I met reported that, for the most part, they avoided seeing Vietnam-themed movies after their return. They also had a particularly hard time watching news coverage of subsequent wars—from Desert

Storm to the twenty-first-century wars in Afghanistan and Iraq. "I try not to watch too much of the war news because that pisses me off so much," said Kettlewell. "I'm seeing the same things happening to these [veterans] as happened to us, despite the fact they're being welcomed home and they're all being told they're heroes. They still have not been able to adjust."

Emotional numbing, self-isolation, and disinterest in once plea-surable activities are also hallmarks of PTSD. Former Navy nurse Kay Bauer hadn't even realized she'd built a wall between herself and her husband until he said he was going to file for divorce: "My husband came to me one day and said, 'We're getting a divorce.' I said, 'We are?'" For over a year, he told her, she had been shutting him out, refusing to talk to him about anything but the most mundane and superficial topics. He presented her with two options: "You either go in for counseling and do something or we have to divorce. I cannot live this way any longer." Bauer was stunned. "I did not know," she said, explaining that this lack of awareness was "one of the severe symptoms" of her PTSD. Her husband's announcement was a wake-up call for her, one that ultimately led to some positive results; she and her husband remain married to this day.

Bauer wasn't the only nurse who isolated herself from loved ones or buried her emotions about the war. In 1999, Lynn Kohl told me that she had only recently begun to feel emotion again. "I just now am starting to get feeling back, where I can have emotion. That's thir-ty years," she said. "That's kind of weird, too, because I never know when all of a sudden that's going to happen. I'll be watching TV and all of a sudden [*sniff, sniff*]." Another common feature of PTSD is that it can wax and wane over the years, appearing, disappearing, and reappearing as new events unearth old memories. Although Kohl described the resurfacing of her emotions with good humor in 1999, when I interviewed her again in 2009, she was more somber, a fact she attributed to the Iraq War. "I'm better right now, but the last two years, maybe even three, I have had such an intense anger. It's just so deep," she said. "I don't even listen to the news anymore, because I just get angry again." She acknowledged that she had isolated herself at home. "I used to have a lot of friends here. I don't see any of them anymore. I talk to one or two now and again; that's it. I don't do any of the healing work I did. I don't do *anything*."

Hyperarousal symptoms affected a number of the nurses I met as well. Having lived for a year in a dangerous, stressful situation, they returned home and found it hard to let down their guard. They felt as if they were always on alert, always ready to jump at the merest hint of danger, ready to take up the fight. Veterans often have a heightened startle response to loud or surprising noises. Kohl said she had desperately missed eating ice cream while overseas, and so once she got home, she and her mother went grocery shopping to get some. "We were walking down an aisle and a lady behind us dropped a can. I was down on the floor like that," she said with a snap of her fingers. "My mom was sitting there; all these people in the aisle are looking at me. She never took me shopping again."[4]

One of the most common manifestations of hyperarousal among the women I interviewed was extreme irritability. Many nurses described themselves as angry after their tours, more combative and prone to arguing than they had been before they went to Vietnam. This took its toll on both their professional and personal lives. Bobby Smith and Penny Kettlewell both quit at least one nursing job because they found themselves arguing with colleagues who neither understood nor respected the nursing work they had done overseas. D-M Boulay got into a shouting match with a resident while working at Hennepin County General Hospital after her return. "I never shout. I don't raise my voice. I don't get angry and have a hissy fit," she said. "I simply don't; that's just not my style." After she and the resident "screamed at one another" that day, she began to realize that "something was wrong with me and nursing." Ann Rudolph described her postwar anger as "a rage just underneath the surface." "You can live this life and be who you are, go to work, do your thing, be with your kids, be not with your kids, just live," she said, "but underneath that surface, this *boom*! 'you're-going-to-explode' type of thing."

Flashbacks, emotional numbing, and hyperarousal—these symptoms of PTSD were problematic enough in and of themselves. But they were joined by other associated difficulties as well, ranging from high blood pressure and panic attacks to anxiety and suicidal thoughts. Depression commonly occurs in conjunction with PTSD, especially among women: almost half of female PTSD sufferers also struggle with depression. More than a third of the women I interviewed either had been diagnosed and treated for clinical depression or described long periods of deep sadness. And, though they may have felt isolated, those with PTSD did not suffer alone. PTSD affected husbands, children, friends, and colleagues, as women seeking retreat from their wartime memories slipped into silence or rage. As such, PTSD is not just an individual issue, but a family and community one as well.[5]

Given what the mental health community now knows about PTSD, it is not surprising that some of the nurses who served in Vietnam fell victim to it. They were young women who endured months of stressful living in which they witnessed, in immediate and intimate ways, the deep suffering of wounded G.I.s. And though they helped save many lives, they also spoke of feeling overwhelmed by the responsibility their jobs entailed and frustrated at their inability to do more to alleviate the pain of those under their care. While many nurses had good individual support systems when they returned home—friends, family, fellow veterans—the general cultural antipathy toward Vietnam veterans inhibited veterans' ability to reconcile their wartime experiences. No wonder, then, that the war didn't end once they left the war zone.[6]

### PTSD and Women Veterans: Confronting the VA in the 1970s and 1980s

If it seems obvious, especially in retrospect, that nurse-veterans would be vulnerable to PTSD, it certainly wasn't so clear at the time—to the military, the VA, the general public, even to the nurses themselves. The nurses I spoke to said they were frightened and confused by their symptoms, often believing they were "crazy" and the only ones having difficulty getting on with things at home. Yet, get on with things they did, hiding their struggles from everyone around them. Friends, family, coworkers—no one knew what was happening to these women, because the women didn't talk about it and no one thought to ask. Eventually, though, the veneer began to crack. As Penny Kettlewell put it, "You feel like you're going to crawl outside of your skin if you can't—you've got to grab something solid." For some nurses, that something solid was the Veterans Administration. Unfortunately, in the 1970s and 1980s, the VA was not doing a very good job of helping veterans with PTSD or of caring for women veterans, period.[7]

From its founding in 1930, the VA has been responsible for coordinating the disbursement of benefits and services to American veterans under the motto, "To care for him who shall have borne the battle." It was the VA, then, that should have taken on the task of caring for the physical *and* psychological well-being of former soldiers. Caught in the political debate over the legitimacy of Vietnam veterans' need for "readjustment counseling," however, the VA stood back and forced veterans and their allies to take the lead in securing the help they needed. When, after years of lobbying by a group of committed male Vietnam veterans and independent mental health professionals, in 1978 the American Psychiatric Association (APA) included post-traumatic stress disorder as a diagnostic category of mental illness in the draft version of the *DSM-III,* VA clinicians finally had a tool to connect their patients' psychological distress to their wartime experiences. In 1979 Congress passed Public Law 96-22, which allocated $12 million to the VA to establish a network of Vet Centers where veterans could obtain readjustment counseling in a more welcoming, less bureaucratic setting than the VA.[8]

Though establishment of the Vet Centers and the addition of PTSD to the *DSM-III* were victories for male Vietnam veterans, their benefits to women who had served were less clear. Those who had worked so hard to secure psychiatric help for ailing veterans were male veterans and their therapists, and so their understanding of war-related stress was based on the paradigm of combat trauma. Nurses came home with many of the same problems that combat veterans did, but no one seemed to make the connection between their war service and their depression, memory difficulties, and relationship problems because they had not served in combat.

This blindness reflected a larger cultural ignorance about women veterans as well. The general psychiatric community didn't see women veterans' problems as related to their war service because it didn't see women as veterans in the first place. Although the feminist movement had, by the 1980s, made great strides in debunking the myth that women were best and only suited for domestic duties in the home, it had done little to dislodge the association between soldiering and masculinity and men. The U.S. census had polled men about their veteran status since 1910, but it wasn't until 1980 that it inquired as to whether or not a female respondent had served her country. In 1970, women constituted 1.9 percent of all U.S. veterans. By 1982, thanks in part to post–Vietnam era efforts to recruit women to the All-Volunteer Force, just over one million women identified themselves as military veterans, doubling their share of the total veteran population to 3.8 percent. Despite these rising numbers, however, women veterans were still largely invisible on the national landscape.[9]

Women veterans absorbed these cultural messages even when they flew in the face of their own experiences. Edy Johnson had to be convinced by others that she was eligible for a veteran's bonus. "I thought you had to have been in combat to be considered a veteran," she recalled. She remembered thinking, "I guess I do consider myself a veteran, but it isn't really fair. I didn't have to be out there shooting people or anything." Johnson was one of the lucky ones who adjusted relatively easily to life after war, and so she never sought counseling. But even those few women who saw therapists for depression or marital problems didn't see the link to their service in Vietnam— either because they failed to identify themselves as Vietnam veterans to their counselors or because the counselors dismissed their war experiences as irrelevant to the issues at hand.[10]

In 1978, Mary Beth Crowley saw a civilian psychiatrist for help in dealing with a deep sadness and inexplicable bouts of crying. "I would just cry for no reason," she said. "I had no reason to be depressed. I was thirty-two. I wasn't married, but that had never really been an issue for me." Apparently it was an issue for her psychiatrist, however: "He asked me, 'Is it because you're not married?' I said, 'I don't think so.' 'Then, why are you crying?' 'I don't really know.'" It was Crowley's mother who first suggested that Crowley's year in Vietnam might be at the root of the issue or at least germane in some way. When presented with this possibility, however, the psychiatrist dismissed it out of hand: "He said, 'Absolutely not.' It wasn't really spoken of then." The whole experience was a "big waste of money" for Crowley. Crowley's psychiatrist wasn't the only mental health professional who failed to understand the ramifications of women's war service, however. When Ann Rudolph began having trouble in her marriage, she saw three or four different counselors over the course of several years. Even though each of them knew that she was a Vietnam veteran, "*no one ever* thought or knew what to do with my Vietnam experience and how that might have had anything to do with any of the problems."

If civilian doctors didn't know what to do with women veterans, the VA wasn't doing much better. It was barely providing the most basic of medical care to its female clientele, let alone any special readjustment counseling for women with PTSD. In September 1982—three months after the Equal Rights Amendment went down to defeat—the General Accounting Office (GAO) released a report on the VA's record of service to female veterans, including its response to the psychological needs of women who had served in Vietnam. The report discussed a number of discrepancies in the treatment of men and women veterans, especially with regard to the provision of medical care, and concluded (rather tepidly) that women veterans "have not always received recognition as veterans and VA benefits equal to those given to male veterans." Kay Bauer put it more directly: "It's a very, very anti-woman organization. . . . The whole Veterans' Administration is geared to men, period." On the rare occasion that she sought any care from the VA, she confronted an attitude among staff members that women and their troubles didn't belong at the VA. "That's a perception that we got, that it wasn't worthwhile," she said. "Who are you to have problems?"[11]

But many women veterans were having adjustment problems, and in some ways, the VA was only adding to them. The same year that the GAO revealed a gender-based inequality in the VA's provision of services, Lynn Kohl joined an in-patient PTSD treatment program at the VA in Tomah, Wisconsin. "They didn't know what to do with me," she recalled, because "they had never had females." All the men in the program slept in the same area in the hospital, but the unit did not have any rooms for women. Instead, Kohl was assigned to a locked psychiatric ward, where she ended up watching over an enlisted woman veteran who had attempted suicide. The men in her group insisted that she belonged with them, however, and so hospital staff cleaned out a utility closet in the PTSD unit for her to use as a bedroom.[12]

After emerging from her makeshift sleeping accommodations each day, Kohl attended the male-dominated PTSD therapy group, where "they talked about guns" but "didn't know what to do for me." When group members were asked to identify the specific incident that contributed to their postwar stress problems, Kohl was unable to respond. The guys "weren't in fights every day," she told me. "They'd be on patrol for sometimes even weeks before they'd have a firefight. And so there were one or two things in their year that they could identify [as the likely origin of their PTSD]." In contrast, she said, "Every day was a trauma for me." The narrow view that combat was the only source of wartime trauma meant that nurses, whose caretaking duties in the war had demanded that they repress their own emotional needs, were once again left to fend for themselves. Doctors and her fellow group members interpreted Kohl's inability to fit her experiences into the male paradigm as a sign that she was not cooperating with the prescribed treatment strategy. She left the group before its completion.[13]

Even the heralded Vet Centers didn't quite know what to do with women veterans, at least in the early years of their existence. The program had proved invaluable to Vietnam veterans, and when President Ronald Reagan threatened to halt all funding and close the ninety-one Vet Centers in 1981, male veterans rallied to save the centers. Still, it would take another year for the Vet Center program to take notice of women. In September 1982, it established a Working Group on Women Vietnam Veterans that suggested "a whole range of reforms to make the Vet Centers more helpful and congenial to women." Despite such efforts, however, nearly ten years later the Vet Center counseling groups still focused primarily on men, as former Vietnam Veterans of America National Women's Director Lynda Van Devanter Buckley pointed out in a congressional hearing in 1991.[14]

Lynn Bower discovered this lack of balance firsthand. When the nightmares and exhaustion finally became too much to bear, she sought help at the Vet Center on University Avenue in St. Paul in the early 1980s. The therapist and male veterans at the Vet Center were very welcoming, Bower recalled, and simply admitting that she was a veteran who was having trouble and taking steps to address it made her feel better. She attended several group sessions with friendly male Vietnam veterans but never felt that she fit in. "They had their own story to tell, and I didn't say anything in the groups, because my story isn't their story," she explained. "*I'm* the one that held their hand. I'm the one that held their head when they weren't going to breathe anymore. So I couldn't talk about firefights and I couldn't talk about that kind of stuff." She left the group and went to individual counseling for a short time: "Then I didn't go back again, because it just seemed like they were really busy with the real people."

The rocky road women Vietnam veterans had to travel to find help for their postwar difficulties was beginning to smooth by the mid-1980s. Although the early attempt to treat PTSD in Vietnam veterans focused on men and Vet Center efforts on behalf of women failed to live up to their potential, gender-specific outreach and programming eventually helped struggling women veterans find the camaraderie that began to shape their recovery. ANC veteran Diane Evans started processing her war experiences through poetry, on the recommendation of her counselor at the Vet Center. Evans's guest appearance at the Vet Center in the late eighties, after she had begun work on the Vietnam Women's Memorial, prompted Penny Kettlewell to first identify herself as a Vietnam veteran. She had read of Evans's upcoming visit in the newspaper and decided to visit the center the same day in hopes that doing so would help combat her depression and suicidal thoughts. "It took all the courage I have ever had to muster in my life. I could have gone to Vietnam ten times without as much effort as it took me to drive to that Vet Center," recalled Kettlewell. "There just happened to be a parking place right smack in front. There's never a parking place in front. I got out, and I walked in there, and I thought, 'I can't. Fuck it. I can't walk in.' Finally, I got in through the door, and just as I was about ready to tear out, Diane saw me, and she ran over and grabbed me. And she wouldn't let me go. And she talked to me for about a half hour." It was at this meeting that Evans told Kettlewell about the women veterans' group that by that time was running out of the Minneapolis VA.[15]

### On Their Own: The Minneapolis Nurses' Group

By the mid-1980s, Kay Bauer had been in military service in one form or another—as a student, as an active-duty Navy nurse, as a Reservist—for twenty-five years. After her tour in Vietnam, she had cared for war-wounded Marines at Quantico, recruited for the Navy Nurse Corps, gotten married and started a family, dealt with the aftermath of a bomb blast in the office building where she worked, been spurned by the Veterans of Foreign Wars, implemented a Tri-Service Nurses Program to coordinate nursing practice in the three military services, helped establish an advocacy group for women who had served their country (the Minnesota Association of Civilian and Veteran Women, or MACVW), and begun working on behalf of the project to build a memorial to women Vietnam veterans in Washington, D.C. Nicknamed "the Admiral" by her friends and fellow nurses, Kay Bauer was a take-charge woman: when she saw something that needed doing, she did it. As she got to know other Vietnam nurses through her work with MACVW and the memorial project, she saw a need for them to talk about the war and its impact on their postwar lives. "I realized that they had never had a chance to experience any closure, which I did, because I'd been talking all these years on television and the radio, to groups of people in front of me," she said. Bauer continued to support the memorial but turned most of her attention to helping the nurses in "the here and now." And so she started a support group for nurses who had served in Vietnam.[16]

It wasn't easy. After meeting with these fellow nurses informally for some time and realizing that they needed the input of professionals, Bauer called the Minneapolis VA. The main VA directed her to the Post-Traumatic Stress Recovery unit, where she met Kay Ryan, a therapist whom many of the nurses I met now credit with rescuing them from the downward spiral of PTSD. Ryan told Bauer that a previous attempt to establish a women veterans' PTSD group had failed but that she would offer whatever support she could if Bauer wanted to try it again. Bauer definitely wanted to take another chance, and so she asked ANC veteran Mary Beth Crowley, who was working at the VA at the time, for help in contacting other women Vietnam veterans in the area. "Let's start calling them, see if they'd be willing to get together," Bauer suggested. "Then we pulled in Penny Kettlewell. We pulled in Air Force nurse [Bobby Smith]. Then we pulled in Lynn Kohl. We pulled in [another woman] from Wisconsin. We pulled in all of these people." Soon Joan Paulson and Ann Rudolph and Mary Lu Brunner were part of the group.[17]

One by one, the nurses drew each other in, convincing each new member that there was an alternative way of coping with postwar stress that involved neither silent suffering nor the task of trying to fit in with men's groups. The group met weekly with Kay Ryan for "six or seven years," its membership varying from year to year, month to month. Some stayed for only a short while; some stayed for the duration. The group existed on the periphery of the main VA, associated with it but never clearly part of it. Bauer described it as a "dichotomy between the VA and the PTSD unit" in which "you could never coalesce the two, and you could never travel from one to the other." Nevertheless, the group provided its members with a safe place to talk about their war experiences, the camaraderie of other women veterans, and the dedicated support of a skilled therapist. For Penny Kettlewell, the group was "an absolute lifeline" and Kay Ryan an "angel in disguise."

Kay Ryan was born and raised in Butte, Montana. Like everyone else in this study, she was a nurse: she earned a three-year nursing diploma from St. Patrick's School of Nursing in Missoula, Montana, in 1963. While Kay Bauer and Penny Kettlewell were putting their nursing skills to the test in Vietnam, Ryan married, moved to South Carolina, had two children, and worked in "all-black hospitals" there. In 1975 she earned her bachelor's degree in nursing from the University of South Carolina and, in 1977, her master's degree in psychiatric nursing. After several years of teaching and doing clinical work with the wives and children of military personnel in South Carolina, she moved to Minneapolis in 1985. In 1986 she took a job at the VA, where she joined a team of therapists who had begun an outpatient program for male Vietnam veterans with PTSD. The program offices were located in an outbuilding detached from the main VA hospital. The stigma of being part of a controversial, lost war in Vietnam had, by the 1980s, morphed into the stereotype of the dangerous, volatile, crazy Vietnam veteran, a stereotype to which even VA staffers were not immune, according to Ryan. Even at the VA, "there's always been such fear and disdain for combat vets," Ryan said in explaining the off-site location of the PTSD unit. "They don't look good. They swear. They drink. They carry knives and guns." Ryan and her fellow therapists were stigmatized by association as well. "We were renegades," she said, regarded by other VA staffers as "pretty crazy" for working with the "wild and wooly" Vietnam vets.[18]

But Ryan was committed to helping these "wild and wooly characters." For her first couple of years in the Post-Traumatic Stress

Recovery unit at the VA, she worked with male Vietnam veterans in a seven-week outpatient program. Then she and an occupational therapist began a group for the female partners of Vietnam veterans. She listened to the stories of the war's impact on those who had served and those who had stayed behind, and she took them to heart. Despite traditional professional standards that required maintaining an objective, clinical distance between therapist and patient, Ryan became attached to veterans she met. "I just couldn't distance completely and not have the connection," she said, "because I didn't think I would be effective." For their part, she said, the veterans appreciated her "willingness to take a chance and to trust them when nobody else had." She took this same willingness to connect with her patients to her work with the women Vietnam veterans Kay Bauer and Mary Beth Crowley had rounded up as well. And although doing so would take a significant emotional toll on Ryan herself, the benefits to the nurses were tremendous. She knew just how to engage women who were scarred by their war experiences, skittish about identifying themselves as Vietnam veterans, and scared at what they might face if they did.

Indeed, it was Kay Ryan who gently lured Kettlewell into the group that became her lifeline. Although Diane Evans had told Kettlewell about the group during their conversation at the Vet Center, Evans's attention was focused primarily on the memorial project, and so she gave Kettlewell the name and phone number of a social worker who cofacilitated a support group for women veterans. When Kettlewell contacted her, the social worker said that the group had already been formed and she wasn't sure that Kettlewell could join. Had the social worker not taken her phone number, Kettlewell may have disappeared into the northern Minnesota woods for good. But then Kay Ryan called. "She just said all the right things to encourage me," Kettlewell recalled. It was December 1989, and Ryan invited Kettlewell to the group's Christmas party. "I said, 'I don't do Christmas parties. I don't do social affairs. Forget it, I'm not coming.'" Instead, she agreed to attend the January 1990 meeting: "I told them at work I needed that time off. I drove to Minneapolis. Sat in the parking lot for two or three hours, sitting there psyching myself up to come in."[19]

As Kettlewell steeled her nerves in the parking lot at the VA, Kay

Ryan, Air Force veteran Bobby Smith, and the rest of the group waited for her. Kettlewell and Smith recalled the event during a joint
interview nearly a decade later. "Meanwhile, we knew that she was
coming down," said Smith. "We were sitting in the cafeteria of the
VA, which is where she was supposed to meet us. And Kay [Ryan] is
a wreck because she didn't want to lose a nurse," Smith said. "Pretty
soon . . . I see this head come around the corner and these big eyes.
You know what a deer looks like when they get caught in the head-
lights? And Kay leapt, ran to her, grabbed her, pulled her over. And
then we went to our room and had the meeting, and the next thing
you know, she's telling everybody her life story." Kettlewell continued: "I couldn't believe it. I hadn't told anybody for years, and then
I couldn't stop. It was so nice. Because I had listened to all of them,
and I thought, 'Oh my God, they've all been through it.'" As she listened to Kettlewell open herself to others that day in 1990, Smith
kept thinking, "It's okay, you're safe here, you're safe here. Don't wor-
ry, you're safe. You're safe."

That feeling of safety—of being surrounded by women who had
experienced similar things and who would not cast judgment on one
another—was critical to the group's success. As word of the group
spread from one woman to another, new members were drawn in.
Of the fifteen women I interviewed for this study, eleven were part
of this support group for at least a short time; at least seven of them
participated for more than a few meetings. Bobby Smith and Penny
Kettlewell (who were by this time roommates) were mainstays of the
group, traveling from northern Minnesota for the meetings. Lynn
Kohl—who had been accused of not working hard enough in the in-
patient PTSD group at the Tomah, Wisconsin, VA—drove from central Wisconsin to Minneapolis several times a month to meet with
her fellow nurse-veterans. Ann Rudolph found the group when she
finally contacted the VA after her previous counselors didn't know
what to do with the fact that she was a Vietnam veteran. Immediately,
she felt a bond with the others in the group: "You're a sisterhood
regardless of what your experiences were out there. There's an empathy and a knowing."

Nurses brought different issues and needs to the group. Joan
Paulson attended the group when Kettlewell, with whom she had
roomed in Vietnam, got in touch with her and invited her to a meet-

ing. Paulson had had a chance to digest some of her war experiences with interested friends after her return but still found the support group to be warm and welcoming, even if the other members' "pain was greater than my pain was." Valerie Buchan went to a few meetings, until her work schedule conflicted with the group's meetings. Mary Breed was active in the MACVW group and working for the memorial project but only attended the PTSD support group for a short time. She had worked through much of her postwar anger before the group began meeting, simply by talking to friend and coworker Mary Beth Crowley. "By the time this group started," she explained, "I didn't want to go back to that anger."

In many ways, the nurses' support group functioned much like the rap groups begun two decades earlier by male combat veterans searching for a way to deal with their post-traumatic stress. The women came together in a safe, nonjudgmental setting to talk, mostly to each other, about their experiences in and after the war. "We'd talk about what they did in Vietnam, what they saw, what was bothering them about it," Kay Bauer said, "what kinds of things happened when they came home." The going wasn't always easy; there were occasional tensions as volatile subjects and misunderstandings over the purpose and function of the group arose. Still, the women persevered and worked with each other to tackle such difficulties. For women who felt the larger VA system had rendered them voiceless, it was critical that each participant had a say in the group's operation. Some women underwent individual therapy with Kay Ryan as well. Under the guidance of Ryan and an occupational therapist, the nurses used art—poetry, painting, drawing—to give voice to otherwise unspeakable feelings.

For four weeks in 1991, six women—Bobby Smith, Penny Kettlewell, Ann Rudolph, Lynn Kohl, Kay Bauer, and another woman—attended a more intensive PTSD group that met four days a week in a hotel. The Gulf War had just started, and the women needed help dealing with emotions triggered by this new war. Bauer had arranged for the participants to receive continuing education units (CEUs)—credits for ongoing training required to maintain nursing licensure—so it would be easier for them to take time off from work. Kay Ryan headed the group but called other mental health experts in for specific sessions. During the day, the women attended lectures, did therapeutic art projects, and delved even further into their war-based trauma. During the evening, they had fun. "We had good bonding," Rudolph recalled. "Just cool sisterhood stuff." The benefits of both the larger support group and the more intensive PTSD retreat group were significant: Lynn Kohl stopped having nightmares once she started attending the group. Ann Rudolph let go of the rage that had been simmering just below the surface. More importantly, nurses found in each other the support and understanding that helped them cope with their residual war trauma.

It wasn't only Minnesota women who were coming together to build a network of support for those who had served in Vietnam. Spurred on by increasing awareness of PTSD and women's wartime service in general and the efforts of some committed counselors and veterans in particular, women veterans' support groups began springing up across the country in the 1980s. Although the Minneapolis group was their primary home for support and camaraderie, a number of the women in this study participated in other groups as well. In 1988, for instance, Kay Bauer was one of six women Vietnam veterans to participate in an Outward Bound program in Rockland, Maine, run by a former Green Beret Vietnam veteran. For a week, the women tackled physical, mental, and emotional challenges on Hurricane Island and, in the process, began to "learn again lessons of love and trust." In September 1990, counselors from the Springfield, Illinois, Vet Center organized an intensive weekend program for women Vietnam veterans. Ann Rudolph, Penny Kettlewell, and Diane Evans all took part in the group at one time or another. The National Women's Trauma Recovery Program—the VA's first residential PTSD program for women—opened in Menlo Park, California, in 1992. These groups featured counselors and participants who understood the specific nature of women's war trauma, the unique ways in which women veterans were disenfranchised after the war, and the specific ways in which PTSD manifested itself in women. Most importantly, they helped women recover from war trauma by fostering connections with other women war veterans.[20]

The formal Minneapolis support group disbanded in the mid-1990s when, according to Kay Bauer, it asked to be transferred to the main VA hospital. "That was the end of our group," she said. "The VA said, 'Forget it,' and we were all dropped. So our group never existed

again." It only existed in the first place because the nurses themselves saw to it that the VA provide them with some kind of help.
"We stood up and picked up the VA on our shoulders and drug them
along," Penny Kettlewell explained. "We just were sort of an unstop-
pable force. We saw there was hope, we saw there was help, they
had the capacity to do it, and we basically pushed them to do it."
The nurses found their ally within the VA in Kay Ryan, and together
they gave form and shape to women Vietnam veterans' suffering. "We
were *all* nurses over there," explained Lynn Kohl. "Even though we
might have been in different areas, we all had similar experiences.
A lot of the feelings were the same, the emotions." She found the
women's group to be more useful than any of the male-dominated
veteran groups she had attended over the years. In 2007, having difficulty with the wars in Iraq and Afghanistan, Kohl went back to one
such group in Wisconsin that she had originally attended in the early 1980s. "The same guys are there," she said. "They're talking about
their guns and the same things as they were back in 1982. Nothing
has changed. But the women moved on. We moved ahead."[21]

The support group that Kay Bauer and Kay Ryan started became
Penny Kettlewell's lifeline. It meant everything to her to find other
women who understood what she had gone through in Vietnam
because they had experienced it, too: "Every one of them was so
accepting and encouraging. We all were so much alike." That sense
of connection and support helped Kettlewell survive. "That group
gave me another ten years of being able to work and function," she
said. "I didn't collapse under the strain." The group was still meeting in 1993 when the Vietnam Women's Memorial was dedicated in
Washington, D.C. Kettlewell traveled across the country with others
from the group to attend the festivities. And there, on the National
Mall in front of a crowd of women Vietnam veterans and their supporters, she read a poem that she had written as part of her therapy.
If the support group had saved Penny Kettlewell's life, reconciled her
to her past, the Vietnam Women's Memorial took that healing to another level: it reconciled women Vietnam veterans with the nation.

# 6

## *"Before You Can Forget, You Need to Remember"*

### The Vietnam Women's Memorial

**TWO DAYS AFTER VETERANS' DAY** in 1982, Diane Carlson Evans stood with approximately 150,000 others to participate in the dedication ceremony for the newly unveiled Vietnam Veterans Memorial, commonly known as "the Wall." She stood in the sea of faces as senators, veterans' organization representatives, and political dignitaries offered a long-overdue "thanks" and "welcome home" to the three million U.S. troops who had served in Vietnam. More than fifty-eight thousand of those troops never made the journey home. Their names—among them the names of the eight military women killed in Vietnam—were etched into the black granite of the Wall. D-M Boulay was in Washington, D.C., that November, too, for a meeting of the American Association of Nurse Attorneys. She didn't attend the dedication ceremonies for the Wall, however. "I couldn't bear the thought of being there on the dedication day with all those people," she said. "Crowds are not my favorite place. So I waited until the next day." After visiting the Wall, she returned to Minneapolis and went back to work at her law practice.[1]

If both Evans and Boulay had been moved by the Wall, they both were also chagrined to learn, in 1983, that a statue of three male soldiers was to be added to the Vietnam Veterans Memorial in 1984. "The Wall was complete," Evans explained later, "because the men and women who died in Vietnam were together on the Wall." But now that visitors to the memorial would see, in Evans's words, "men in the flesh and blood and portrayed visibly as men," she worried that women's contributions to the war would be erased. So Evans contacted Minneapolis sculptor Rodger Brodin and asked him to create a statue for nurses who had served in Vietnam. At the same time, Boulay and her associates at the Vietnam Veterans Leadership Program in Minneapolis were discussing the implications of adding a statue of only men to the Wall. In late 1983, Boulay, Evans, Brodin, and three Marine veterans of the war met to discuss the possibilities for honoring women veterans. Brodin brought a sketch of the nurse statue he and Evans had envisioned, and a plan was born. As Boulay put it at the time, "They're putting up a statue of the men, for the guys who served. What if we do the same for women?" Thus began a collaboration that prompted the formation of the Vietnam Women's Memorial Project, Inc. (VWMP) in 1984 and ultimately led to the dedication of the Vietnam Women's Memorial in 1993.[2]

Although Evans and Boulay were the prime movers behind the original idea to build a memorial to women who had served in Vietnam, it was the collective efforts of women Vietnam veterans from across the country that made the project a success. And a colossal effort it was. In contrast to the speed with which the Wall and statue of three men were proposed, built, and dedicated (roughly a two-year process for each), the effort to build a memorial for women spanned ten years and three presidential elections, required the approval of three federal commissions and two acts of Congress, involved hundreds of women veterans in a national grassroots publicity campaign, generated an often heated public debate over the significance of gender to military service and national memorials, and witnessed two distinct design models. Because the project was based in Minneapolis for the first few years of its existence, Minnesota's women veterans played an especially important role in the campaign, and most of the fifteen nurses I interviewed for this project contributed in some way to its success. This chapter focuses on their contributions and the healing effects that this work, and the Memorial itself, eventually had for so many of them. As Diane Evans put it, "Before you can forget, you need to remember."[3]

*From the Wall to* Rambo *to* Three Fighting Men*:*
*The Origins of the Vietnam Women's Memorial Project*

The Wall is a place of healing for many Vietnam veterans. It was for
Evans, who captured the effect of her visit to the Wall in 1982 in a
poem she wrote a year later.

*That beautiful black granite*
*Wall, now carries the burden*
*For me*
*And for us all.*[4]

That the Wall plays such a redemptive role for so many Vietnam veterans belies its troubled origins in the decade after the war's end. If
for much of the 1970s Vietnam veterans were an invisible population,
by the end of the decade some were breaking their silence by lobbying for a memorial. Vietnam veterans Jan Scruggs, Jack Wheeler, and
Robert Doubek cofounded the Vietnam Veterans Memorial Fund
(VVMF) in 1979, not long after Scruggs saw *The Deer Hunter* and came
to the disturbing realization that "no one remembers [the] names" of
those who had served and died in Vietnam. In 1980, President Jimmy
Carter signed legislation authorizing construction of a memorial for
Vietnam veterans on two acres of land on the Mall in Washington,
D.C. From the moment Maya Lin's design was chosen for the memorial, it became clear that deciding how to remember the war and
those who fought it would ignite as many passionate political and
personal debates as had the war itself.[5]

     When Valerie Buchan first saw pictures of the Wall, its long, black
arms descending into the earth, she felt insulted. "Well, they're giving us one more kick," she remembered thinking. "A black slab in
the ground? This is going to be our memorial?" She was not the
only one who found Lin's design wanting. Critics deplored its col-
or, shape, and design, comparing it unfavorably to the grand white
marble sculptures that would surround it on the Mall and calling
it a "wailing wall" for antiwar protesters. They condemned the process by which the design had been chosen and lobbed ad homi-
nem attacks against Maya Lin, a young Chinese American student
from Yale University. So powerful were these critics—among them

former VVMF supporters such as Vietnam veteran Tom Carhart, millionaire H. Ross Perot, and former Vietnam POW Admiral James J. Stockdale—that they effectively held hostage the construction of the memorial by withdrawing their political and financial support of the VVMF until their concerns had been addressed. Indeed, the Wall would not have been built had not its supporters agreed to appease its detractors by adding a U.S. flag and a more realistic and sufficiently "heroic" statue to the site. In May 1982, six months before the Wall's dedication, the VVMF chose Frederick Hart's larger-than-life-sized bronze sculpture of three infantrymen to join the Wall as part of the Vietnam Veterans Memorial. The figures bear all the marks of the typical Vietnam infantryman: boonie hats and dog tags, rifles and bandoliers, characteristics of white, black, and brown skin. Most importantly and obviously, they are all men.[6]

By the time Hart's statue was built in 1984, the male Vietnam veteran had already become a familiar character in American popular culture. As Diane Evans recalled of the early eighties, "Every time I pick up a newspaper or a magazine, I am seeing my brother veteran, and I am glad to be doing that . . . but they weren't talking about the women." From memoirs of male Vietnam veterans such as Tim O'Brien, Ron Kovic, and Philip Caputo to films featuring soldiers and veterans as principal characters, the Vietnam War story of the seventies and eighties, whether told in bronze, celluloid, or print, was the story of the male combat grunt. When, in 1983, Evans heard Frederick Hart describe the three figures in his forthcoming statue as "consistent with history," she was offended. Hart's statement "reflected the belief that only men serve and therefore are portrayed." It was time for a change.[7]

Although women Vietnam veterans had begun making inroads into the public consciousness in the mid-1980s—with the publication of Lynda Van Devanter's memoir, *Home Before Morning,* in 1983; an article in *MS* magazine about "Vietnam nurses" in 1984; the release of *Purple Hearts,* a film starring Cheryl Ladd as an Army nurse in Vietnam, in 1984; and Keith Walker's oral history, *A Piece of My Heart,* in 1985—several of the nurses in this study said they felt excluded by the overwhelming focus on male veterans. They were particularly attuned to developments regarding the memorials in Washington, D.C. Once the Wall's understated elegance began drawing visitors after its dedication in 1982, Valerie Buchan became a fan, describing it as "wonderful," "thought-provoking," and "dignified." Edy Johnson found it "inspired" when she visited in 1984. She liked "the fact that you could see the reflections of the people in the material of the wall and the names." But Kay Bauer felt there was no place for her at either the Wall or the men's statue. "Definitely not," she said when I asked if the Wall meant anything to her when it first opened. "That was not for women, to the extent that I wouldn't even go there."[8]

Luckily for her, Evans and Boulay had set the wheels in motion to build a memorial that women veterans would find more relevant and welcoming. Realizing they would need to raise a significant amount of money to accomplish their goal, they incorporated as a nonprofit organization with three specific goals: to identify women who had served in Vietnam, to educate the public about women's service during the war, and to build a memorial on the grounds of the existing Vietnam Veterans Memorial in Washington, D.C. Boulay and Evans sat on its board, along with former Marine Jerry Bender and Hamline University Law School dean Stephen Young. The statue of a young Army nurse holding a helmet in her hands that Brodin had crafted after Evans first contacted him became the focal point for what was, at first, known as the Vietnam Nurses Memorial Project. As word of the project began to spread, Evans said they began hearing from women who had served in Vietnam in capacities besides nursing. "I was not a nurse in Vietnam," they would write. "What about us? What about our service?" As a result, the Vietnam Nurses Memorial Project became the Vietnam Women's Memorial Project (VWMP). "We didn't want to leave anyone out," Evans explained.[9]

The early years of the VWMP were filled with hard work as Boulay and Evans cut their teeth in the fields of political lobbying, fundraising, public relations, and grassroots organizing. Neither of them had any prior experience dealing with the politicking that would become essential if the project were to succeed, but they each brought with them other professional skills, important networking contacts, and a fierce tenacity that sustained them in even the darkest hours of the battle, for a battle it would become. Fortunately, they were not in it alone. Their work was buffeted by a growing network of supporters, including politicians, veterans' organizations, male Vietnam veterans, and, most importantly, an ever-expanding web of women Vietnam veterans from across the country, many of whom had never before admitted their veteran status.

### A Gathering of Forces: Building Support for the VWMP, 1984–87

On August 12, 1984, Mary O'Brien Tyrrell went with her son to the Landmark Center in St. Paul to see the model of Brodin's statue, titled, simply, *The Nurse.* The display of the statue was the focus of an event signifying the public launch of the nationwide memorial campaign. As Tyrrell stood in the crowd that day, she started crying. "My son said, 'What's the matter with you, Mom?'" she recalled. "'I don't know. I don't know.' It was just the peeling of the onion." The layers of that onion continued to peel in 1986 when she was working at the VA hospital in St. Cloud and a colleague, himself a Vietnam veteran, thanked her for her service during the war. "The feeling I had when he said 'thank you' to me was that the top of my head came off. And I mean that from a physical point of view. It felt like my head opened up!" she exclaimed. "All of a sudden these feelings of grief and stress and anger and of being overwhelmed and fear and all that stuff was there."

She began writing poetry after her encounter with this grateful man. One poem, called "Saving Lives," honored the corpsmen with whom she had worked, tracing the bond she had developed with these young medic-soldiers and the horror she felt upon finding one of their names on the Wall. During a visit to the Wall in 1986, she left a copy of this poem there. Tyrrell hadn't been part of the nurses' support group in Minneapolis; she had never sought counseling to help her deal with her wartime memories. Instead, writing poetry became her therapy, her way of dealing with whatever PTSD she may have had. Then, after seeing Brodin's *The Nurse* in St. Paul in 1984 and giving voice to her wartime experiences in poetry, Tyrrell was ready to start talking about her eighteen months on Guam. She was ready to identify herself as a veteran. She was ready to go to work for the VWMP.[10]

The VWMP needed women like Tyrrell. The success of the project depended on its supporters' ability to convince the American public that what women had done in Vietnam was significant enough to warrant honoring them on the National Mall. The best way to do this was to convince women veterans to share their stories—no small task given the generally disinterested response they had received when they came home and their subsequent retreat into silence about their military experiences. Diane Evans had only just begun talking about Vietnam herself: in a 1983 speech at a Lions Club, she spoke about nurses' tender caregiving during the war and the beauty, but incompleteness, of the Vietnam Veterans Memorial. Although D-M Boulay had discussed her Vietnam experience with her veteran-physician husband, it was her work with the VWMP that brought her story into public view. "I had to explain to people that I was a Vietnam vet and listen to the response, 'I didn't know women were there,'" she explained. "That made me explain more and more to more and more people." Now the trick was to get other women Vietnam veterans to do the same.[11]

The event at the Landmark Center in 1984 was the VWMP's first public event, and Evans was not at all certain beforehand that it would be a success. She remembered one nurse veteran from Minnesota who called her after seeing a press release about the unveiling. "Do you think anybody will give a damn?" she asked Evans. "That struck me because I was worried that maybe people wouldn't," Evans admitted. "But how could they care if they didn't even know what women did?" As it turned out, she needn't have worried. The event was well attended and generated two front-page articles in the *St. Paul Pioneer Press and Dispatch.* "The place was absolutely filled," Evans recalled. "There was standing room only. All these motorcyclists, these guys who were Vietnam vets, came roaring in on their motorcycles in their black leather, and they stood in the back to show support for the nurses and the women who served. The press came and some very good stories were done." In addition, "ten or fifteen Minnesota women veterans were there."

Mary O'Brien Tyrrell was there. So were Valerie Buchan, Kay Bauer, and Edy Johnson. Johnson spoke at the ceremony, and all three of them—along with D-M Boulay and Diane Jaeger, a nurse from Wisconsin who had also served in Vietnam—shared their stories in a feature article in the *St. Paul Pioneer Press and Dispatch.* Mary Breed wasn't able to attend the festivities that day, but she soon got in-

*Mary Beth Crowley (shown here in 1970–71) encouraged others to share their Vietnam War experiences, assembling slide shows and speaking at schools and in front of veterans groups.*

volved in the project at the behest of Mary Beth Crowley, who served as the North Central Regional Coordinator for the VWMP. "Mary Beth got me into speaking engagements," Breed said. She spoke at schools and in front of veterans' groups, and she and Crowley put together a slide show of their Vietnam experiences. Sometimes, it felt like too much, and she didn't want to talk about Vietnam anymore. "You get tired of talking about it," she said, but her name was often the last on the list, and so if she didn't agree to speak, no one would. It was through her work on the project that Crowley first began talking about Vietnam, too. "In the seventies, I never would have said anything," Crowley noted. Even as late as 1985, Crowley told a reporter for the *Minneapolis Star and Tribune* that she rarely dealt with her memories from Vietnam. She remembered dancing to "Save the Country" by the Fifth Dimension before starting her shifts in Vietnam, but for the most part, "I tune out Vietnam," she told the newspaper's readers. But as she became more involved with the VWMP, she spoke more frequently about her war experiences.[12]

Recruiting women to the project through word-of-mouth helped the VWMP work toward achieving its goal of building a network of sister veterans. As the Minnesota State Coordinator in the mid-1980s, Mary O'Brien Tyrrell remembered D-M Boulay telling her that part of her job was to contact a woman Vietnam veteran in another state so that they could exchange their war stories with each other. Tyrrell described this strategy as a "genius idea" because it reassured her that she was not alone in struggling to make sense of her wartime experiences, that she hadn't "exaggerated" their intensity or their impact on her life. Once found, many women contributed what they could to the project. Valerie Buchan was involved from the beginning, helping to raise funds by selling pins and buttons, until she lost track of the project when it "got very big." Joan Paulson contributed money to the project, and Mary Lu Brunner helped with fund-raising. Lynn Kohl served as an area advisor for the VWMP in central Wisconsin for a while and helped raise $5,000 for the cause. Although neither Bobby Smith nor Penny Kettlewell were up to speaking publicly about their own wartime experiences, they "did what [they] could" to lend their support. Kay Bauer helped locate other women veterans through her contacts in the Reserves and participated in letter-writing, pin-selling, and fund-raising campaigns for the memorial, all the while helping to get the PTSD group up and running. Mary O'Brien Tyrrell served as Minnesota State Coordinator for the VWMP until 1988.[13]

While many women veterans gave generously of themselves in support of the VWMP, the project consumed the lives of D-M Boulay and Diane Evans. Evans quit her part-time job and "gave up everything but my family" to work as chair of public relations and board liaison to veterans organizations. Five major veterans organizations—the American Legion, the Veterans of Foreign Wars (VFW), Paralyzed Veterans of America, Disabled Veterans of America, and Vietnam Veterans of America—had cast their lot with the project by the end of 1985. She also continued expanding the network of women veterans. While some women refused to open the Pandora's box of their war memories by working for the VWMP, many others volunteered to share their stories at events where models of *The Nurse* were on display. Male Vietnam veterans, too, were among the project's biggest supporters, according to Evans.[14]

Boulay worked the political side of the project. Though busy with her law practice and the Agent Orange Veterans Payment Program Advisory Board (the team responsible for distributing the proceeds of the class-action lawsuit filed on behalf of Vietnam veterans against the manufacturers of the herbicide), she also acted as VWMP chair and CEO. Her work on the Agent Orange lawsuit led to helpful contacts in Washington, D.C.—such as Chuck Hagel, who had extensive lobbyist, political, and business connections in Washington (and would later serve two terms as a Republican senator from Nebraska). Hagel "got me pointed in all the right directions for who to see on the Hill," Boulay recalled, and served as VWMP treasurer for a time. Soon she had wooed Senator Dave Durenberger (R-MN), Representative Sam Gejdenson (D-CT), and VVMF Chair Jack Wheeler to the project's ever-growing list of supporters.[15]

By August 1987, the VWMP had raised $290,000 of an estimated total of $1.2 million and had set its sights on dedicating the memorial on Veterans Day 1988. Before it could do so, however, it would have to pass muster with several federal agencies whose job it was to oversee the public and artistic development of the nation's capital. In September 1987, Secretary of the Interior Donald Hodel gave his stamp of approval to the VWMP. The next stop was a hearing before the Commission of Fine Arts (CFA).

On October 22, 1987, Diane Evans, D-M Boulay, Rodger Brodin, Senator Dave Durenberger, and a handful of fellow VWMP board members and supporters gathered in the CFA offices in Washington, D.C. The CFA had been established in 1910 to "advise the government on matters pertaining to the arts"; in 1987 it had been under the leadership of the patrician J. Carter Brown for more than fifteen years. As gatekeeper for the arts scene in the nation's capital, Brown did his best to protect, as he saw it, the integrity of the Vietnam Veterans Memorial from the threat posed to it by the VWMP. Although VWMP supporters argued vehemently that the Vietnam Veterans Memorial—the Hart statue, specifically—was incomplete in its portrayal of those who had served, Brown and three other members of the CFA sided with the project's opponents; the meeting concluded with a 4–1 vote against the VWMP. In a letter to Hodel dated October 28, 1987, Brown explained the reasoning behind the vote. "First and foremost," he wrote, "the Commission views the memorial in its present form as complete." The three male figures of Hart's statue represented all who had served, "the part standing for the whole."[16]

The specific part that was chosen to represent the whole was very telling, however. When Evans heard that the Hart statue was "universally intended to include the women," she remembered thinking, "Well, which one of those men is a woman?" Hart's statue did not, in fact, represent everyone—it represented men; accordingly, the Vietnam Women's Memorial would represent women, and it would use *The Nurse* to do so. [17]

These arguments would carry the VWMP from the offices of the CFA to the halls of Congress. Outraged that "five people on a commission" had the power to veto what they saw as a mandate of the American people to honor women who served in Vietnam, Evans and Boulay returned to VWMP headquarters in Minneapolis frustrated but determined. Durenberger suggested that the best way to ensure the project's success would be to secure explicit legislative support, and so in November 1987 he introduced a bill to "authorize the Vietnam Women's Memorial Project, Inc., to construct a statue at the Vietnam Veterans Memorial in honor and recognition of the women of the United States who served in the Vietnam conflict" and to locate it on the grounds of the existing Vietnam Veterans Memorial. In February 1988, the Senate Subcommittee on Public Lands, National Parks and Forests held hearings on S. 2042 at which Durenberger explained his support for *The Nurse:* "Infantryman has always represented all of the MOS [military occupational specialties], if you will, but it has also stood for man, and this stands very clearly for woman. It stands more for woman . . . than it stands for nurse." The combat grunt was supposed to epitomize manhood, just as the nurse was assumed to represent womanhood, thus balancing the representation of Vietnam veterans at the memorial site.[18]

*Losing* The Nurse, *Gaining a Memorial:*
*Commissions, Congress, and the VWMP, 1988–93*

In 1984, Mary Lu Brunner had written a poem called "To My Unknown Soldier Boy." It was an homage to one of the nameless young men who died under her care. "I regret I didn't know you. / I can't tell your mother I was there," she wrote. Seven years later, her poem—along with others written by Diane Evans, Penny Kettlewell, Mary O'Brien Tyrrell, and other women Vietnam veterans appeared in *Visions of War, Dreams of Peace: Writings of Women in the Vietnam War.* The volume's contributors agreed to donate the royalties from sales of the book to the Vietnam Women's Memorial Project as the struggle to build the memorial continued and costs increased. Durenberger's bill had passed the Senate by a vote of 96 to 1 in June 1988, and on November 15, 1988, President Ronald Reagan had signed Public Law 100-660. Although the VWMP had secured long-sought approval to build its memorial, the law only *recommended* that it be located on the grounds of the Vietnam Veterans Memorial. So, on Veterans Day 1988, there was still no statue and the project needed another $600,000 to meet its new goal of $1.3 million.[19]

From 1988 to 1993, the VWMP redoubled its efforts. It ramped up its publicity campaign, drawing actress Loretta Swit of *M\*A\*S\*H* fame to the cause and delivering to members of Congress a poster-petition with the motto, "Not all women wore love beads in the sixties." By July 1988, the VWMP had relocated its central offices from Minneapolis to Washington, D.C., to allow for better access to legislators and commissioners who would decide the project's fate. The move followed a "management shakeup" at the project that resulted from a falling-out between Rodger Brodin, Diane Evans, another board member, and D-M Boulay over finances and general control of the project's operation. Evangeline Jamison—an Army nurse veteran of World War II, Korea, and Vietnam—replaced Boulay as chair, while Evans continued to volunteer full time for the VWMP, sat on its board of directors, and served as chair of the Committee on Veterans Affairs and of public relations. Evans and the VWMP continued to do battle with J. Carter Brown as well, taking issue with his apparent equation of women's wartime service to that of scout dogs, his description of *The Nurse* as looking as if she were about to "upchuck," and his portrayal of the women of the VWMP as hysterical, myopic, Minnesota women pushing their personal agenda down the throat of the nation.[20]

Brown's comments did not go over well with the women who had, by then, devoted five years of their lives to the VWMP. Kay Bauer remembered how distressed Diane Evans and others were by Brown's "terrible demeaning put-down words" that made them "feel like all of us women were useless human beings." Brown's remarks found little support in the mainstream media, however, especially as women Vietnam veterans in general became increasingly visible. In 1988, ABC television introduced *China Beach,* a Vietnam War drama whose lead character was Army nurse Colleen McMurphy (Dana Delany). Delany's McMurphy bore a striking resemblance to Diane Evans who, by 1989, had become the public face of the VWMP. That year, Evans took part in two significant television events featuring women Vietnam veterans. On February 26, 1989, she appeared in a *60 Minutes* episode about women Vietnam veterans and, less than a month later, in a special episode of *China Beach* in which interviews with actual women veterans were interspersed with footage from the show.[21]

Combined with the diligent work of VWMP activists and ongoing congressional wrangling, such publicity helped build momentum for the Memorial. On November 28, 1989, President George H. W. Bush signed the second piece of legislation on behalf of a memorial to women Vietnam veterans. Public Law 101-187 guaranteed the VWMP a spot on the Mall, if not on the 2.2-acre Vietnam Veterans Memorial site. Final approval for that specific location followed in spring 1990 with the consent of the CFA, National Capital Planning Commission (NCPC), and National Capital Memorial Commission (NCMC).[22]

With approval granted and site secured, the next task facing the VWMP was deciding on a final design for the memorial. Brodin's *The Nurse* had been controversial from the beginning. Longtime opponents found the artistic merits of the statue wanting and suggested that the Memorial might take the form of a plaque, bench, or bas relief. These options, of course, would not do for women veterans what Hart's statue did for men—depict them "in the flesh and blood." More worrisome criticism came from a group that the VWMP very much wanted to satisfy: enlisted women veterans. Women who had served in Vietnam in capacities other than nursing were among the first to voice complaints about Brodin's model. "I didn't like the Memorial," recalled Women's Army Corps Vietnam veteran Carol Lincoln. *The Nurse* "made everybody think that everybody's a nurse," she told me in an interview for another project. "It didn't portray me." Such complaints signaled the trap within which the VWMP was caught: if Hart's statue represented symbolic man, the Women's Memorial would have to represent symbolic woman, and symbolic woman does not, cannot possibly, represent the diversity of actual women.[23]

The VWMP took pains to try to accommodate the views and experiences of nonnurse women veterans once it realized that Brodin's *The Nurse* would not satisfy the CFA, which retained artistic oversight of the project. When the CFA launched a national open design competition in August 1990, it declared that the winning design would have to represent the "various occupational specialties" and racial backgrounds of women who had served. In June 1991, the VWMP board decided that a sculpture by Glenna Goodacre met all these criteria. On March 11, 1993, the NCPC and CFA granted their approval on the final design for the Vietnam Women's Memorial.[24]

Goodacre's sculpture depicts three military women: one supports a wounded man (the largest figure in the composition) lying prostrate across her lap, another looks skyward, and a third kneels on the ground with an empty helmet before her. Evans explained that it was the latter figure that was the heart of the piece: "The kneeling woman embodies the totality of the dramatic experiences of war—the intensity, fatigue, anguish and isolation. Her despair speaks to the pain of war and need for solace." Despite the VWMP's attempts to broaden the depiction of women to include nonnurses, the statue highlights the caretaking, emotional work that nurses did and is often described as "the nurses memorial."[25]

Still, many of the nurses I met were disappointed that *The Nurse* would not be installed near the Wall. "We supported that other one for so long," Lynn Kohl said. "So that was hard. But this one is moving, too." Valerie Buchan thinks the Goodacre statue is "beautiful, but it's not reality at all. No nurse sat on a chair and held a sick soldier across her lap." Nevertheless, she appreciates the statue's depiction of "the way that the women cared for the soldiers." Mary O'Brien Tyrrell and Edy Johnson also preferred the original statue, in part because it spoke to them more directly as nurses. "I thought it was so great," Johnson said of *The Nurse.* The Memorial "got to be more than just the nurse statue. It got to be women in general. So the emphasis was a little bit different from what I had." Tyrrell, too, had been attached to Brodin's sculpture. "It makes my heart ache that it wasn't

[*The Nurse*]," she said, "but it was politics, you know. What are you going to do?"

On July 29, 1993, General Colin Powell, Vietnam War veteran and Gulf War hero, spoke at groundbreaking festivities for the new Vietnam Women's Memorial. He described women's bravery, strength, and courage, mentioned the numerous duties they performed in Vietnam, and said that "for too long" society had "ignored the vital and endless work that falls to women and is not appreciated as it should be." "How much of your heart did you leave there?" he asked the women in attendance. "How often were you the mother for a kid asking for Mom in the last few seconds of his life? How many nineteen-year-old sons did you lose?" In building the Memorial, he said, women who served in Vietnam would be honored for "the hope and the strength, the tenderness and the power, the kindness and the passion" that they brought to war. The Memorial, he said, will remind America that "even in the depths of horror and cruelty there will always beat the heart of human love." If nurses had broken the midcentury mold for women by joining the military and going to war, the work they did there was familiar in its emotional overtones, and it was that familiarity that the Vietnam Women's Memorial captured.[26]

### Dedication Day 1993: The Vietnam Women's Memorial

On a crisp, sunny November day in 1993, Vice President Al Gore joined Diane Evans, Glenna Goodacre, and the entire VWMP board of directors on the grounds of the Vietnam Veterans Memorial for the unveiling and dedication of the Vietnam Women's Memorial. Women Vietnam veterans came from around the country to attend the ceremony the VWMP called "A Celebration of Patriotism and Courage." They came in boonie hats and combat boots, in business suits and motorcycle leather, in sweatshirts saying "Real China Beach Nurses." They came to remember and to be honored, to meet old friends and heal old wounds. Penny Kettlewell was there. And it was there, in front of the gathered crowd, that she read one of the poems she had written as part of her therapy in the PTSD group run by Kay Ryan. "I Hold Them" it was called, and it spoke of the care she provided young G.I.s in Vietnam. It described her enduring concern for these men, twenty years after war's end, as she stood in front of their names etched on a long black wall. It also gave voice to a nurse's lingering wartime trauma.[27]

> *They have become such a part of me*
> *When you look at me, who do you see?*
> *Can I live if I set them free?*
> *Who will hold them*
> *And salvage me?*[28]

Kettlewell wasn't the only nurse from Minnesota, or from the group whose stories form the core of this book, to attend the dedication of the Memorial in 1993. Of course Diane Evans, by this time chair of the VWMP, was there, playing general host of the festivities. Kay Bauer, Bobby Smith, and Penny Kettlewell drove together from Minnesota to Washington, D.C., where they then met up with "the Marys" (Breed and Crowley), Mary Lu Brunner, Lynn Kohl, and Ann Rudolph. Lynn Bower—who for so long had carried a sense of guilt for having cut her tour in Vietnam short due to her pregnancy—was there, too. Although she'd met some of the other Minnesota veterans before, she was feeling uncertain about her role in the group of "real" Vietnam veterans: "I don't know if they'll want me, this group," she remembered thinking. But, she said, "they were wonderful. That's really when I met them all, and they all just opened their arms and it was like it's okay. It's okay. We've all got our own story and it's okay." Mary Lu Brunner and Valerie Buchan also made the journey across the country. A friend from Guam convinced Mary O'Brien Tyrrell to make the trip. "I wasn't planning to go because I couldn't afford it," Tyrrell explained. But when her friend insisted that she come, she managed to find the money for a plane ticket and a shared hotel room.[29]

After arriving and settling into their hotels, the women turned their attention to the slate of activities scheduled for November 10–12. From hospital reunions to musical tributes to panel discussions, it was three full days of sometimes painful, sometimes joyful celebration. But the main events took place on Veterans Day, November 11, with the official dedication of the Memorial in the afternoon and an evening candlelight ceremony. For the women I met, however, the morning parade down Constitution Avenue was the emotional highlight of the day.

Constitution Avenue runs along the northern side of the National Mall, from the Capitol building on the east end to the Lincoln Memorial on the west end. Women Vietnam veterans took their place at the head of the parade as it gathered between Seventh and Fourteenth streets. As they marched westward toward the Wall and the site for their new memorial, the women passed hallmarks of national honor: the American History Museum, the Washington Monument, the White House, Constitution Gardens. They entered the grounds of the Vietnam Veterans Memorial at Twenty-first Avenue at the eastern end of the Wall and made their way toward a tree-lined plaza where Glenna Goodacre's statue awaited. All along the way, they were cheered, thanked, and hugged by the supporters who thronged the parade route.

In all, twenty-five thousand people flocked to the city for the occasion; even if every military woman who had served in Vietnam had shown up in Washington that day, they still would have been outnumbered more than two to one by their admirers. The media was there, too, in force. The *New York Times, Washington Post, St. Paul Pioneer Press,* CBS *Sunday Morning,* and C-SPAN sent cameras and reporters to cover the festivities. Twin Cities' WCCO television captured Penny Kettlewell and Kay Bauer walking arm in arm along the parade route, Kettlewell clasping a photo of her lost friend, Heddy Orlowski. Local camera crews scanned the row of Minnesota nurses—Mary Breed, Mary Lu Brunner, Ann Rudolph, Valerie Buchan, and Lynn Bower among them—as they basked in the warmth of the moment.[30]

But it wasn't the attention of the media that moved the women; it was the thanks of the citizens lining the street that warmed their hearts. "The *best* part of that whole thing was the parade and the 'thank you' signs," Ann Rudolph recalled. "I didn't know I needed that." Lynn Bower agreed: "When we walked down that street, these women and men on the street, all they had to say was, 'Welcome home.' We were all walking with just tears streaming, because, finally, somebody wanted us home." Lynn Kohl explained that it wasn't the recognition per se that mattered to her and other women veterans. "It's not so much about saying 'hey, look what I did, I'm wonderful,'" she explained. "It's healing." For Mary Lu Brunner, the parade provided her the welcome home she had needed: "When we were in that parade and they were clapping, I thought, 'Oh, my God!' I mean, it was . . . I can't find the words to describe that. That was definitely enough of a welcome and thank you." Brunner received a more personal thank-you that day as well. Awaiting her at the end of the parade was a former G.I. who had spent time in Brunner's hospital in Vietnam. The two of them had been writing letters for some time, after he had contacted her to see if she had, perhaps, been his nurse. And there he was that day in November 1993, waiting to thank the nurse who had helped send him home.

Mary O'Brien Tyrrell had a "wonderful weekend in Washington" that November. She reunited with old friends from the U.S. Naval Hospital on Guam, marched in the parade, and attended the dedication of the Memorial. She also discovered that her poem, "Saving Lives," was part of an exhibit of artifacts left at the Wall that was on display in the Smithsonian National Museum of American History. And although she had loved *The Nurse* and despite the fact that she had stopped working for the VWMP in the late 1980s, she appreciated the significance of the Memorial. "I'm *so* grateful that we have that statue, so, so grateful," she said, "because then I can talk about it. . . . It sets a whole different feeling about what we did compared to what had been before, when we really weren't allowed to talk about it." For Tyrrell and others like her, the Vietnam Women's Memorial opened doors that had long been shut and signaled an important step in their recovery from war.[31]

If healing was the main benefit women veterans derived from the Memorial, that healing came from the long-overdue recognition of their wartime service. Nurses wanted the public to know that they did their best to provide excellent medical care, to save lives, and, if all else failed, to provide as much comfort as possible to dying soldiers. "I just wanted to tell all the moms and the wives, the children, how we tried our best to be with their sons, their husbands, and their brothers," Penny Kettlewell said at the candlelight ceremony. Others saw the Memorial as a much-needed tribute to women's service in general. "It was the very first time that this nation had said, 'Yes! Women have been involved in war, had to put up with the same things,'" Kay Bauer said. "We didn't shoot people. That wasn't our job. But we had to be there and take care of the aftermath of what went on."[32]

*Vietnam Women's Memorial, Washington, D.C.*

The cultural mechanisms that had redeemed male Vietnam veterans in the 1980s had also erased women veterans from the story. Diane Evans wanted to correct this record and saw in the struggle to do so the larger issues at stake. "Who gets to decide?" she asked. "Who gets to make decisions about who in your country will be honored and remembered and given great significance by being visibly portrayed on . . . the most prestigious ground in your nation?" The VWMP wanted to ensure that women Vietnam veterans would have the power to remember as well as the honor of being remembered. "Let no one ever forget you again and what you did for this nation," Evans told the crowd on dedication day. "And don't ever hide the fact again that you are a veteran of the Vietnam War."[33]

D-M Boulay and Diane Evans devoted a significant part of their lives to helping their sister veterans become visible to the nation. Their commitment to the project did not come without cost. Boulay remembered the hostile phone calls she received at project head-quarters: "Occasionally, the phone would ring and we would get some person vomiting verbal abuse upon us, everything from, 'You're a woman. How could you serve in war?' 'How could you defend our country when we were doing such nasty things?' 'Were you a whore?'" Evans was attacked as a "femi-nazi" and derided as a "woman coming out of the cornfields." She also missed some important moments in the lives of her four young children as she mustered all of her energy for the project. "I missed piano recitals. I missed tennis matches. I missed Little League. I missed parent-teacher conferences," she said. "It was a very painful ten years. I wouldn't go through it again, but I'm glad I did it."

Still, both of them take pride in the Memorial and in their roles in spreading the word about women's service in Vietnam. Although she left the Vietnam Women's Memorial Project in 1988 under stressful conditions and did not attend the dedication in 1993, Boulay said her work with the VWMP "enriched my life immensely." She recalled, "I met such wonderful people. I met people I hadn't seen in a million years. I learned how to be a lobbyist and get a major piece of legislation through." She also takes comfort in knowing that "when I leave this world, there'll be something behind that's tangible that talks about an issue that I care about and that's women's service to their country." Evans is still associated with the Vietnam Women's Memorial (now) Foundation, which continues with its education and research missions. "I have stepped back a lot," she said. "I feel like I should step back more, but . . . I still have responsibilities toward the public and my sister veterans." Despite the moments with her family that she sacrificed for the VWMP, Evans described dedication day as one of the happiest of her life: "Just looking out in the crowd and seeing my sister veterans out there hugging, laughing, crying was like the pinnacle. It was like *the* moment I'd been waiting for all those years, to see them come together and see them recognized. That was a happy moment for me. It was like America came around."

# Conclusion

For all the American wild flowers that were in Vietnam
They gave us humanity in an inhuman place
With love & respect, Paul
> (note left at the Vietnam Women's Memorial)

One day I met a stranger
He was a major
Nothing he said or did impressed me
Two weeks later he was dead
A helicopter blade had severed his head.
> (poem left at the Vietnam Women's Memorial,
> presumably by a nurse veteran)[1]

**MORE THAN FIFTEEN YEARS** after the dedication of the Vietnam Women's Memorial, visitors still leave personal mementos at its base. Objects don't appear as frequently as they do at the Wall, but they do appear, many of them attesting to the compassion, strength, and exhaustion with which women rendered their service to the nation. The many notes of thanks left by male veterans highlight women's emotional and caretaking labor; the reminiscences of women veterans foreground the horrors of war, emotional suffering, and need for healing. This, then, may be the Memorial's greatest success: that it lends itself to a variety of interpretations for those who visit it. Women veterans can be honored for performing caretaking duties that traditionally defined women's place in the nation, and they can also be remembered as war heroes in their own right.

It's been forty or more years since the fifteen women whose stories are told in this book came home from Vietnam. They now have spent the majority of their lives as war veterans. As young women of the 1960s, they swam against society's currents by joining the military and going to war. At the same time, however, they rode the waves of social change that redefined who women were and what they could be. Ultimately, they washed ashore in the turbulence of their generation's defining political battle, weathered survivors of the nation's longest and most controversial war. Just as the Vietnam War was a transformative event in the life of the United States, so it was in the lives of these women. The twelve months they spent tending to the war wounded changed their view of the war, their country, and themselves. They came home as more confident nurses but less certain citizens, confused by the turmoil that greeted them upon their return. Their wartime selves lay dormant while they tried to resume the lives they had left before the war and the country tried to right itself. But dormancy is not resolution, and eventually the emotional remnants of war began surfacing in frightening ways. When their gender became the grounds on which they were excluded from the psychological and social recovery made possible by the recognition of PTSD and the memorializing of male veterans, their passions flamed and their spirits ignited. They stepped out of the shadows, took each other by the hand, and marched toward a healing of their own.

For many of these women, however, healing is an ongoing process rather than a finite state of being. The war is still a part of them and always will be. "There's not a day that I don't think about [the war]," Mary Lu Brunner said. "It might be fleeting, but it's there. It's always there. It's always with me. It's part of me." The role the war plays in their daily lives varies from woman to woman, and for each individual woman, from year to year and month to month, even day to day. When I first met her in spring 2000, Penny Kettlewell was doing all right. She had found her lifeline in the nurses' PTSD group and attended the dedication of the Vietnam Women's Memorial several years earlier and was still working as a nurse in Duluth. Later that year, however, the flashbacks returned, and by spring 2001, she was in an outpatient PTSD program at the VA hospital in St. Cloud. This time, however, the VA came through for her. "*Everybody* was so kind," she said. "It was like, hey, this cannot be a VA hospital. They were bending over backwards for everybody." As of early summer

2009, the war was "in the back forty" of Kettlewell's life, along with nursing; she now co-owns and -operates a glass craft shop in central Wisconsin.[2]

Lynn Kohl, too, had suffered some setbacks after our first meeting in 1999. In 2005, she returned to Vietnam with a study group of veterans and students. She had hoped the trip would provide her with some closure, and in some ways it did. Among the cities her group visited was Pleiku, where she had worked in an Army hospital in 1969 and 1970 and which, in 2005, was home to "the best hospital in all of the Central Highlands." Throughout her trip, she said, she was treated with warmth and respect by the vast majority of the Vietnamese people she met. She got into a minor tussle with a guard at Ho Chi Minh's mausoleum in Hanoi, however, over whether she could bring a water bottle into the building. The water bottle was in a special, handmade bottle holder that she wore over her shoulder. The guard tried to pull it off her shoulder and ended up pointing his gun at her with "this look on his face like 'I could kill you on the spot.'"

She ended up without her water and with her holder, and the incident left her feeling unsettled about the long-term effects of American involvement in Vietnam. Witnessing the restrictions on free speech by the Vietnamese communist government and the poverty that has persisted since her first visit to the country also made her feel as if the war "was all for nothing." Moreover, unlike Kettlewell, Kohl continued to be disappointed by her experiences with the bureaucracy of the VA. Adding all of this to her frustrations with the U.S. wars in the Middle East and the relatively recent suicide of her Vietnam veteran ex-husband made for a combustible mix. "I'm questioning all my beliefs, everything," she told me in June 2009.

Wounds still remain, then. Time may heal, but it does not entirely erase. Yet the passage of time has dulled the edge of anger—about the war, the antiwar movement, the ill treatment of women who served—in many of these women. It also has softened the sharpness of memories now more than four decades old. Indeed, *Sisterhood of War* is a record not only of what these fifteen women did during and after the war but also of how they continue to narrate those experiences to themselves and others. In some instances, memories of the war have faded or taken on new meaning; in others, they have become frozen in the story's retelling.

"Every day was a trauma for me," Lynn Kohl told me in 1999, echo-ing the sentiment if not the exact wording she had used when tell-ing her story for Keith Walker's 1985 oral history. Ten years after our interview, she told medical journalist Kay Schwebke the same thing: "Every day was a trauma for me." Over a span of almost twenty-five years, then, trauma remained the central prism through which Kohl viewed her time in Vietnam. The precise repetition of this phrase also says something about the relationship between memory and language and the human desire for expediency and self-protection, however. Using the same words to describe the same emotions and events may have become an understandable shortcut for women like Kohl who were asked repeatedly to delve into some of the most pain-ful experiences of their lives. Perhaps it allowed them to tell their stories honestly without having to feel them as deeply each time, without having to find new words for old pain. Or, perhaps each re-telling opened old wounds again, adding layer upon layer of scar tis-sue as the cycle of telling, healing, and retelling continued. Perhaps it is some of both.[3]

Overall, both individually and collectively, these women's stories moved in the direction of closure. They expressed an awareness of the passing of generations and a desire to add their stories to the public record, not for personal acclaim but for historical preserva-tion. They sacrificed their own comfort to once again journey back to war in order that women's service be given its due. They wanted to honor the current generation of soldiers and veterans to ensure that service to country is imbued with the honor it deserves. And, ulti-mately, they wanted to make sense of their lives, for themselves and their families, their state and their country. "It's good to sit down and listen to veterans and people who had to put up with some trauma in their [lives]," said Kay Bauer. But she insisted that it wasn't just veterans who have important stories to tell and that listening is as important as speaking: "We have so many heroes in our daily life that we don't pay attention to and we don't listen to. We don't listen to our spouses, our children, our close friends. We need to pay better atten-tion to them and listen to them."[4]

Kay Bauer, Lynn Kohl, Penny Kettlewell, and the other Minnesota women who formed the nurses group and worked on behalf of the

VWMP continue to meet informally about twice a year entering the second decade of the twenty-first century. It was part of this group that traveled to Washington, D.C., in November 2008 to celebrate the Vietnam Women's Memorial's fifteenth anniversary. What began as a desperately needed support group for nurse-veterans with PTSD has morphed into a social gathering of women who, long ago, served their country in Vietnam. Instead of undergoing therapy, the women now meet to socialize or to attend veterans' functions together. Fourteen of the fifteen women I interviewed are part of this incarnation of the group, and they continue to welcome new members into the fold, offering them the same comfortable camaraderie that proved so crucial to their own survival years before. Some of the intimacy of the original group has been lost, in part because the group's size has expanded, in part because the intensity of the need for a support group has diminished over the years. People have come and gone and come back again. When the women gather now, they are as likely to talk about grandchildren and retirement plans as they are about Vietnam and PTSD. If Vietnam was the only thing they had in common, said Joan Paulson, getting together once every few years would be enough. "For me, it's so long ago," she explained. But "it turned into friendships." As Lynn Bower described this group of war survivors, "We're gray-haired ladies with grandchildren." She laughed. "Who would think that we had any of [these experiences]? It kind of puts a different spin on older people. What stories do they have to tell? What are we missing by not getting their stories? . . . What are these wrinkles covering?"[5]

In Bower's case, they're hiding six weeks she spent in a war zone in 1971, a brief period that turned into a life-altering experience, one that continues to shape her life forty years later. Near the end of our interview, she told me about a young G.I. she had cared for one night in Vietnam. He had proposed to her, and after she politely refused, he asked her to make him a promise: "He said, 'You have to promise me that you will live . . . that you will use your senses, you'll smell the flowers.'" Her voice caught. "I've been trying to live that promise," she said, "for all those eighteen-year-olds that never got past eighteen." To her, "every day is a gift," and living her life as fully as possible is her final gift to the boys she had cared for when she was barely more than a girl.

# Acknowledgments

**MANY PEOPLE HAVE CONTRIBUTED** to the success of this project, and I am happy to have the chance to thank some of them by name. This book had its origins as my PhD dissertation for the American Studies program at the University of Minnesota. My dissertation committee—co-advisers Sara Evans and Maria Damon, Lisa Disch, and Elaine Tyler May—shepherded me through the transformation from student to scholar with the right blend of professionalism, moral support, good grace, and potluck dinners. Writing group peers Margot Canaday, Kate Kane, and Mary Elizabeth Strunk provided wise but gentle feedback on each chapter, and Karen Connelly-Lane, the late Josie Fowler, Anita Gonzalez, Gaye Johnson, and Anne Martinez helped me survive the triumphs and tribulations that graduate school brings.

A host of other professionals deserve thanks as well, among them John Baky, curator of the special collection of Imaginative Representations of the Vietnam War at LaSalle University; Duery Felton, curator of the Vietnam Veterans Memorial Collection at the National Park Service; Joan Furey and her staff at the Center for Women Veterans in the Department of Veterans Affairs; Sue

Kohler at the Commission of Fine Arts in Washington, D.C.; and Nancy Young of the National Capital Memorial Commission and National Park Service. I also appreciate the feedback provided by fellow participants at the annual meetings of the American Studies Association, the Columbia University Summer Institute in Oral History, the Oral History Association, and the Popular Culture Association. Crucial financial support was provided by the University of Minnesota as well as by the National Women's Studies Association, the P.E.O. Sisterhood, and the Woodrow Wilson National Fellowship Foundation.

I don't know of anyone who has had so smooth a beginning to a book project as did I with the Minnesota Historical Society and the Minnesota Historical Society Press. James E. Fogerty's interest in my work with women Vietnam veterans first brought me into the MHS fold, and he introduced me to Greg Britton, then director of the MHS Press. Marilyn Olson-Treml's management of the interview recordings and printed transcripts and Beverly Hermes's exemplary transcription work made my life incredibly easy. Editors Shannon Pennefeather, Ann Regan, and Marilyn Ziebarth shaped my thinking and writing in invaluable ways. Prior to my work with them, independent editor Jeanne Barker-Nunn helped me turn the earliest drafts of these chapters into something worth reading.

I also thank my students and colleagues at St. Catherine University for providing me with a collegial intellectual atmosphere. My students, especially, remind me anew how important it is to make women a central part of our nation's history and how effectively oral history can make the past come alive.

It goes without saying that I am most indebted to the women featured in *Sisterhood of War*. They *are* the book, and their willingness to give of themselves in such personal and profound ways has inspired me far beyond the confines of this project. Although they were all unfailingly generous, a few deserve special mention: Kay Bauer, who acted as my main point of contact with the women veterans community in Minnesota; Kay, Diane Evans, Penny Kettlewell, Lynn Kohl, and Joan Paulson, who stuck with me as this project developed from dissertation to book; Kay, Joan, Mary Breed, Mary Beth Crowley, and Mary O'Brien Tyrrell, who shared their war stories with my students; and Mary O'Brien Tyrrell, who not only was a wonderful interviewee but also has become a good friend and mentor.

Finally, a brief but sincere thanks to my family: my husband Steve, my son Tu, and my brother Eric. I only wish my parents, Matti Theodore Wikstrom and Sharon Lee Moore Wikstrom, were still here to share in my joy at seeing this project come to fruition.

# *Interviewees*

| NAME | INTERVIEW DATE(S) | LOCATION OF RECORDING AND TRANSCRIPT |
|---|---|---|
| Catherine "Kay" Bauer | 28 April 2005<br>24 November 1999 | MHS; author's personal collection |
| Donna-Marie "D-M" Boulay | 10 June 2005 | MHS |
| Lynn Bower | 20 June 2006 | MHS |
| Mary Breed | 23, 25 September 2006 | MHS |
| Mary Lu Brunner | 23 May 2006 | MHS |
| Valerie Buchan | 27 October 2005 | MHS |
| Mary Beth Crowley | 25 May 2005 | MHS |
| Diane Carslon Evans | 8 May 2007<br>3 April 2001<br>10 May 2000 | MHS |
| Edythe "Edy" Johnson | 7 June 2005 | MHS |
| Penelope "Penny" Kettlewell | 2 June 2009<br>26 March 2000 | Author's personal collection |
| Lynn Kohl | 2 June 2009<br>1 October 1999 | Author's personal collection |
| Joan Paulson | 5 March 2009<br>1 December 1999 | Author's personal collection |
| Ann Rudolph | 26 May 2005 | MHS |
| Barbara "Bobby" Smith | 26 March 2000 | Author's personal collection |
| Mary O'Brien Tyrrell | 23 May 2006 | MHS |

All information about or attributed to the above women comes from these interviews unless otherwise noted. Recordings and transcripts held at the Minnesota Historical Society (MHS) are available to patrons of the library at the Minnesota History Center in St. Paul.

| SERVICE BRANCH | DATES OF SERVICE IN VIETNAM |
| --- | --- |
| Navy Nurse Corps | January 1966–January 1967 |
| Army Nurse Corps | February 1967–March 1968 |
| Army Nurse Corps | August 1971–September 1971 |
| Army Nurse Corps | September 1970–June 1971 |
| Army Nurse Corps | June 1968–July 1969 |
| Army Nurse Corps | September 1968–September 1969 |
| Army Nurse Corps | February 1970–February 1971 |
| Army Nurse Corps | August 1968–August 1969 |
| Army Nurse Corps | April 1968–April 1969 |
| Army Nurse Corps | September 1967–September 1968 |
| | July 1970–July 1971 |
| Army Nurse Corps | June 1969–June 1970 |
| Army Nurse Corps | August 1967–August 1968 |
| Army Nurse Corps | September 1965–July 1966 |
| Air Force Nurse Corps | August 1966–August 1967 |
| Navy Nurse Corps | June 1967–December 1968 (Guam) |

Unless otherwise noted, photographs were supplied by their subjects.

# Notes

## Notes to Introduction

**1.** Diane Carlson Evans, "Our War" (1983), in *Visions of War, Dreams of Peace: Writings of Women in the Vietnam War,* eds. Lynda Van Devanter and Joan A. Furey (New York: Warner Books, 1991), 95–97. Tim O'Brien, *The Things They Carried* (New York: Broadway Books/Houghton Mifflin, 1990).

**2.** These figures are taken from the following sources: U.S. Department of Veterans Affairs, Women Veterans Statistics, "Women Veterans Population, October 2009"; U.S. Department of Veterans Affairs, Demographics, Veteran Population 2007, VetPop2007 State Tables 2L, "Veterans by State, Period, Age Group, Gender, 2000–2036"; Vietnam Women's Memorial Foundation website, http://tinyurl.com/4tdggsz; Women in Military Service for America Memorial Foundation, Inc., website, http://tinyurl.com/4urqhum; Celebration of Patriotism and Courage: Dedication of the Vietnam Women's Memorial, November 10–12, 1993 (Washington, D.C.: Vietnam Women's Memorial Project, 1993); "Vietnam," author and veteran Noonie Fortin's website, http://www.nooniefortin.com/vietnam.htm.

**3.** Some of the women were born and raised in Minnesota but now live elsewhere, while others grew up in other states but moved here after the war ended. One woman grew up and still lives in Wisconsin but is a central member of the core group of Minnesota nurses whose stories are featured here. Another woman didn't serve in Vietnam itself, but on Guam, where she treated casualties coming from Vietnam.

**4.** The group that I contacted was Vietnam Women Veterans, an organization for nonnurse veterans of the war. They formed their group to bring attention to the experiences of women who served in capacities besides nursing—as enlisted women or line officers. For more information on enlisted or line officer women veterans, see ch. 1 of my dissertation, "G.I. Gender: Vietnam War–Era Women Veterans and U.S. Citizenship" (PhD diss., University of Minnesota, 2002), 42–107.

**5.** The idea of the "loyalty of the shared ordeal" comes from B. J. Phillips, "On Location with the WACs," *MS Magazine* (November 1972): 55.

**6.** I am using the word "soldier" here in its most general sense, to refer to anyone who serves in any branch of the military.

**7.** Though there are no official membership rolls or organizational charts for this group, I realize that I have not interviewed every nurse veteran from Minnesota who has been part of, or knows the members of, this group.

The military, VA, and veteran communities often carefully distinguish between "Vietnam veterans" (those who served in the Republic of Vietnam [South Vietnam]) and "Vietnam era veterans" (those who served during the war but were stationed elsewhere) to clarify who is eligible for which kinds of services, benefits, and honors. As the women's Vietnam veteran community took shape in organizing for the Vietnam Women's Memorial, however, such distinctions became less important. Mary O'Brien Tyrrell, for instance, had served on Guam, not in Vietnam, but was actively involved in the Vietnam Women's Memorial Project.

All quotes, ideas, and actions attributed to these women in the text are taken from these interviews unless otherwise noted. See Interviewees section for information on these interviews.

**8.** See, for example, Keith Walker, *A Piece of My Heart: The Stories of Twenty-Six American Women Who Served in Vietnam* (Novato, CA: Presidio Press, [1985] 1997); Elizabeth Norman, *Women at War: The Story of Fifty Military Nurses Who Served in Vietnam* (Philadelphia: University of Pennsylvania Press, 1990); Kara Dixon Vuic, *Officer, Nurse, Woman: The Army Nurse Corps in the Vietnam War* (Baltimore, MD: Johns Hopkins University Press, 2010).

**9.** O'Brien, *The Things They Carried,* 179–80.

**10.** Alessandro Portelli, *The Death of Luigi Trastulli and Other Stories: Form and Meaning in Oral History* (Albany: State University of New York Press, 1991), 50, and *The Order Has Been Carried Out: History, Memory, and Meaning of a Nazi Massacre in Rome* (New York: Palgrave MacMillan, 2003), 16.

**11.** O'Brien, *The Things They Carried,* 225.

### Notes to Chapter 1

**1.** In the mid-1960s, 97 percent of new nurses were white, and 99 percent were female. Norman, *Women at War,* 7, 9; Susan Gelfand Malka, *Daring to*

*Care: American Nursing and Second-Wave Feminism* (Urbana and Chicago: University of Illinois Press, 2007), 25; Vuic, *Officer, Nurse, Woman,* 16–17.

Sara Evans, *Born for Liberty: A History of Women in America* (New York: Free Press, 1989), 254; Elaine Tyler May, *Homeward Bound: American Families in the Cold War Era* (New York: Basic Books/HarperCollins Publishers, 1988), 166–67.

**2.** White married women with children increased their rate of participation in the labor force from 17 to 30 percent between 1950 and 1960, according to Sara Evans (*Born for Liberty,* 254, 252, 261).

**3.** See Julia Kirk Blackwelder, *Now Hiring: The Feminization of Work in the United States, 1900–1995* (College Station: Texas A&M University Press, 1997), 241–42; U.S. Census Bureau, 1960 Census of Population United States Summary, Volume I, Part I, Characteristics of the Population Section 6: Detailed Characteristics, Table 194, "Employment Status by Age, Color, and Sex, for the United States, Urban and Rural, 1960," 1–487.

**4.** Most of the newly employed women of the postwar period found jobs in female-dominated fields considered to be appropriate for women. William H. Chafe, *The Unfinished Journey: America Since World War II,* 6th ed. (New York: Oxford University Press, 2007), 80; U.S. Department of Education, "Title IX: 25 Years of Progress," June 1997, http://tinyurl.com/4kydu7h.

Florence Nightingale, *Notes on Nursing: What It Is, and What It Is Not* (New York: Appleton, 1860), 3, as cited in Malka, *Daring to Care,* 1.

**5.** Malka, *Daring to Care,* 14, 17, 25.

**6.** In 1945, only five percent of new nurses had graduated from four-year institutions; by 1965, 15.6 percent of nursing students graduated from four-year programs, while 77.1 percent trained in hospital diploma programs. Malka, *Daring to Care,* 26–27, 48, 29, 41. Eleven of the fifteen women I interviewed attended hospital diploma schools; only Kay Bauer (College of St. Catherine), Mary Beth Crowley (University of Minnesota), Mary O'Brien Tyrrell (St. Scholastica), Ann Rudolph (St. Olaf), and D-M Boulay received their BSNs. (Boulay received her BSN from Boston College after having also completed a three-year diploma program.)

See Malka, *Daring to Care,* chs. 2 and 3, for more of the debate over the goals of nursing education.

**7.** For more on the ways in which nursing schools reinforced gender stereotypes, see Malka, *Daring to Care,* ch. 2.

**8.** Historian and retired Air Force Major General Jeanne Holm argued that military nurses were accepted during the interwar years when enlisted women were not because "nursing was accepted as women's work, and nurses were considered a necessary evil." Jeanne M. Holm, *Women in the Military: An Unfinished Revolution* (Novato, CA: Presidio Press, 1992), 17.

**9.** Linda K. Kerber, *Women of the Republic: Intellect and Ideology in Revolutionary America* (Chapel Hill: University of North Carolina Press, 1980).

Holm, *Women in the Military,* 71–72, 109, 289–304; Vuic, *Officer, Nurse, Woman,* ch. 5; Mary T. Sarnecky, *A History of the U.S. Army Nurse Corps* (Philadelphia: University of Pennsylvania Press, 1999), 367, 269–71; Connie L. Reeves, "Invisible Soldiers: Military Nurses," in Francine D'Amico and Laurie Weinstein, ed., *Gender Camouflage: Women and the U.S. Military* (New York: New York University Press, 1999), 19.

The Army Nurse Corps' campaign was termed Operation Nightingale. For more information, see Vuic, *Officer, Nurse, Woman,* 22–26.

**10.** By 1960, more than half of all new Army nurses joined by way of the Student Nurse Program; by 1966, the proportion had jumped to more than 80 percent. Sarnecky, *A History of the U.S. Army Nurse Corps,* 323, 338.

Doris M. Sterner, *In and Out of Harm's Way: A History of the Navy Nurse Corps* (Seattle, WA: Peanut Butter Publishing, 1997), 339.

**11.** Vuic, *Officer, Nurse, Woman,* 26–33.

**12.** By 1958, notes historian William Chafe, 97 percent of Americans said they believed in God and 110 million of them belonged to some type of church (*Unfinished Journey,* 115). Although such associations were promoted by politicians, they also were part of American popular (religious) culture. For more on the link between communism and religion in U.S. popular culture, see Thomas Aiello, "Constructing 'Godless Communism': Religion, Politics, and Popular Culture, 1954–1960," *Americana: The Journal of American Popular Culture (1900 to Present)* 4.1 (Spring 2005).

**13.** Recruiting commercial, U.S. Army Public Affairs, Los Angeles Branch, NW Ayer, Inc., n.d., as it appears in Elizabeth Bouiss, dir., *No Time for Tears,* Mitch Wood, prod. (New York: West End Films; Boston: Fanlight Productions, 1993).

The *American Journal of Nursing* was the publication of the American Nurses' Association. It also featured articles on the financial and professional benefits of joining the military nurse corps. See, for example, "The Army Nurse," *American Journal of Nursing* 66 (February 1966): 291–92; "Army Nurses to be Featured in the 'Big Picture,'" *American Journal of Nursing* 66 (January 1966): 17; Martha Belote, "Where to Go for an Education: ANC, NNC, AFNC," *American Journal of Nursing* 67 (June 1967): 1250–53.

"Back From Vietnam," *American Journal of Nursing* 67 (October 1967): 2120–23; "Mercy Mission to Saigon," *American Journal of Nursing* 70 (September 1970): 1946–49. See also Aline E. Morin, "Navy Hospital in Saigon," *American Journal of Nursing* 66 (September 1966): 1977–79; "Nurses in the News," *American Journal of Nursing* 67 (December 1967): 2478; Sandra

Kirkpatrick, "Battle Casualty: Amputee," *American Journal of Nursing* 69 (May 1968): 998+; Frances C. McKown and Annelle Lee, "International Ward," *American Journal of Nursing* 69 (April 1969): 772–73.

**14.** Betty J. Antilla, "Nurse Corps Needs Aid," *American Journal of Nursing* 69 (October 1969): 2113–14. By 1968, the Army Nurse Corps had appointed thirty-three ANC officers to recruiting duty throughout the country. Antilla was in charge of recruiting in the Midwest. For more on the ANC's struggle to recruit nurses in the context of antiwar sentiment, see Vuic, *Officer, Nurse, Woman,* 21–22.

**15.** Although Evans's two brothers served in the military, neither of them went to Vietnam.

**16.** For more on the Army's Officer Basic Course for nurses, see Vuic, *Officer, Nurse, Woman,* 43–46.

**17.** Although she volunteered to serve in Vietnam, Mary O'Brien Tyrrell was told she was too young (and of too low a rank) to be assigned to Vietnam. Instead, she spent eighteen months at a Navy hospital in Guam, caring for Marines who had been wounded in Vietnam.

**18.** See, for example, William Broyles, "Why Men Love War," *Esquire* (November 1984): 55–65.

## Notes to Chapter 2

**1.** Kohl told this story both years before and years after the 1999 interview in which she described it to me. See, for example, Walker, *A Piece of My Heart,* 193, and Kay E. Schwebke, "The Vietnam Women's Memorial: Better Late than Never," *American Journal of Nursing* 109.5 (May 2009): 34–40. Holm, *Women in the Military,* 322.

**2.** Kohl's hoochmate was Lynda Van Devanter, coauthor, with Christopher Morgan, of *Home Before Morning: The Story of an Army Nurse in Vietnam* (New York: Warner Books, 1983) and coeditor, with Joan Furey, of *Visions of War.* Van Devanter died at age fifty-five in November 2002, reportedly of an illness related to exposure to Agent Orange.

**3.** The high heels nurses wore on the flight to Vietnam proved the downfall of Edy Johnson, literally. As she descended the steps from plane to tarmac in her heels, she tripped and broke her ankle. Thus, nurse Johnson spent her first week in-country as a patient at the 93rd Evacuation Hospital at Long Binh. She recalled the event with good humor and said that most of the other medical personnel she met during that week also found the situation to be humorously ironic.

Some women were fortunate to travel to Vietnam with their stateside hospital colleagues. Edy Johnson and D-M Boulay, for example, traveled with their hospital units and so were in the company of other women en route to Vietnam.

**4.** Breed left Vietnam before her twelve-month tour was up because her father died. After his funeral, the Army wanted to send her back to Vietnam, but she requested and was granted assignment to a stateside military hospital.

**5.** Most Navy nurses either had specific orders for their ground duty stations before they left the United States or served aboard the ships on which they sailed to Vietnam, and so there was no equivalent processing center for them.

**6.** Other casualty staging units were located at the Tan Son Nhut and Da Nang air bases. For more information on the various military medical facilities in operation in Vietnam, see Mary T. Sarnecky, *A History of the U.S. Army Nurse Corps,* 361–62; Susan H. Godson, *Serving Proudly: A History of Women in the U.S. Navy* (Annapolis, MD: U.S. Naval Institute Press, 2001), 219; Jeanne M. Holm and Sarah P. Wells, "Air Force Women in the Vietnam War," in Diane Carlson Evans, ed., *The Dedication of the Vietnam Women's Memorial: A Celebration of Patriotism and Courage* (Vietnam Women's Memorial Project, 1993), 46.

**7.** E. R. Baker, "Caregivers as Casualties," *Western Journal of Nursing Research* 11.5 (1989): 628–31, as cited in Iris J. West, "The Women of the Army Nurse Corps during the Vietnam War," in Evans, *Dedication of the Vietnam Women's Memorial,* 1.

Patients were more often admitted to Army hospitals for diseases than for battlefield injuries, in fact; 69 percent of hospital admissions from 1965 to 1969 were for diseases (West, "The Women of the Army Nurse Corps," 3). Navy nurse Kay Bauer, who was part of a Forward Surgical Team stationed in Rach Gia and whose main patients were local Vietnamese, encountered diseases in her patients that had been virtually eliminated in the United States, such as tuberculosis, tetanus, and polio. Part of her team's responsibility was to inoculate the local population against such things if possible.

**8.** This comes from my interview with Bower in June 2006, but the story about the scissors is also recounted in Schwebke, "The Vietnam Women's Memorial."

**9.** Triage was the process by which patients were classified according to the severity of their needs and their likelihood of survival. Those who would likely survive with immediate attention were given first priority, followed by those whose condition required attention but could wait. The "walking wounded" were those whose wounds were less serious and lower priority. "Expectants" were those who were so seriously injured that death seemed imminent. They were given lowest priority in terms of order of care. Many nurses describe triage as one of the most difficult assignments they faced.

**10.** Mary O'Brien Tyrrell estimated that between 20 and 30 percent of the patients she treated at the U.S. Naval Hospital on Guam were African American. Valerie Buchan and D-M Boulay both said it seemed that the majority of their patients were black. This was in contrast to the predominantly white nursing staff. Buchan, for example, remembered only four African American nurses of the sixty who worked at her hospital.

**11.** The incident that Evans described was re-created for the television series *China Beach* in 1989. The show's producers had contacted Evans (and others) after the show's female veteran viewers criticized it for oversexualizing their experiences. They interviewed Evans and intercut clips from the interview with scenes from an episode in which Army nurse Colleen McMurphy (Dana Delany) spends the night by a dying soldier's bed. See "Vets," *China Beach,* dir. John Sacret Young, written by John Wells and John Sacret Young, ABC, 15 March 1989. For more information on *China Beach,* the Vietnam Women's Memorial Project, and the postwar representation of women Vietnam veterans, see ch. 3 of my dissertation, "G.I. Gender."

**12.** White phosphorous (WP, or "Willie Peter") is an incendiary chemical used to both illuminate and provide smoke cover during battle. It was also used against enemy personnel. WP causes bone-deep, extremely painful burns that cannot be extinguished with water.

**13.** For more information on anti-Vietnamese racism among American personnel, see, for example, Darrell Y. Hamamoto, *Monitored Peril: Asian Americans and the Politics of TV Representation* (Minneapolis: University of Minnesota Press, 1994), 156; Robert Jay Lifton, *Home From the War: Vietnam Veterans—Neither Victims nor Executioners* (New York: Basic Books, [1973] 1985), chap. 7, "Gooks and Men"; Byron G. Fiman, Jonathan F. Borus, and M. Duncan Stanton, "Black-White and American-Vietnamese Relations Among Soldiers in Vietnam," *Journal of Social Issues* 31.4 (1975): 39–48.

For examples of anti-Vietnamese sentiment of both kinds among nurses, see the testimony of Leslie McClusky (57–58), Ann Powlas (123), and Jill Mishkel (143) in Kathryn Marshall, *In the Combat Zone* (New York: Penguin Books, 1987); Lorraine Boudreau (30–31), Lois Johns (51), Laura Radnor (133), and Joan Waradzyn Thomas (147) in Dan Freedman and Jacqueline Rhoads, *Nurses in Vietnam: The Forgotten Veterans* (Austin: Texas Monthly Press, 1987). Elizabeth Norman reported that five of the fifty women she interviewed "were never able to work comfortably with either enemy or civilian Vietnamese" (*Women at War,* 42).

**14.** The official name for the Viet Cong was the National Liberation Front (NLF), but most Americans referred to these guerrilla forces as the Viet Cong or VC.

**15.** For a vivid account of how difficult the balancing act was for villagers in South Vietnam, see Le Ly Hayslip, with Jay Wurts, *When Heaven and Earth Changed Places: A Vietnamese Woman's Journey from War to Peace* (New York: Doubleday, 1989).

**16.** For more on these MEDCAP programs, see Sarnecky, *A History of the U.S. Army Nurse Corps,* 340–44, and Norman, *Women at War,* 22–23.

**17.** Penny Kettlewell knew one of the other nurses who died in Vietnam, Hedwig "Heddy" Orlowski. Official military records indicate that Orlowski and fellow Army nurses Eleanor Alexander, Jerome Olmstead, and Kenneth Shoemaker and SP5 Phillip Ogas (and twenty-one others) were killed when their plane crashed in bad weather in November 1967. But Kettlewell said that when the plane was finally recovered, it was filled with bullet holes. She believes their deaths should rightly be numbered among those killed by enemy fire.

**18.** Technically, there was no such thing as the North Vietnamese Army, or NVA. The official name for the North's military force was the People's Army of Vietnam (PAVN). "NVA" was the term more frequently used by Americans, however.

**19.** Sarnecky, *A History of the U.S. Army Nurse Corps,* 370.

## Notes to Chapter 3

**1.** Civilian nursing was also a female-dominated profession. Although there once had been nursing schools designed solely for men, as the health care profession became increasingly stratified by gender in the early twentieth century, men dominated the field of doctoring while women dominated the field of nursing. By 1966, men constituted less than one percent of all registered nurses and less than two percent of all students in and graduates of registered nursing programs. For more information, see Christine L. Williams, *Gender Differences at Work: Women and Men in Nontraditional Occupations* (Berkeley and Los Angeles: University of California Press, 1989); Vuic, *Officer, Nurse, Woman,* 47–52; Malka, *Daring to Care;* Sarnecky, *A History of the U.S. Army Nurse Corps,* 395; Sterner, *In and Out of Harm's Way,* 12–13, 19. Vuic notes that between 20 percent and 30 percent of army nurses who served in Vietnam (1,000–1,500) were men and that once the Army Nurse Corps began accepting men in 1955, it had a higher percentage of male nurses than did civilian nursing (47, 50–51, 103). Although the Army and Air Force Nurse Corps offered reserve commissions to male nurses after Congress passed legislation in 1955, the Navy did not do so until 1964. Godson, *Serving Proudly,* 210–11; Sterner, *In and Out of Harm's Way,* 306.

   **2.** Maj. Gen. Delk Oden (U.S. Army Support Group, Vietnam) to Mildred Clark (chief of Army Nurse Corps), 30 December 1968, telegram, cited in Sarnecky, *A History of the U.S. Army Nurse Corps,* 345, 346. See Williams, *Gender Differences at Work,* 88–130, for ways in which civilian male nurses have benefited from their gender.

   Althea Williams (USARV chief nurse), "End of Tour Report," 16 January 1969, cited in Sarnecky, *A History of the U.S. Army Nurse Corps,* 346. For more on the ANC's policies regarding assignments in Vietnam for male and female nurses, see Vuic, *Officer, Nurse, Woman,* 105–11.

   **3.** From 1965 to 1972, only 379 men served in the Navy Nurse Corps (Godson, *Serving Proudly,* 211). In 1966, because of the ongoing nurse short- age in the services, the Selective Service attempted to draft seven hundred male nurses for the Army and two hundred for the Navy; this measure yield- ed only about 150 male nurses for the Army. Sarnecky, *A History of the U.S. Army Nurse Corps,* 339; Vuic, *Officer, Nurse, Woman,* 51. Sarnecky notes that the Selective Service had prepared a plan to draft female nurses but never implemented it because the ANC opposed such a measure.

   Often, the men were nurse anesthetists, a nursing specialty that drew higher pay in civilian life if not in the military, where pay is based on rank. Christine Williams argues that male nurses try to elevate their status as nurses to preserve their sense of masculinity and that one way of doing this is to work in higher-paying nursing specialties, such as nurse-anesthetists (*Gender Differences at Work,* 129). See also Vuic, *Officer, Nurse, Woman,* 102.

   Edy Johnson, personal e-mail communication, 25 August 2009.

   **4.** Kay Bauer, personal e-mail communication, 24 August 2009; Mary O'Brien Tyrrell, personal conversation, 24 August 2009.

   **5.** There has never been one single umbrella policy or law excluding women from combat duty. Instead, the service branches have defined their own policies, often citing the 1948 Women's Armed Services Integration Act as justification for excluding women from any duty defined as "combat" or "combat-related." Such policies apply to all women in uniform, not just nurs- es. For more information, see Holm, *Women in the Military,* chap. 26.

   **6.** Vuic points out that ANC policy was to provide female nurses with three hours of weapons training on the .45 pistol. Male nurses, on the other hand, received those three hours of training, plus another seven hours of rifle and firing training, as well as thirteen hours on simulated combat ma- neuvers (*Officer, Nurse, Woman,* 45–46).

   Joan Paulson, personal e-mail communication, 5 August 2009; Penny

Kettlewell, personal e-mail communication, 28 July 2009; Mary Beth Crowley, personal e-mail communication, 29 July 2009.

Bauer speculated that she and her team may have been issued weapons due to their remote location at a Vietnamese provincial hospital. Legally, any nurse could have carried a weapon: the Geneva Convention allowed non-combatant medical personnel to carry weapons for use in self-defense or in defense of their patients. Geneva Convention for the Amelioration of the Condition of the Wounded and Sick in Armed Forces in the Field, Chapter III, Article 22 (Geneva, 12 August 1949), from International Committee of the Red Cross website, International Humanitarian Law, Treaties and Documents, 1949 Conventions and Additional Protocols, http://tinyurl.com/4ouypcs. Standard practice, however, was to leave the defense of the hospital and its patients and personnel to already-armed soldiers, including corpsmen.

**7.** Except for Mary O'Brien Tyrrell and Lynn Kohl, all the women I met said they received combat pay. Tyrrell served in Guam, not Vietnam, and so was not entitled to combat pay. Kohl remembered that no women received combat pay because they were not issued weapons. According to Connie L. Reeves, however, all nurses who served in Vietnam received combat pay. "Invisible Soldiers," 23.

**8.** Penny Kettlewell, personal e-mail communication, 28 July 2009. Elizabeth Norman asserts that "each hospital ward had a shelf with helmets and flak jackets" for nurses to use, but Kettlewell said there were not enough flak jackets for both the nurses and the men during Tet, and so the men got first dibs on them. Norman, *Women at War,* 81.

**9.** For more on racial exclusions in military nursing, see Holm, *Women in the Military,* 109; Sarnecky, *A History of the U.S. Army Nurse Corps,* 269–71; Reeves, "Invisible Soldiers," 19; Cynthia Enloe, *Maneuvers: The International Politics of Militarizing Women's Lives* (Berkeley: University of California Press, 2000) 215–17.

Sarnecky, *A History of the U.S. Army Nurse Corps,* 292; Godson, *Serving Proudly,* 171; Vuic, *Officer, Nurse, Woman,* 114–15, 116. For a thorough discussion of ANC policies regarding marriage, pregnancy, and motherhood, see Vuic, *Officer, Nurse, Woman,* chap. 5.

As of January 1970, "certain" ANC officers were allowed to remain on duty after giving birth (Sarnecky, *A History of the U.S. Army Nurse Corps,* 367). In January 1971 the ANC offered married women who became mothers or gave birth the possibility of remaining in the military but did not extend the privilege to single women (Vuic, *Officer, Nurse, Woman,* 127). In June 1974, the Department of Defense told all services that separation from duty due to pregnancy would become voluntary only, beginning in May 1975 (Holm, *Women in the Military,* 300). For more general information on military family policy, see Holm, *Women in the Military,* chap. 20; Vuic, *Officer, Nurse, Woman,* 123–34.

Husbands and children were considered dependents of servicewomen (and so entitled to benefits such as on-base family housing, medical services, and family separation pay) only if the woman could prove her family relied on her income for one half or more of their support; no such proof was required for a serviceman's family to be considered his dependents. This policy was overturned by the U.S. Supreme Court in 1973 in *Frontiero vs. Richardson,* 411 U.S. 677 (1973). See Holm, *Women in the Military,* 290–91; Vuic, *Officer, Nurse, Woman,* 121–22.

**10.** Ann Rudolph, personal e-mail communication, 27 July 2009.

**11.** See Vuic, *Officer, Nurse, Woman,* 129, for a discussion of ANC policy regarding pregnant nurses in Vietnam, the goal of which was to return them to the United States as quickly as possible. Bower went on to serve twelve years in the Reserves and felt she fulfilled her obligation to the military. Still, her sense of guilt over leaving Vietnam after only six weeks lingered.

**12.** Sarnecky, *A History of the U.S. Army Nurse Corps,* 377. From March 1962 to March 1973, about five thousand Army nurses served in Vietnam. West, "The Women of the Army Nurse Corps." Approximately four thousand Air Force nurses served in the Vietnam theater from 1965 to 1972. (Col. Consuella Pockett, "Commentary: Air Force Nursing: 60 years, still counting," 11, 14 May 2009, Charleston Air Force Base website, http://tinyurl.com/4fxhbuf. Approximately five hundred WACs and five hundred WAFs (Women in the Air Force), thirty-six Women Marines, and only a handful of WAVEs served in Vietnam over the duration of the war. (Godson, *Serving Proudly,* 212). Jean Ebbert and Marie-Beth Hall, "Women in the Navy," at Vietnam Women's Memorial Foundation site, http://tinyurl.com/4swah5s.

Voegele quoted in Holm, *Women in the Military,* 227.

Westmoreland quoted in Sarnecky, *A History of the U.S. Army Nurse Corps,* 347, based on an interview she conducted with Catherine Betz on 23 May 1992, the transcript of which is housed at the U.S. Army Nurse Corps Oral History Program at the Center for Military History in Washington, D.C. For more on the ways in which female soldiers are constructed as accessories to and morale boosters for male soldiers, see Edna Levy, "Women Warriors: The Paradox and Politics of Israeli Women in Uniform," in *Women, States, and Nationalism: At Home in the Nation?* ed. Sita Ranchod-Nilsson and Mary Ann Tétreault (London and New York: Routledge, 2000), 181–95; Williams, *Gender Differences at Work,* 36–41; Vuic, *Officer, Nurse, Woman,* 95; Joshua S. Goldstein, *War and Gender: How Gender Shapes the War System and Vice Versa* (Cambridge, NY: Cambridge University Press, 2001), 306–9.

ANC advertisement appearing in the *American Journal of Nursing* and *Glamour* in 1970, reprinted and discussed in Kara Dixon Vuic, "'Officer, Nurse, Woman': Army Nurse Corps Recruitment for the Vietnam War," *Nursing History Review* 14 (2006): 111–59, at 135–36.

**13.** For more on racist and sexist images of Asian women, see Yen Le Espiritu, *Asian American Women and Men: Labor, Laws, and Love* (Thousand Oaks, CA: SAGE Publications, 1997); John Baky, "White Cong and the Black Clap: The Ambient Truth of Vietnam War Legendry," in Kalí Tal and Dan Duffy, *Nobody Gets Off the Bus: The Vietnam Generation Big Book* 5 (Woodbridge, CT: Vietnam Generation, 1994), esp. para. 21–24.

Punjis are sharpened spikes that the NLF would hide in and along trails through the jungle. Both limericks are from Ken Melvin, *Sorry 'Bout That!: Cartoons, Limericks, and Other Diversions of G.I. Vietnam* (Tokyo: The Wayward Press, 1966). For a first-person account from the perspective of a Vietnamese woman who was caught up in these dynamics, see Hayslip with Wurts, *When Heaven and Earth Changed Places.*

**14.** Rudolph worked at Walter Reed Army Medical Center in late 1964, during which time she also served as a model for Army Nurse Corps publicity materials and as a representative of the Army in the patriotic pageant "Prelude to Taps."

**15.** Penny Kettlewell is of mixed-race heritage, both Caucasian and Native American.

This racial imbalance was a result of the fact that nursing schools were still dominated by white women. African Americans constituted only five percent of nursing students in the early 1960s; by the early 1970s, the proportion had risen only to seven percent. As late as 1980, nearly 87 percent of all registered nurses in the United States were white. See Vuic, *Officer, Nurse, Woman,* 120; Evelyn Nakano Glenn, "From Servitude to Service Work: Historical Continuities in the Racial Division of Paid Reproductive Labor," in *Unequal Sisters: A Multicultural Reader in U.S. Women's History,* 3rd ed., ed. Vicki L. Ruiz and Ellen Carol DuBois (New York: Routledge, 2000), 436–65, at 450. Glenn points out that white women are overrepresented as RNs, while African American women are overrepresented as licensed practical nurses (LPNs) and nurse's aides. Asian Americans of both sexes made up only one percent of total U.S. armed forces during the Vietnam War; 34,600 served in Vietnam. See Chalsa M. Loo and Peter Nien-chu Kiang, "Race-related Stressors and Psychological Trauma: Contributions of Asian American Vietnam Veterans," in *Asian Americans: Vulnerable Populations, Model Interventions, and Clarifying Agendas,* ed. Lin Zhan (Sudbury, MA: Jones and Bartlett Publishers, 2003): 19–42, at 20. Just over sixty-one thousand American Indians went to war against the communists in Vietnam.

See Troy Johnson, Duane Champagne, and Joane Nagel, "American Indian Activism and Transformation: Lessons from Alcatraz," in *American Indian Activism: Alcatraz to the Longest Walk,* ed. Troy Johnson, Joane Nagel, and Duane Champagne (Urbana: University of Illinois Press, 1997): 9–44, at 21.

Italian-Chinese American Army nurse Lily Adams, whom I interviewed for another project, said she sometimes received attention of a more threatening nature when G.I.s mistook her for a Vietnamese prostitute. In a setting where Vietnamese women were, at best, treated as sex objects and, at worst, victims of sexual violence, this was a precarious situation for Adams: "Guys would come up to me and say stuff and [I]'d just keep on walking because if you said anything, you might piss them off. And before you know it, they'd be dragging my body somewhere. So I had to handle myself differently than maybe a Caucasian woman would, walking through the compound." Most G.I.s posed no threat to Adams, however, and she, too, was revered as a round-eye, even though her eyes "aren't that round." Lily Lee Adams, personal interview, 11 January 2000. I interviewed Adams for my dissertation, but since she has no connections to Minnesota, she is not included among the group of nurses upon whom I am focusing here. For accounts of the sexual abuse (and sometimes murder) of Vietnamese women, see Jacqueline E. Lawson, "'She's a Pretty Woman . . . for a Gook': The Misogyny of the Vietnam War," *Journal of American Culture* 12 (Fall 1989): 59; Daniel Lang, *Casualties of War* (New York: McGraw-Hill, 1969); Mark Baker, *Nam: The Vietnam War in the Words of the Men and Women Who Fought There* (New York: Berkley, 1981), 187, 211–15; Michael Bilton and Kevin Sim, *Four Hours in My Lai* (New York: Penguin Books, 1992).

**16.** Holm, *Women in the Military,* 227.

**17.** Vuic, *Officer, Nurse, Woman,* 135–137. Kay Bauer, personal e-mail communication, 25 August 2009.

**18.** Sarnecky, *A History of the U.S. Army Nurse Corps,* 334, 360. For more on the significance of the debates over uniforms, see Enloe, *Maneuvers,* 261; Vuic, *Officer, Nurse, Woman,* 90–99; Elizabeth L. Hillman, "Dressed to Kill? The Paradox of Women in Military Uniforms," *Beyond Zero Tolerance: Discrimination in Military Culture,* ed. Mary Fainsod Katzenstein and Judith Reppy (Lanham, MD: Rowman & Littlefield Publishers, Inc., 1999), 65–80.

**19.** Vuic points out, however, that four Army hospitals in Vietnam had beauty salons for women. The chief nurses at the 3rd Field Hospital in Saigon and 67th Evacuation Hospital in Qui Nhon requested beauty salons for their nurses in part because they viewed it as a matter of fairness, since men had access to barber shops on base. But the salons also helped women achieve the feminine appearance that both they and their male officers and patients desired. Vuic, *Officer, Nurse, Woman,* 97–99.

Westmoreland quoted in Sarnecky, *A History of the U.S. Army Nurse Corps,* 348.

**20.** The movie *M\*A\*S\*H* came out in 1970, and the television series of the same name ran from 1972 to 1983. While both movie and series thus appeared after many women had already served in Vietnam, the "'Hot Lips' Houlihan" character provided a widely identifiable figure for images of nurses, military women, and military nurses that had been circulating long before.

**21.** Not only was such sexual behavior an affront to the military (and the culture in which it operated), but so too was the apparent confusion over proper gender identity. See Enloe, *Maneuvers,* 263. For more on the history of homosexuality and the U.S. military, see Leisa D. Meyer, *Creating GI Jane: Sexuality and Power in the Women's Army Corps During World War II* (New York: Columbia University Press, 1996), chap. 7; Allan Bérubé, *Coming Out Under Fire: The History of Gay Men and Women in World War Two* (New York: Plume/Penguin, 1990); John Costello, *Virtue Under Fire: How World War II Changed Our Social and Sexual Attitudes* (Boston: Little, Brown and Company, 1985); Melissa S. Herbert, *Camouflage Isn't Only for Combat: Gender, Sexuality, and Women in the Military* (New York: New York University Press, 1998); Randy Shilts, *Conduct Unbecoming: Gays and Lesbians in the U.S. Military–Vietnam to the Persian Gulf* (New York: St. Martin's Press, 1993); Margot Canaday, *The Straight State: Sexuality and Citizenship in Twentieth Century America* (Princeton, NJ: Princeton University Press, 2009).

**22.** For more information on female nurses' experiences with sexual harassment and assault in Vietnam, see Vuic, *Officer, Nurse, Woman,* 142–49. A 1997 article about a study based on the National Vietnam Veterans Readjustment Survey found that of 396 female Vietnam veterans who had served in-country (as nurses or otherwise), one percent reported incidents of sexual assault, while 25 percent reported incidents of sexual harassment. The study also found that war trauma and sexual trauma "made approximately equal contributions to the probability of developing chronic posttraumatic stress disorder," even though women reported experiencing sexual trauma less frequently than war trauma. Alan Fontana, Linda Spoonster Schwartz, and Robert Rosenheck, "Posttraumatic Stress Disorder among Female Vietnam Veterans: A Causal Model of Etiology," *American Journal of Public Health* 87.2 (February 1997): 170, 173.

**23.** Lynn Bower falls somewhere between these two groups. She was in a long-term relationship with a military man before she went to Vietnam. They served in Vietnam at the same time and married when they returned, after he and his first wife divorced.

**24.** Finding statistics on the incidence of sexual assault and harassment experienced by military women who served in Vietnam is difficult, but a

2003 study found that 30 percent of women who served during the Vietnam era or later experienced sexual assault while in uniform. See Department of Veterans Affairs Employee Education System, "Veterans Health Initiative: Military Sexual Trauma," Independent Study Course Released January 2004, 2–3, http://tinyurl.com/4kout3e.

**25.** Staff Sgt. Barry Sadler, "Salute to the Nurses," *Ballad of the Green Berets,* RCA, 1966.

**26.** I visited the National Park Service's Vietnam Veterans Memorial Collection (VVMC) in Bethesda, MD, in February 2001. Among the many items that had been left at the Vietnam Women's Memorial were notes of thanks from male veterans, "Thank You, Ladies" buttons, poems, photographs, Combat Infantryman Badges, Combat Medics Badges, Purple Heart ribbons, and other unit insignia. For an example of web page tributes to nurse veterans of the Vietnam War, see "Touched by an Angel," a tribute site by Jeff "Doc" Dentice, http://www.war-veterans.org/Angels.htm. For an example of a YouTube video tribute, see "A Salute to the Nurses of Vietnam," posted by djay72 (Jeff), http://tinyurl.com/4over7h. Kay Ryan was a social worker in the Post Traumatic Stress Recovery unit at the Minneapolis VA from 1986 to 2001. She ran several therapy groups for male combat veterans of the war and said that the men shared many "endearments" about nurses they had encountered in Vietnam. They recounted stories of nurses helping them write letters to family at home, protecting their patients from incoming rounds by sheltering them with mattresses, holding patients while they died, and many other instances of commitment and sacrifice. Kay Ryan, personal e-mail communication, 12 January 2011. For an example of a veteran writing to his former nurse years after the war, see the account by Judy Crausbay Hamilton in Xiaobing Li, *Voices From the Vietnam War: Stories from American, Asian, and Russian Veterans* (Lexington: University Press of Kentucky, 2010), 153–54.

An example of this evolution in recollection occurred in research I conducted for my dissertation. Former Army nurse Lily Lee Adams told me in 2000 that she did not like it when other American personnel in Vietnam referred to the Vietnamese as "gooks." Lily Lee Adams, personal interview, 11 January 2000. But in a 1985 book, Adams herself uses the term when describing her reaction to having to care for a Vietnamese prisoner of war: "I didn't come here to take care of gooks" (Walker, *A Piece of My Heart,* 320). That Adams herself is of Asian heritage probably made her more sensitive to the term even while she was in Vietnam, but that she was American still separated her from the Vietnamese enemy.

"American wild flowers" from a note left at the Vietnam Women's Memorial, in the VVMC. "Angels" is a term that many male Vietnam veterans have used to describe the nurses. See "Touched by an Angel" website and letter to Hamilton in Li, *Voices From the Vietnam War,* 154; Vinny Alestra, "They Were Angels," in Jan Hornung, *Angels in Vietnam: Women Who Served* (Lincoln, NE: iUniverse, Inc., 2002), 41–42.

**27.** Such stereotypes echo the general "Madonna-whore" dichotomy that has long characterized sexualized imagery of women. For an example of how such stereotypes (and others) function with regard to nurses and nursing, see Jacqueline M. Bridges, "Literature Review on the Images of the Nurse and Nursing in the Media," *Journal of Advanced Nursing* 15.7 (July 1990): 850–54.

**28.** I interviewed ten nurses and ten enlisted or line officer women for my dissertation and found that the latter group experienced relatively more hostility from male peers than did the nurses. The further away from "feminine" jobs they worked, the more difficulties they seemed to encounter from the men around them. For more on my findings about enlisted women who served, see chap. 1 of my dissertation, "G.I. Gender," 42–107.

**29.** This role playing is covered in the existing literature by and about Vietnam nurses as well. See, for example, Vuic, *Officer, Nurse, Woman,* 149–54; Norman, *Women at War,* chap. 6; Walker, *A Piece of My Heart;* Freedman and Rhoads, *Nurses in Vietnam;* Marshall, *In the Combat Zone;* Olga Gruhzit-Hoyt, *A Time Remembered: American Women in the Vietnam War* (Novato, CA: Presidio Press, 1999); ABC News/The Learning Channel's *Women at War* television documentary and companion book, Ron Steinman, *Women in Vietnam: The Oral History* (New York: TV Books, 2000).

## Notes to Chapter 4

**1.** Penny Kettlewell and Bobby Smith both recounted hearing such a story during their joint interview in 2000, but the quote from Kettlewell comes from a personal e-mail communication, 11 February 2011. According to Mary Reynolds Powell, Army nurse Wendy Wall said that a male soldier who she had assumed was guarding her and other nurses during a firefight in 1969 told her that he had actually been instructed to "shoot the nurses if we got overrun." Wall in Mary Reynolds Powell, *A World of Hurt: Between Innocence and Arrogance in Vietnam* (Chesterland, OH: Greenleaf Enterprises, 2000), 143–44.

**2.** The *New York Times* reported on the use of "pep pills" as early as 1968. See, for example, "U.S. Troops in Vietnam Are Said to Get Pep Pills," 6 March 1968; "Pentagon Explains G.I.'s Get Pep Pills To Diet and Survive," 7 March 1968.

**3.** Breed was surprised when, years later, some of the corpsmen with whom she had worked told her that they had used marijuana while in Vietnam, though never while on duty. "I had no idea!" she said.

**4.** "Pentagon Steps Up Fight on Drug Use in Vietnam: Sharp Rise Noted in Inquiries Into Marijuana Cases for G.I.'s in Last 2 Years," *New York Times,* 16 February 1968; Iver Peterson, "Deaths From Drug Abuse Rise Among Vietnam G.I.'s," *New York Times,* 31 October 1970; Alvin M. Shuster, "G.I. Heroin Addiction Epidemic in Vietnam," *New York Times,* 16 May 1971; James M. Naughton, "President Gives 'Highest Priority' to Drug Problem: Pledges a National Offensive on Addiction Among Both G.I.'s and Civilians," *New York Times,* 2 June 1971.

Jeremy Kuzmarov, *The Myth of the Addicted Army: Vietnam and the Modern War on Drugs* (Amherst: University of Massachusetts Press, 2009). Kuzmarov suggests that the media was too quick to rely on exaggerated reports that confused drug use with drug abuse to sell papers; that the Nixon administration's War on Drugs was an attempt to deflect attention from the failure of—and increasing dissatisfaction with—its policies in Vietnam; and that the Democratic Party and antiwar movement perpetuated the "myth of the addicted army" for their own political purposes.

**5.** Several months after Kettlewell left Vietnam, her former colleagues wrote a letter to Senator Mike Mansfield (D-MT) expressing their discontent with the war. See "Doctors in Vietnam," *New York Times,* 10 December 1971.

According to Richard Moser, between eight hundred and one thousand fragging attempts had been made with explosive devices by the end of the war (48). Fraggings and other forms of resistance to military authority—and sometimes the war itself—were emblems of the antiwar G.I. movement. For more information, see Richard Moser, *The New Winter Soldiers: G.I. and Veteran Dissent During the Vietnam Era* (New Brunswick, NJ: Rutgers University Press, 1996); David Cortright, *Soldiers in Revolt: The American Military Today* (Garden City, NY: Anchor Press/Doubleday, 1975); H. Bruce Franklin, *Vietnam and Other American Fantasies* (Amherst: University of Massachusetts Press, 2000); Robert Buzzanco, *Masters of War: Military Dissent and Politics in the Vietnam Era* (New York: Cambridge University Press, 1996); Harry Haines, ed., "G.I. Resistance: Soldiers and Veterans Against the War," *Vietnam Generation* 2.1 (1990).

**6.** The Central Highlands area of Vietnam also had red clay dirt. However, Bower, who worked at the 24th Evacuation Hospital in Long Binh outside of Saigon (quite a distance south of the Highlands), specifically recalled being instructed to get rid of these soldiers' uniforms because they would somehow indicate that they had been wounded beyond the borders of Vietnam.

**7.** Buchan recalled that the hospital received a special commendation for having treated the most patients in its emergency room of any Army hospital in Vietnam that year.

**8.** Joan Paulson speculated that perhaps this was the military's way of foreclosing the possibility of any alliance between the veterans and the anti-war activists. "Maybe we would have voiced an agreement" with the protesters, she said.

**9.** "Minneapolis Building Hit," *New York Times,* 18 August 1970. Bauer recalled that the dynamite was placed by students from the University of Minnesota, whom police eventually identified. Kay Bauer, e-mail communication, 8 October 2009.

**10.** "Shoreview Home Blast May Have Been Bomb," *St. Paul Pioneer Press,* 3 December 1970, 1. See also "House Blast Kills Shoreview Couple," *St. Paul Pioneer Press,* 5 October 1970, 1.

Kay Bauer, e-mail communication, 6 January 2011. Edwin and Irene Gallagher were killed in the blast. Their son, Donald, remembered that his parents' house and the Bauers' house were almost identical. In following up on this story, I contacted the Ramsey County Sheriff's Department Investigations Division. Sgt. Rollie Martinez went to great lengths to find records of the case—in the sheriff's department, the Shoreview Fire Department, and the state fire marshal's office—but discovered that none of these organizations' archives dated back as far as 1970. As far as he could determine, no suspects were identified or arrested in the matter, and no official records indicate that the Bauers' home was the intended target—or not. Donald Gallagher, telephone conversation, 4 February 2011; Sgt. Rollie Martinez, personal e-mail, voicemail, and telephone conversations, 7, 10, 20 January, 4 February 2011.

**11.** George Herring, *America's Longest War: The United States and Vietnam, 1950–1975,* 3rd ed. (New York: McGraw-Hill, Inc., 1996), 267.

**12.** Jerry Lembcke, *The Spitting Image: Myth, Memory, and the Legacy of Vietnam* (New York: New York University Press, 1998).

**13.** Lynda Van Devanter (with Christopher Morgan) recorded her own experiences in her book, *Home Before Morning: The True Story of an Army Nurse in Vietnam.* For a detailed description of her return to the United States, see chap. 17, "Welcome Home, Asshole!" 245–61.

**14.** B. Drummond Ayres Jr., "The Vietnam Veteran: Silent, Perplexed, Unnoticed," *New York Times,* 8 November 1970.

**15.** Valerie Buchan spent more than sixteen years in the Reserves, while Kay Bauer and Edy Johnson devoted more than twenty years of their lives to the Navy and Army Reserves, respectively.

**16.** Nursing scholar Elizabeth Norman also noted this unease between a veteran wife and nonveteran husband in *Women at War,* 137.

**17.** Edy Johnson, personal e-mail communication, 30 October 2009.

**18.** Mary O'Brien Tyrrell, personal e-mail communication, 30 October

2009. Before she joined the Navy, however, Tyrrell had taken some interest in the ideas of Betty Friedan as they were being discussed on her all-female college campus. Already surrounded by accomplished young women who were seeking higher education, Tyrrell felt it "unnecessary" to participate in "protest marches or bra-burning sessions."

**19.** The VFW opened its doors to women in 1978.

## Notes to Chapter 5

**1.** For more on the evolution of terminology and diagnoses for war veterans' postwar adjustment problems, see the documentary film *The Soldier's Heart,* written, produced, and directed by Raney Aronson (Frontline with A Little Rain Productions, 2005), http://tinyurl.com/4vj75wq. For more on World War II veterans' adjustment difficulties, see Thomas Childers, *Soldier from the War Returning: The Greatest Generation's Troubled Homecoming from World War II* (Boston: Houghton Mifflin, 2009), especially chap. 9, "Picking Up the Pieces."

In one of the earliest academic discussions of women Vietnam veterans, nurse-scholar Sara McVicker described similar feelings in the nurses she interviewed. See Sara J. McVicker, "Invisible Veterans: The Women Who Served in Vietnam," *Journal of Psychosocial Nursing* 23 (October 1985): 16–17.

**2.** American Psychiatric Association, *The Diagnostic and Statistical Manual of Mental Disorders, Third Edition* (Washington, D.C.: American Psychiatric Association), 1980. Jessica Hamblen, "What is PTSD?" [handout], National Center for PTSD, http://tinyurl.com/4nl7an4. See also U.S. Department of Veterans Affairs, "DSM-IV-TR Criteria for PTSD," National Center for PTSD, http://tinyurl.com/4fpotl6. For more on the history of this debate and changing definitions of PTSD in the *DSM,* see Robert L. Spitzer, Michael B. First, and Jerome C. Wakefield, "Saving PTSD from Itself in DSM-V," *Journal of Anxiety Disorders* 21 (2007): 233–41.

**3.** Richard A. Kulka, et al., *Trauma and the Vietnam War Generation: Report of Findings from the National Vietnam Veterans Readjustment Study* (New York: Brunner/Mazel, 1990), 53, 67. Margaret A. Carson, et al., in "Psychophysiologic Assessment of Posttraumatic Stress Disorder in Vietnam Nurse Veterans Who Witnessed Injury or Death," *Journal of Consulting and Clinical Psychology* 68.5 (2000): 890–97. For more on women Vietnam veterans and PTSD, see Jenny Ann Schnaier, "Women Vietnam Veterans and Their Mental Health Adjustment: A Study of Their Experience and Post-Traumatic Stress," unpublished master's thesis, University of Maryland, 1982; Linda Spoonster Schwartz, "Women and the Vietnam Experience," *IMAGE: Journal of Nursing Scholarship* 19.4 (1987): 168–73; Janet Ott, "Women Viet Nam

Veterans," in *The Trauma of War: Stress and Recovery in Vietnam Veterans,* ed. Stephen M. Sonnenberg, Arthur S. Blank, and John A. Talbott (Washington, D.C.: American Psychiatric Press, 1985), 309–19; Norman, *Women at War,* 44–54. "Women, Trauma, and PTSD," National Center for PTSD, U.S. Department of Veterans Affairs website, http://tinyurl.com/4sy72uk.

**4.** Ice cream was available at military bases throughout Vietnam during the war. Whether it was available on Kohl's base or she availed herself of it, the memory of having missed it was central to her story about adjusting to life after the war. Ice cream signified the creature comforts of home that Kohl had missed while in Vietnam and represented the failed potential of simply picking up where she had left off once she returned to the United States.

**5.** Hamblen, "What is PTSD?" 4. For more on the effect of PTSD on families and interpersonal relationships of Vietnam veterans, see ch. 10, "PTSD Among Vietnam Veterans: A Family Perspective," in Kulka, et al., *Trauma and the Vietnam War Generation,* 236–57; Candis M. Williams and Tom Williams, "Family Therapy for Vietnam Veterans," in Sonnenberg, Blank, and Talbott, *The Trauma of War,* 193–209. Most of these early studies of PTSD and the family focused on male veterans and their spouses and children.

**6.** See Dave Grossman, *On Killing: The Psychological Cost of Learning to Kill in War and Society* (New York: Back Bay Books, 2009), sec. 7, "Killing in Vietnam: What Have We Done to Our Soldiers?" for a discussion of the relevance of social support to veterans' postwar adjustment and how the lack of such support contributed to PTSD among Vietnam veterans.

**7.** The VA became the cabinet-level Department of Veterans Affairs in 1989, but from 1930 until 1989 it was the Veterans Administration. I use "VA" to refer to both incarnations of the agency.

**8.** For more on the struggle for readjustment counseling for Vietnam veterans, see Wilbur J. Scott, *Vietnam Veterans Since the War: The Politics of PTSD, Agent Orange, and the National Memorial* (Norman: University of Oklahoma Press, [1993] 2004), esp. chap. 2 and 3; Gerald Nicosia, *Home to War: A History of the Vietnam Veterans' Movement* (New York: Crown Publishers, 2001), esp. chap. 4 and 6; Lifton, *Home From War.*

Though the official *DSM-III* was not published until 1980, the draft version of the manual circulated and provided legitimacy to Vietnam veterans' postwar struggles, once known as "Post-Vietnam Syndrome."

The relationship between the Vet Centers and the VA was not an amicable one, according to Nicosia. He notes that the VA was "initially so reluctant to provide logistical support to the Vet Centers . . . that one congressman . . . actually talked of moving the program to the Forestry Service under the Department of Agriculture, where there was more sympathy for Vietnam vets" (*Home to War,* 518).

**9.** These figures include women who served in the military prior to the Vietnam era as well. They come from a VA Department of Medicine and Surgery White Paper, "Female Veterans," 28 December 1982, 1, in the records of the Center for Women Veterans, Department of Veterans Affairs, Washington, D.C.

**10.** Ott found that women Vietnam veterans were often reluctant to admit to their veteran status unless asked directly by clinicians ("Women Viet Nam Veterans," 314–17).

**11.** U.S. General Accounting Office, *Actions Needed to Insure That Female Veterans Have Equal Access to VA Benefits* (Washington, D.C.: Government Printing Office, 24 September 1982), 2, in the records of the Center for Women Veterans, Department of Veterans Affairs, Washington, D.C. I obtained these materials via a Freedom of Information Act request. Thanks to Joan Furey and her staff at the center for providing me with the information. The study identified a lack of "full gynecological and obstetrical care" as one of the most pervasive problems in the VA health care system, followed closely by a lack of private facilities for women Most of the women I interviewed had relatively little contact with the VA medical system as patients, either because they enjoyed good health, worked at the VA and didn't want to seek care there, or had private insurance through their own or their husbands' employment. A 1984 Louis Harris and Associates study confirmed that 75 percent of women veterans had a private health insurance plan. See U.S. Veterans Administration, *Survey of Female Veterans: A Study of the Needs, Attitudes and Experiences of Women Veterans* (Washington, D.C.: Government Printing Office, August 1985, reprinted September 1985), 118–19.

For more on the history of women veterans and their claims to veterans' benefits and VA services from 1930 to the 1960s, see June Willenz, *Women Veterans: America's Forgotten Heroines* (New York: Continuum Publishing Co., 1983); Richard Severo and Lewis Milford, *The Wages of War: When America's Soldiers Came Home–From Valley Forge to Vietnam* (New York: Simon and Schuster, 1989), 301–4; Holm, *Women in the Military;* Meyer, *Creating G.I. Jane;* Bettie J. Morden, *The Women's Army Corps, 1945–1978* (Washington, D.C.: Center of Military History, U.S. Army, 1990); Yvonne C. Pateman, *Women Who Dared: American Female Test Pilots, Flight-Test Engineers, and Astronauts, 1912–1996* (N.p.: Norstahr Publishing, 1997); Reeves, "Invisible Soldiers," 15–30.

**12.** The GAO report confirmed that Kohl's experiences were not unique. See U.S. GAO, *Actions Needed,* 4. Kohl said that she was worried about her suicidal roommate, especially since no medical staff checked on her throughout the night: "So all night I'm sitting there listening to her breath, you know, watching her chest rise . . . and I'm the patient!" Once she moved to her new accommodations, however, she lost access to the women-only showers. For a while, her male groupmates would stand guard for her as she used the men's facilities; eventually, a sympathetic VA nurse gave her a set of keys for the women's staff locker room.

**13.** Though these quotes are taken from my interview with Kohl in 1999, she also recounts the story, using very similar language, in Walker, *A Piece of My Heart,* 198–99, and in Schwebke, "The Vietnam Women's Memorial."

**14.** See Nicosia, *Home to War,* 397–401, 537; David Bonior, Steven M. Champlin, and Timothy S. Kolly, *The Vietnam Veteran: A History of Neglect* (New York: Praeger Publishers, 1984), 76–77. The existence of this Working Group led the GAO to its only positive report on the VA's service for women veterans. The Readjustment Counseling Program, it noted, "was specifically addressing female veterans' needs." U.S. GAO, *Actions Needed,* 14.

Lynda Van Devanter Buckley, U.S. Congress, House Veterans Affairs Committee Subcommittee on Oversight and Investigations Hearing on Women Veterans, Women Veterans' Benefits and Services Field Hearing, 21 August 1991 (Washington, D.C.: Government Printing Office, 1992), 135–37.

**15.** For more on the positives and negatives for women veterans in the Vet Centers, see Brenda Denzler, "Acceptance and Avoidance: The Woman Vietnam Vet," *Minerva: Quarterly Report on Women and the Military* 5 (30 June 1987): 72+; "Post Trauma Treatment Center Offers Aid to Vietnam Nurses," *Minerva: Quarterly Report on Women and the Military* 2 (31 December 1984): 24.

A Vet Center also acted as the go-between for Diane Evans and Bobby Smith when Smith telephoned the center after seeing a television program about nurses in Vietnam. No one at the center was able to help Smith at the time, but center staff contacted Evans, who then contacted Smith.

**16.** Several different women veteran groups operated in Minnesota in the 1980s and 1990s, with some overlap in membership and mission among them. The Vietnam Women's Memorial Project (now Vietnam Women's Memorial Foundation) incorporated in 1984. The Women Veterans Project was meeting in the early to mid-1980s and became MACVW in late 1984. By 1989 or so, some of the women involved in both of these groups had become part of the PTSD support group headed by Kay Ryan. As of 2011, the VWMF is still in operation, MACVW has become Women Veterans of Minnesota, and the PTSD support group has disbanded but continues to meet at least twice a year on an informal, social basis with even more women Vietnam veterans involved.

**17.** Crowley herself did not participate in the group because she was an employee of the VA and didn't want staff or colleagues to have access to any of her private records.

**18.** Kay Ryan, personal interview, 28 January 2009.

**19.** Ann Rudolph also recalled the cautious way in which new members were admitted to the group. She said she "did some kind of an intake thing" with Kay Ryan, who then invited her to join the group. "I think she had to tell them about me, and they had to kind of accept me. I mean, it wasn't just a drop-on-by type of a thing." This procedure was no doubt designed to ensure the smooth and respectful functioning of a group whose purpose was to delve into particularly difficult, personal, and often controversial topics.

**20.** Denise Goodman, "Letting the Pain Come—and Go," *Boston Globe,* 25 September 1988, 27–28.

**21.** I could not locate any administrative records about the group through the Minneapolis VAMC. Dr. Michael Dieperink, PTSR Medical Director at the Minneapolis VAMC, indicated that the PTSR unit did not keep such records about therapy groups, only patient charts, and that Kay Ryan would be the person with the most information about the group. Neither Dieperink nor any of the other current and former staff members he contacted could comment on how or if this group affected subsequent care and treatment of women Vietnam veterans at the Minneapolis VAMC. Dieperink, e-mail communication, 26 January 2011.

## *Notes to Chapter 6*

**1.** The number of people at the dedication ceremony comes from Jan C. Scruggs and Joel L. Swerdlow, *To Heal a Nation: The Vietnam Veterans Memorial* (New York: Harper & Row, 1985), 152.

The eight military women killed in Vietnam are 2nd Lt. Carol Ann Drazba, U.S. Army Nurse Corps (US ANC), d. 18 February 1966; 2nd Lt. Elizabeth Ann Jones, US ANC, d. 18 February 1966; 1st Lt. Hedwig Diane Orlowski, US ANC, d. 30 November 1967; Capt. Eleanor Grace Alexander, US ANC, d. 30 November 1967; 2nd Lt. Pamela Dorothy Donovan, US ANC, d. 8 July 1968; Lt. Annie Ruth Graham, US ANC, d. 14 August 1968; 1st Lt. Sharon Ann Lane, US ANC, d. 8 June 1969; Capt. Mary Therese Klinker, U.S. Air Force, d. 9 April 1975.

**2.** The Vietnam Veterans Leadership Program (VVLP) was a national, federally funded program initiated in 1981 whose main goal was to help Vietnam veterans with job training, employment, and small business development. Boulay's law office was near the office of the VVLP, which was how she got to know Marine Vietnam veterans John Field and Steve Markley.

**3.** Diane Evans as quoted in Kate McCarthy McEnroe, "Vietnam Nurse Battles for Fitting Tribute," *St. Paul Pioneer Press and Dispatch,* 13 April 1986.

**4.** Diane Carlson Evans, "Thanks, Nurse," in *Visions of War,* 95–97.

**5.** Scruggs and Swerdlow, *To Heal a Nation,* 7. Vietnam Veterans Memorial Fund, Inc., Pub. L. No. 96-297, 94 Stat. 828 (1980).

**6.** Scott, *Vietnam Veterans Since the War,* 147. See also Marita Sturken, *Tangled Memories: The Vietnam War, the AIDS Epidemic, and the Politics of Remembering* (Berkeley: University of California Press, 1997); Daphne Berdahl, "Voices at the Wall: Discourses of Self, History and National Identity at the Vietnam Veterans Memorial," *History & Memory* 6 (Fall/Winter 1994): 90–97; John Bodnar, *Remaking America: Public Memory, Commemoration, and Patriotism in the Twentieth Century* (Princeton, NJ: Princeton University Press, 1992); Kristin Ann Hass, *Carried to the Wall: American Memory and the Vietnam Veterans Memorial* (Berkeley: University of California Press, 1998); Fred Turner, *Echoes of Combat: The Vietnam War in American Memory* (New York and London: Anchor Books/Doubleday, 1996); Elizabeth Hess, "Vietnam: Memorials of Misfortune," in *Unwinding the Vietnam War: From War Into Peace,* ed. Reese Williams (Seattle, WA: Real Comet Press, 1987), 262–72; Franklin Ng, "Maya Lin and the Vietnam Veterans Memorial," in *Chinese America: History and Perspectives* (San Francisco, CA: Chinese Historical Society of America, 1994): 201–21; Catherine M. Howett, "The Vietnam Veterans Memorial: Public Art and Politics," *Landscape* 28.2 (1985): 1–9; Karal Ann Marling and Robert Silberman, "The Statue Near the Wall: The Vietnam Veterans Memorial and the Art of Remembering," *Smithsonian Studies in American Art* 1 (Spring 1987): 5–29.

Vietnam veteran Tom Carhart even went so far as to refer to Lin as a "gook." Scott, *Vietnam Veterans Since the War,* 140.

Hart had been part of a team that submitted an entry to the original VVMF design competition. They placed third. The VVMF awarded Hart $330,000 for his winning design in the sculpture competition; Maya Lin earned $20,000 for her design in the original competition. Mary McLeod, "The Battle for the Monument," in *The Experimental Tradition: Essays on Competitions in Architecture,* ed. Hélène Lipstadt, Barry Bergdoll, Architectural League of New York., et al. (New York: Princeton Architectural Press, 1989), 127. *Three Fighting Men* is the popular title of the work, but National Park Service Vietnam Veterans Memorial Collection curator Duery Felton Jr. told me that the statue is officially untitled. Duery Felton Jr., personal conversation, 21 February 2001. Since the same legislation (Pub. L. 96-297) authorized construction of all three memorials (the Wall, Hart's, and the Vietnam Women's Memorial), they, together, constitute the Vietnam Veterans Memorial. Thus, "Vietnam Veterans Memorial" refers to the collection of memorials. I use the specific names of the works when referring to them individually.

**7.** Tim O'Brien, *If I Die in a Combat Zone: Box Me Up and Ship Me Home*

(New York: Delacorte Press, 1973); Ron Kovic, *Born on the Fourth of July* (New York: McGraw-Hill, 1976); Philip Caputo, *A Rumor of War* (New York: Henry Holt and Company, Inc. 1977); Paul Schrader, *Taxi Driver,* directed by Martin Scorsese (Columbia Pictures, 1976); Robert C. Jones, Waldo Salt, Nancy Dowd and Rudy Wurlitzer, *Coming Home,* directed by Hal Ashby (United Artists, 1978); Michael Cimino and Deric Washburn, *The Deer Hunter,* directed by Michael Cimino (MCA/Universal, 1978); John Milius and Francis Ford Coppola, *Apocalypse Now,* directed by Francis Ford Coppola (United Artists, 1979); William Sackheim, Michael Kozoll, and Q. Moonblood, *First Blood,* directed by Ted Kotcheff (Orion, 1982); David Morrell, Kevin Jarre, Sylvester Stallone, and James Cameron, *Rambo: First Blood, Part II,* directed by George P. Cosmatos (Warner Communications, 1985); Oliver Stone, *Platoon,* directed by Oliver Stone (Orion, 1986); Stanley Kubrick, Gustav Hasford, and Michael Herr, *Full Metal Jacket,* directed by Stanley Kubrick (Warner Brothers, 1987); Ron Kovic and Oliver Stone, *Born on the Fourth of July,* directed by Oliver Stone (Universal, 1989). For more on the gendered nature of Vietnam War films and literature, see Susan Jeffords, *The Remasculinization of America: Gender and the Vietnam War* (Bloomington and Indianapolis: Indiana University Press, 1989); Lorrie N. Smith, "'The Things Men Do': The Gendered Subtext in Tim O'Brien's *Esquire* Stories," *Critique* 36.1 (1994): 16–39.

Diane Carlson Evans, "Moving a Vision: The Vietnam Women's Memorial," (n.d.), Vietnam Women's Memorial Foundation website, http://tinyurl.com/4llllkg.

**8.** Van Devanter with Morgan, *Home Before Morning;* Sidney J. Furie and Rick Natkin, *Purple Hearts,* directed by Sidney J. Furie (Warner Bros., 1984); Myra MacPherson, "Vietnam Nurses: These Are the Women Who Went to War," *MS Magazine* (June 1984): 52–56, 104–6, excerpted from MacPherson's book, *Long Time Passing: Vietnam and the Haunted Generation* (New York: Doubleday and Company, Inc., 1984); Walker, *A Piece of My Heart.*

**9.** This organizational history of the VWMP comes from interviews and e-mail communication with Evans and Boulay, as well as Evans, "Moving a Vision."

**10.** Mary O'Brien Tyrrell, "Saving Lives" ([1986] 2003). This poem also appeared in *VA Practitioner* (October 1987): 80–81, and Van Devanter and Furey, *Visions of War,* 60. Tyrrell recounted this series of events to me in our interview. She also describes them in an article she wrote: Mary M. Tyrrell, "The Unseen Veteran," *VA Practitioner* (October 1987): 73–81.

**11.** Evans, "Moving a Vision," 2.

**12.** "Veteran Nurses Remember 'Endless Parade' of Wounded," *St. Paul Pioneer Press and Dispatch,* 12 August 1984. Gordon Slovut, "Memories of

Vietnam Stay with Nurse," *Minneapolis Star and Tribune,* 3 December 1985. Crowley and Diane Evans also shared their stories in a documentary for KTCA in 1985: *And A Time To Heal,* produced and written by Gary Gilson, Twin Cities Public Television, Inc., 1985.

**13.** Mary O'Brien Tyrrell, personal conversation, 21 January 2010.

**14.** Evans, "Moving a Vision," 6.

**15.** Other prominent figures who held advisory, honorary, or active roles within the VWMP included U.S. Senators Alan Cranston (D-CA) and Rudy Boschwitz (R-MN); Lt. Col. Evangeline Jamison (USA, Ret.); Maj. Gen. Jeanne M. Holm (USAF, Ret.); former director of the Navy Nurse Corps, Rear Adm. Frances Shea Buckley (USN, Ret.); former chief of staff, U.S. Army, Gen. William Westmoreland (USA, Ret.); and entertainer and troop favorite Martha Raye. This partial list of VWMP members taken from a 31 December 1987 letter from VWMP Chairman and CEO D-M Boulay to VWMP supporters, included in the VWMP newsletter, *The Legacy* (Fourth Quarter 1987): 6. The newsletter was in the personal files of Mary O'Brien Tyrrell.

**16.** Sue A. Kohler, *The Commission of Fine Arts: A Brief History 1910–1995* (Washington, D.C.: Government Printing Office, 1996), 1. Brown headed the National Gallery from 1969 to 1992 and served on the CFA from 1971 until shortly before his death in June 2002. Though he came from a moneyed family—Brown University in Providence, Rhode Island, bears his family's name—he was often referred to as a "populist" for his efforts at making art accessible to the general public. See J. Carter Brown, "Introduction" for Rings of Passion Project website, 1996 (site retired; URL unavailable); Chuck Conconi, "Remembering J. Carter Brown," *Washingtonian People OnLine,* June 2002 (URL unavailable); David D'Arcy, "In Memory of J. Carter Brown," *The Art Newspaper.com,* June 2002 (URL unavailable).

Minutes of the Meeting of the Commission of Fine Arts, 22 October 1987, 2, 5, in the records of the CFA. Frederick Hart was a member of the CFA at this time. Recognizing the conflict of interest that his presence represented, he abstained from voting on the proposed women's memorial. He did, however, offer his opinion on the matter: he claimed that his work was "fully symbolic of all who had served" and that any further additions to the memorial "could demolish its impact and balance." Minutes, 4. So, at the end, Brown, Carolyn Deaver, Neil Porterfield, and Diane Wolf voted against the VWMP, Roy Goodman for the VWMP, with Hart abstaining. Maya Lin, who had also opposed the Hart statue, sent a letter to the CFA expressing her vehement opposition to another addition to her original memorial design. Maya Ying Lin, letter to the Commission of Fine Arts, 20 October 1987, included as Exhibit A-1 in Minutes, 22 October 1987, in the records of the CFA. For local press coverage of the VWMP and CFA debates, see Benjamin Forgey, "Women and the Wall: Memorial Proposal: Honor Without Integrity," *The Washington Post,* 22 October 1987; Forgey, "Commission Vetoes Vietnam Women's Statue," *The Washington Post,* 23 October 1987.

J. Carter Brown, letter to Donald P. Hodel, 28 October 1987, in the records of the CFA.

**17.** Diane Carlson Evans, "The Vietnam Women's Memorial Project, Inc." testimony at the 22 October 1987 CFA meeting, in the records of the CFA.

**18.** Sen. Dave Durenberger (R-MN), U.S. Congress, Senate Committee on Energy and Natural Resources, Vietnam Women's Memorial Hearing, 23 February 1988 (Washington, D.C.: Government Printing Office, 1988), 9.

**19.** Mary Lu Ostergren Brunner, "To My Unknown Soldier Boy," in Van Devanter and Furey, *Visions of War,* 107–8. Evans, "Moving a Vision," 10–11. By 1990, the project had raised $1.75 million but was in need of an additional $2 million. These figures are taken from press accounts about the VWMP and its ongoing campaign to build the memorial. See, for example, "Reagan OKs Viet Statue for Servicewomen," *St. Paul Pioneer Press and Dispatch,* 16 November 1988; Ben Chanco, "Army Nurse Statue to Become Part of the Vietnam Memorial," *St. Paul Pioneer Press,* 11 November 1990; "Women in the Military: Saluting the Past, Facing the Future," *St. Paul Pioneer Press,* 9 November 1993. See also Vietnam Women's Memorial Project, "Budgeted Expense for the Years Ending December 31, 1987 and 1988," in "Invisible Veterans: A Legacy of Healing and Hope," (n.d.—late 1988 or early 1989), Appendix E, E-1. This report is from the personal collection of Mary O'Brien Tyrrell.

**20.** "Join Loretta's Team!" in the VWMP newsletter, *The Legacy* (First Quarter 1988): 4; "Remember the Women; Star Pleads for Salute to Female Vietnam Vets," *USA Today,* 22 June 1988.

According to the *St. Paul Pioneer Press and Dispatch,* VWMP board members Diane Evans and Karen Johnson filed a lawsuit in early May 1988 charging Boulay with financial mismanagement and demanding the removal of six other board members. Brodin had "threatened to withdraw from the Project if Boulay wasn't removed." Boulay denied all allegations against her. After the board replaced Boulay as chairwoman (naming her and Evans as honorary cochairwomen), the lawsuit was dropped. In June 1988, the paper reported that an audit by Ernst & Whitney had cleared Boulay of the charges against her, noting that the original allegations "stemmed from concerns [by Evans and Johnson] that financial records were unavailable for their inspection." This accounting of this "shakeup" comes from the following articles: David Shaffer, "Memorial Board Replaces Chairman," *St. Paul Pioneer Press and Dispatch,* 10 May 1988; Louis Porter II,

"Ex-Viet Memorial Chief Defends Self," *St. Paul Pioneer Press and Dispatch,* 11 May 1988; "Fund-Raiser Says Audit Clears Her," *St. Paul Pioneer Press and Dispatch,* 22 June 1988. Neither Evans nor Boulay—nor any of the other women I interviewed—discussed this incident in any of our interviews. Instead, their recollections about the VWMP centered on the hard but rewarding work of mobilizing support for the Memorial and women Vietnam veterans.

Just after the CFA hearing in October 1987, Brown had said the CFA wanted to avoid a proliferation of "special interest" memorial proposals, noting that "The Park Service even heard from Scout Dogs Associations." Evans and Boulay both recounted this comment in our interviews. Quote taken from Fred T. Abdella, "Memorial to Women Veterans is Sought," *New York Times,* 10 April 1988. See also J. Carter Brown, letter to James C. Murr, Assistant Director for Legislative Reference, Executive Office of the President, 2 November 1988, in the records of the CFA; Brown as quoted in Betty Cuniberti, "Nurses Face Monumental Frustration," *Los Angeles Times,* 14 February 1989.

**21.** "The Forgotten Veterans," *60 Minutes,* produced by Marti Galovic Palmer, anchor Morley Safer, CBS, 26 February 1989 (New York: CBS News Transcripts, 1989), 7; John Wells and John Sacret Young, "Vets," *China Beach,* directed by John Sacret Young, ABC, 15 March 1989, in LaSalle University's special collection Imaginative Representations of the Vietnam War. For a more detailed discussion of *China Beach,* see Kim Heikkila, "'What Women Really Did': Truth and Authority in *China Beach* and the Vietnam Women's Memorial," *Vietnam War Generation Journal* 1 (August 2001): 44–66.

**22.** Joint Resolution (Vietnam War Women Veterans' Memorial), Pub. L. No. 101-187, 103 Stat. 1350 (1989). The job of the National Capital Memorial Commission (NCMC), on which J. Carter Brown held a seat as chair of the CFA, was to ensure that the Memorial proposal met the conditions of the 1986 Commemorative Works Act, which required that any memorial to be built on the Mall commemorate something that is of "preeminent historical and lasting significance to the nation." Evans recalled asking just one question at the NCMC meeting: "Is not saving the lives of 350,000 wounded soldiers in Vietnam of lasting, preeminent significance?" The NCMC voted 5-2 in favor of the VWMP. Transcript of the 9 March 1989 NCMC meeting, in the records of the National Capital Memorial Commission.

**23.** Such suggestions were made at the 1987 and 1990 CFA and 1989 NCMC meetings. Carol Lincoln, personal interview, 25 June 1999.

**24.** Evans in the Minutes of the Meeting of the Commission of Fine Arts, 19 September 1991, 2, in the records of the CFA; Evans interview. Civilian women who served in Vietnam, though not visually represented in the Memorial's figures, are also honored by the VWMP in its mission and activities.

Goodacre's model did not win the competition; she took an honorable mention. But, as Evans recalled in May 2000, the nine-member jury ("five professional sculptors, artists, and architects, and four veterans") split 5-4 in their choice for the memorial, the professionals favoring an abstract design, the veterans a realistic statue. The right to make the final decision was reserved for the VWMP board, and it chose the Goodacre design.

**25.** According to Evans, Goodacre's original design included a figure of a woman holding a wounded or sick Vietnamese baby. Fearing that including it would make the memorial too political, that figure was replaced by the kneeling woman. Diane Evans, letter to Robert G. Stanton of the National Park Service, 18 February 1992, in CFA records.

A brief perusal of newspaper coverage of the dedication ceremonies supports the notion that, despite VWMP's intention to include all women veterans, the Memorial is in fact viewed as one for and about nurses. Most reports described the figures as nurses, focused their human-interest pieces on nurse veterans, and relegated enlisted women to an anonymous group of "and others" who served with nurses in Vietnam. See, for example, Cindy Loose, "Vietnam Women's Memorial Dedicated Before 25,000," *Washington Post,* 12 November 1993; Linda Wheeler, "Relieving the Pain by Reliving the Past; Female Veterans, Workers Remember Vietnam," *Washington Post,* 12 November 1996; Lily Dizon, "The War Within," *Los Angeles Times–Orange County Edition,* 12 November 1993; Michael Kranish, "A Day of Tributes and Pleas," *The Boston Globe,* 12 November 1993; Jim Gogek, "Women Saw Combat Horrors, Public Snubs," *San Diego Union-Tribune,* 21 November 1994; Megan Rosenfeld, "The Angels of Vietnam; For Two Navy Nurses, a Memorial to a Time They Won't Forget," *Washington Post,* 11 November 1993; Leslie Kinsey, "At Vietnam Women's Memorial," [Cleveland] *Plain Dealer,* 6 December 1993; "Women's Memorial is Unveiled Amid Tears and Thanks," Minneapolis *Star Tribune,* 12 November 1993; Mark Bousian, "Statue Honors Female Vietnam Veterans; Memorial: Many at capital unveiling say it is part of the healing process," *Los Angeles Times,* 12 November 1993. Even scholars treat the Memorial as a nurses' memorial. See Enloe, *Maneuvers,* 226–29; G. Kurt Piehler, *Remembering War the American Way* (Washington, D.C.: Smithsonian Institution Press, 1995), 179.

**26.** General Colin L. Powell, "Remarks at the Groundbreaking Ceremony for the Vietnam Women's Memorial," in *Celebration of Patriotism and Courage: Dedication of the Vietnam Women's Memorial, November 10–12, 1993* (Washington, D.C.: Vietnam Women's Memorial Project, 1993), 31–32.

**27.** At this time, the VWMP board of directors included Diane Evans (chair), Doris Lippman, Judith Helein, Dan Daly, Wilma Blakeman, Jane Carson, Shirley Crowe, and Evangeline Jamison.

**28.** Penny Kettlewell, "I Hold Them," in Van Devanter and Furey, *Visions of War,* 105–6.

**29.** Although D-M Boulay did not attend the dedication ceremony, she said that someone sent her a shovel that was used to break ground for the Memorial.

**30.** Kathy Egan, WCCO-TV, 11 November 1993.

**31.** The National Park Service maintains a collection of artifacts that have been left at the Vietnam Veterans Memorial.

**32.** Kettlewell quotation as recorded by WCCO-TV, 11 November 1993.

**33.** Evans quoted by Kathy Egan, WCCO-TV, 11 November 1993.

## Notes to Conclusion

**1.** Both of these items are in the Vietnam Veterans Memorial Collection (VVMC) at a National Park Service warehouse in Bethesda, Maryland.

**2.** The VA as a whole has come a long way in its programming for women veterans. Women veterans now have a home in the national VA at the Center for Women Veterans (CWV), established in 1994 under the guidance of ANC Vietnam veteran Joan Furey. In November 2009, secretary of Veterans Affairs Eric Shinseki announced a major new effort to study the long-term mental and physical effects of women's service in the Vietnam-era military. The Minnesota Department of Veterans Affairs (MDVA) has its own Minnesota Women Veterans program, with a women veterans coordinator in its central office and women veterans and military sexual trauma (MST) program managers at the VAMC facilities in Minneapolis and St. Cloud. Minnesota's women veterans can also seek care at the Minneapolis Women Veterans Comprehensive Health Center at the Minneapolis VAMC or PTSD counseling at the Women's Mental Health Center. The MDVA held a Minnesota Veteran and Military Women's Summit in October 2009 to honor and educate women who have worn—or continue to wear—the uniform. Despite such progress, however, female soldiers and veterans continue to face discrimination and neglect by both the military and the VAMC. For more on such challenges, see Mark Brunswick, "Dismissed: A Series on Women in the Military," Minneapolis *Star Tribune,* 14, 21, 29 November, 18, 29 December 2010.

**3.** In all three instances, Kohl was describing the problems she encountered with the PTSD group at the Tomah, Wisconsin, VA, and how her war experiences did not fit the paradigm of combat-based trauma. See Walker, *A Piece of My Heart,* 198–99; Schwebke, "The Vietnam Women's Memorial."

**4.** For a discussion of life review and oral history, see Harriet Wrye and Jacqueline Churilla, "Looking Inward, Looking Backward: Reminiscence and the Life Review," in *Women's Oral History: The Frontiers Reader,* ed. Susan H. Armitage with Patricia Hart and Karen Weathermon (Lincoln: University of Nebraska Press, 2002), 145–57.

**5.** The group has also included women veterans of other wars, including a couple of World War II veterans, but the main demographic has been Vietnam veterans. Kay Ryan left the VA in 2001.

# Index